A Learning Profession?

STUDIES IN PROFESSIONAL LIFE AND WORK
Volume 10

Editor
Ivor Goodson
Education Research Centre, University of Brighton, UK

Editorial Board
J. M. Pancheco, *University of Minho, Portugal*
David Labaree, *Stanford University*
Sverker Lindblad, *University of Gothenburg*
Leslie Siskin, *NYU/Steinhardt Institute for Education & Social Policy*

Scope

The series will commission books in the broad area of professional life and work. This is a burgeoning area of study now in educational research with more and more books coming out on teachers' lives and work, on nurses' life and work, and on the whole interface between professional knowledge and professional lives.

The focus on life and work has been growing rapidly in the last two decades. There are a number of rationales for this. Firstly, there is a methodological impulse: many new studies are adopting a life history approach. The life history tradition aims to understand the interface between people's life and work and to explore the historical context and the socio-political circumstances in which people's professional life and work is located. The growth in life history studies demands a series of books which allow people to explore this methodological focus within the context of professional settings.

The second rationale for growth in this area is a huge range of restructuring initiatives taking place throughout the world. There is in fact a world movement to restructure education and health. In most forms this takes the introduction of more targets, tests and tables and increasing accountability and performativity regimes. These initiatives have been introduced at governmental level – in most cases without detailed consultation with the teaching and nursing workforces. As a result there is growing evidence of a clash between people's professional life and work missions and the restructuring initiatives which aim to transform these missions. One way of exploring this increasingly acute clash of values is through studies of professional life and work. Hence the European Commission, for instance, have begun to commission quite large studies of professional life and work focussing on teachers and nurses. One of these projects – the Professional Knowledge Network project has studied teachers' and nurses' life and work in seven countries. There will be a range of books coming out from this project and it is intended to commission the main books on nurses and on teachers for this series.

The series will begin with a number of works which aim to define and delineate the field of professional life and work. One of the first books 'Investigating the Teacher's Life and Work' by Ivor Goodson will attempt to bring together the methodological and substantive approaches in one book. This is something of a 'how to do' book in that it looks at how such studies can be undertaken as well as what kind of generic findings might be anticipated.

Future books in the series might expect to look at either the methodological approach of studying professional life and work or provide substantive findings from research projects which aim to investigate professional life and work particularly in education and health settings.

A Learning Profession?

Teachers and their Professional Development in England and Wales 1920-2000

Wendy Robinson
University of Exeter, UK

SENSE PUBLISHERS
ROTTERDAM/BOSTON/TAIPEI

A C.I.P. record for this book is available from the Library of Congress.

ISBN: 978-94-6209-570-0 (paperback)
ISBN: 978-94-6209-571-7 (hardback)
ISBN: 978-94-6209-572-4 (e-book)

Published by: Sense Publishers,
P.O. Box 21858,
3001 AW Rotterdam,
The Netherlands
https://www.sensepublishers.com/

Printed on acid-free paper

TABLE OF CONTENTS

Preface   ix

Acknowledgements   xi

Part 1: Setting the Scene

1. Introduction: Aims, Context and Methodology   3

   Context and Objectives   3
   Methodology and Sources   5
   Organisational Structure of the Book   10
   Notes   12

2. National Policy Mapping   15

   Introduction   15
   Phase One: Initial Development 1914–1945   16
   Phase Two: McNair and the Consolidation of Existing Models
   1945–1960   25
   Phase Three: Challenge and Expansion 1960–1980   29
   Phase Four: Privatisation and Central Control 1980–2000   33
   Notes   35

Part 2: Chronological Case Studies

3. The Vacation Course 1920–1940   41

   Introduction   41
   Historical Context and Vacation Course Outlines   41
   Organisation, Location and Funding   44
   Course Content   48
   Social and Cultural Opportunities   53
   The Vacation Course and Teacher Professionalism   56
   Notes   59

4. Special Advanced Courses for Teachers 1945–1960   63

   Introduction   63
   The Development of 'Special Advanced Courses for Serving Teachers'
   by the Ministry of Education   64

Case Studies: The University of London Institute of Education and the Bristol Institute of Education 70

Chapter Summary 78

Notes 80

5. The Teachers' Centre 1960–1990 85

Teachers' Centres in Context 86

Teachers' Centres: An Overview 88

Teachers' Centre Leaders 94

Teachers' Centres and International Developments 100

Chapter Summary 105

Notes 106

6. Teachers' Experiences of Professional Development 111

Early Career Experiences: 'In at the Deep End' 111

Formal Professional Development: 'Going on Courses' 113

Resourced Professional Development Through Teacher Secondment 117

National Initiatives and Teacher Professional Development 122

Informal/Organic Teacher Development 126

Chapter Summary 129

Notes 129

Part 3: Teachers' Reflections on Professional Development

7. Evaluating Impact: Personal and Professional Perspectives 133

Meanings of Impact 133

Perceptions of Quality 140

Impact for Whom? Motivations and Reach 144

Chapter Summary 149

Notes 150

8. Professional Development and Perceptions of Teacher Professional Identity 153

Personal and Professional Dimensions 153

Perceptions of Status and Accredited Degrees 158

Professional Development and the Wider Professional Community 163

Being a Teacher, Being a Learner 165

Chapter Summary 167

Notes 168

9. Conclusion   171

   Resource, Control and Reach   172
   Professional and Personal Development   184
   Professional Learning and Professional Identity   186
   Notes   189

Select Bibliography   193

PREFACE

Whilst the history of initial teacher education in England and Wales has been fairly well rehearsed in recent years, that of in-service teacher education, or teacher professional development, has received inadequate attention. A distinctive feature of this book is that it moves beyond an analysis of current models of teacher professional development and seeks to locate these within a longer historical perspective. Drawing on original findings from a project funded by the British Academy, the book presents new historical data, both documentary and oral testimony from teachers. It scrutinises the history of teacher professional development across a broad chronological spectrum as well as in some depth and aims to capture both the big picture as well as some of the finer detail – the official 'top-down' story as well as insights into the unique lived experience of practitioners over time.

The book identifies five main conceptual areas: priorities and purpose; funding; scale of teacher engagement; control; and reach, which have shaped ideologies and models of teacher professional development as they have developed over time and against changing education contexts. It argues that the twentieth- century history of teacher professional development in England and Wales, though delivering certain notable examples of excellence, particularly for the individual teachers involved, can broadly be characterised as a history of unfulfilled promise, ongoing problems of underfunding and scarce resource and incoherence. This historical analysis suggests that successive governments have paid lip-service to the idea that a teaching profession requires continuous renewal to maintain both professional and personal standards and quality – as something not just reserved for a small elite group, but for all teachers.

At a time of intense international debate on the primacy of teacher professional development as a lever for sustained educational reform, it is intended that this book might contribute to a fuller understanding of the basis for those unresolved questions and dilemmas about teacher professional development that continue to exercise teachers, professional educators and policy-makers across the world today. It does so in three ways. First, in a field where there is a dearth of detailed historical analysis, it offers a more focussed historical lens through which to better understand the evolution of the current 'problem' of teacher professional development. Secondly, it enriches an understanding of the highly complex dynamic associated with constructions of teacher professionalism and teacher professional development. Thirdly, it suggests scope for further historical analysis of professional development that might be applied to other professions.

Covering such a wide chronological span, it is important to note that the actual terminology used to define and describe activity related to teacher professional development shifted and changed over time and variously included such terms as 'teacher refreshment', 'supplementary training', 'further training of teachers', 'in-service training', 'in-service education', 'continued professional development'. Each of these descriptors contains subtle yet important differences of emphasis and definition. In the book, where specific terms are used in the reported historical data, these are followed – but the more general and current term 'professional development' is used in the commentary.

ACKNOWLEDGEMENTS

The original empirical research that underpins this book would not have been possible without my British Academy Research Development Award 53026, for which I am very grateful. This funded my research project, 'Revisiting Teacher Professional Development: Past and Present Models, 1920-2008', which ran between February 2010 and December 2012 at the University of Exeter, Graduate School of Education, UK. As part of this award I was able to appoint an outstanding Research Fellow, Dr Marie Bryce, who undertook much of the documentary data collection and fieldwork for the project. I fully acknowledge her valued contribution to the research that informs the book. I very much appreciated the interest and wisdom of the project steering group, comprising experts in the field of history of education, Professor Richard Aldrich, Dr David Crook, Dr Peter Cunningham and Professor Gary McCulloch.

My thanks are also due to the archivists and librarians who assisted with access to the various archives and collections in their care. Above all, however, I am indebted to the generosity of the 31 oral history participants who allowed me into their lives and precious professional memories. Their vitality and passion for their own life-long professional development was a real inspiration and I hope that I have done some justice to their testimony.

I would like to thank Jianmei Xie for her invaluable technical assistance in the preparation of the final manuscript for the publishers. Finally, I would like to thank Jim Campbell for his ongoing support, advice and interest in the ideas in the book.

PART 1

SETTING THE SCENE

INTRODUCTION: AIMS, CONTEXT AND METHODOLOGY

CONTEXT AND OBJECTIVES

Globally, the continuing professional development of teachers and its impact on the performance of educational systems are high on political and educational agendas. A well trained, professional, up-to-date, flexible and responsive teaching force, able to make a real difference to the quality of young people's learning, is regarded as a key to educational reform and economic sustainability.[1] Alongside what Neufeld describes as a '*universal international movement to professionalise teachers*'[2] is a growing body of educational research focussed on defining teacher professional development and learning, identifying what works well, and analysing teacher engagement and impact.[3] Nevertheless, this scholarship, supported by numerous large-scale national and international studies, suggests that there is a substantive gap between policy ideals, knowledge and understanding about teacher professional development and the lived reality of teachers across the world.[4] There is debate over which models of professional development are most effective – both in transforming teacher learning and teacher professionalism but also in raising school achievement and pupil performance. There are also important policy-related and research-related questions about the deeper purposes, control, locus, process and impact of professional development on teachers' work and lives and how this should be resourced and managed. There is also real anxiety that teaching is in a state of crisis, reflected in problems associated with attracting, developing and retaining the best graduates into the profession. This is a contested and highly complex field, with some researchers calling for a fundamental rethinking of how teacher professional development should be conceptualised and envisioned.

Recent academic and professional theorising about what makes teacher professional development effective, supports various trends for collaborative and coaching models but raises important questions about the best measurable outcomes for all stakeholders. This generates tension between the different needs of stakeholders – not just those teachers at the heart of the professional development process, whose own needs change and develop throughout the various phases of their professional careers, but also those of pupils, parents and school managers. Current models are impact-driven and impact is measured by improvement in pupil and school performance and not necessarily by enhanced teacher professional identity, capacity and expertise.

3

Yet, although contemporary theorising about teacher professional development has much strength, it is characterised by a lack of historical analysis. There is no sustained analysis of key developments, policy drivers and models of provision over any length of time. The most 'historical' any analysis gets involves some reference to the 1972 James Report on teacher education and training, which is heralded as the real breakthrough for teacher professional development in England, with its official recommendation that teachers should continue their professional training after qualifying.[5] Yet, any cursory review of the standard historical literature on teacher education, hints at a very different story, with a much longer tradition of organised professional development at both central and local levels, and much more sophisticated patterns and networks of provision. Though some well-known historical studies of teaching[6] consider ideas of continuing professional development as part of broader discussions about professionalism, professionalization and initial teacher preparation, there is very limited in-depth, systematic historical research.[7] None of these key works has a defined conceptual framework for teacher professional development as a main focus and one of the key objectives of this book is to redress this fundamental elision in the knowledge-base.

It is from this policy and research context that it is hoped that this book might offer something distinctive to the field. The book presents a new historical analysis of the evolution of organised teacher professional development in England and Wales during the twentieth century. Its approach hopes to open up the wider debate and to contribute to a fuller understanding of the basis for those questions and dilemmas about teacher professional development that have long exercised teachers, professional educators and policy-makers – questions which turn on fundamental issues of priorities and purpose, funding, scale of teacher engagement, control, and reach.

The empirical data on which this book is based draws upon a research project funded by the British Academy, entitled *Revisiting Teacher Professional Development: Past and Present Models, 1920–2000*.[8] The project was developed to address that fundamental gap in our knowledge and understanding of the history of teacher professional development, identified above, and was based on substantive new documentary analysis and original oral history testimony. The core objectives of the project were to undertake a systematic historical review of the development of teachers' continued professional development during the twentieth century, so that current models and practice and new policy initiatives might then be properly contextualised and critiqued. The project was designed around traditional methods of historical investigation, documentary analysis, case-study methodology and oral history. The project was structured in three phases. First, it mapped systematically the historical terrain of teachers' professional development in England and Wales from 1920–2000, and reviewed the various models espoused by key players, including government, local authorities, schools, professional associations, private providers, the teacher unions and teachers themselves. Secondly, it generated a comparative analysis between past and present models of practice with an assessment of what worked, how it worked and why it worked in different contexts and for which stakeholders. Thirdly, through oral history methodology and in-depth case studies, the project examined the experience of teacher professional development from the perspective of teachers and providers.

METHODOLOGY AND SOURCES

Research presented in this book used traditional methods of historical investigation, documentary analysis and case-study methodology, as well as in-depth case studies of the experience of teacher professional development through oral-history interviews with teachers and educationists. The research design aimed to scrutinise the history of teacher professional development across a broad chronological spectrum as well as in some depth. It sought to capture both the big picture as well as some of the finer detail – the official 'top-down' story as well as some insights into the personal lived experience of practitioners over time. There are two important aspects of the methodology to note. The first lies in its breadth and its depth as well as the scope and chronological framework. The second is its analysis of previously unexamined sources. Clearly, there are methodological challenges associated with this kind of historical project. These focus on the nature of historical interpretation and reconstruction as well as issues of reliability and representativeness. Such problems, centring upon the availability of sources, evidential reliability and bias, are to a degree unavoidable, but do not, in consequence, negate the practice or validity of disciplined historical enquiry. Rather, they call for a tempered, prudent and consistently critical approach to the interrogation of sources.[9]

A number of loose research questions informed the selection and analysis of the empirical data, which comprised two broad categories. The first was concerned with the various models of teacher professional development which emerged during the twentieth century, and considered what they were, what the intentions behind them were, who controlled, organised and funded them, what the relationships between key parties, such as central government, local authorities, teacher training institutions, universities, professional and subject associations, and schools, were like. The second category was focussed on the experiences of teachers in terms of their participation and access to different models, how they viewed professional development, whether they valued it, and what the relationship might be between professional development, professional status and professional identity.

The documentary research

Using a traditional approach to documentary research, a range of evidence relevant to the research focus of the project was identified, selected, scrutinised, consulted, interrogated, synthesised and critiqued. A starting point for this part of the research was to consult appropriate official publications, relevant Royal Commissions, Special Inquiries and government Circulars relating to teacher professional development, annual reports of the Board of Education and its successors and annual educational statistics, for the time period under review. The three milestone government reports discussed in Chapter Two: the Departmental Committee Report of 1924–5; the McNair Report of 1944; and the James Report of 1972, together with a careful reading of annual government reports on education, supported a preliminary national mapping exercise. In addition, numerical data on teacher supply and demand, government expenditure on teacher professional development and any relevant data on numbers of teachers participating in courses, found in a piecemeal way across a range of different sources, were cross referenced and collated in an attempt to develop some sort of understanding of the scale of teacher involvement and the costs involved. Though flawed and incomplete, because of the partial nature of the material involved, this piece of analysis was a novel aspect of the study and is discussed further in Chapter Nine.

The UK National Archives at Kew were a rich source of material for the research and around 300 files, representing central government policy on teacher professional development, were consulted. These files were very varied in scope and content and included, for example: Inspectors Reports; different types of communications between civil servants and local authorities, teacher training colleges, universities and other organisations responsible for delivering professional development for teachers; case studies of new models of professional development; prospectuses and materials, local and national surveys; discussions with the Treasury over expenditure; administrative application forms and regulations related to specific training schemes; draft policy documents. The analysis of documents from the UK National Archives enriched the development of the case studies presented in Part Two of the book and also served to stimulate wider historical investigation on specific aspects of teacher professional development using different archives or materials.

Further archival work was conducted at the University of London, Institute of Education, Kings College London and the University of Bristol to develop a deeper understanding of special advanced courses for teachers. Sources included, for example, at the Institute of Education archive, the papers of the Centre for Child Development with annual reports on the Diploma in Child Development directed by Dorothy Gardner during the 1940s to the 1960s. Course prospectuses, programmes, marketing material as well as details of correspondence between Dorothy Gardner and the Ministry of Education during this period revealed much interesting information on the detail of this special advanced course and tensions surrounding its purpose, objectives and funding. Research at Jesus College Oxford, Devon County Record Office, Derby Record Office and the Bodleian Library, Oxford uncovered a range of different primary sources used to build the case study on the vacation course model, described in Chapter Two. Initially discovered in one single file at the National Archives, the City of London Vacation Course (CLVC) stimulated further investigation of the published press, including the *Teachers' World* and *The Times*. As is inevitably the case with historical inquiry of this nature, the research was heavily influenced by what sources were available and often frustrated by evidential gaps. This was particularly the case in the work on the CLVC. A new discovery for this book, and raising all sorts of interesting questions about early forms of privatised teacher professional development and concerns around central government control, this piece of research would have been substantively enriched should an organisational archive of the CLVC been available.

Documentary sources are fully referenced as they are used to illustrate specific themes throughout the book. Where possible, documents were photographed *in situ* (otherwise detailed notes were taken), stored electronically and then analysed and cross-referenced using a series of thematic codes which were developed iteratively during the early stages of data-collection at the National Archives, Kew and which were drawn from the research objectives.

The oral history research

The oral history part of the research reported in the book is both influenced by and will contribute to a growing field of research which has examined teachers' professional lives and practice through the lens of teacher memory, developed over the last two decades by such historians as Cunningham and Gardner in the UK and Altenbaugh and Rousmaniere in the US.[10] Oral histories of teachers' professional lives have emerged as part of a wider interest in the contribution of oral testimony to new forms of social history which seek to privilege the lives and experiences of 'ordinary' people, so often overlooked in standard top-down traditional historical sources. Over time, oral history approaches have come to be regarded as methodologically and epistemologically important in their own right, rather than as add-on embellishments to traditional forms of historical inquiry, which have depended largely on the written documentary record. Oral history approaches are becoming increasingly popular in the field of educational history.[11] There are a range of well-established principles associated with the purpose and practice of oral history, which the proposed study will utilise.[12] These include finding ways to access the sample; identifying willing participants; explaining the aims and outcomes of the project and gaining informed consent; designing a framework for the interviews; conducting, recording, transcribing, translating and analysing the oral history interviews.[13]

A total of 31 participants volunteered to take part in the project – a much larger number than the eighteen originally intended in the original project design. Participants were identified using a convenience and snowball sampling strategy and by disseminating information about the overall research project through various university alumni and other professional networks. Participants were either former teachers or professionals working in the field of teacher professional development. There were 21 women and ten men in the final sample. As a self-selecting group, this gender balance reflects the gender profile of the teaching profession during this period. Their professional roles variously included class teaching, senior management of schools, including departmental headships and overall headships, advisory teachers, inspectors, managers of different types of teacher professional development, particularly teachers' centres wardens. Though not designed to be a fully geographically or professionally representative sample, the spread of participants' professional experience spanned central, southern, eastern, northern and western regions of England, with a stronger bias towards the Midlands and the South West. The oldest participant in the project was born in 1925, though other participants were younger with career experiences mostly covering the late 1960s to the 1990s. Two participants were interviewed twice because their testimony was so rich. Interviews were conducted either in the participants' homes or in meeting rooms at a local university. Prior to interview, participants were given a briefing document which outlined the purpose of the project and described how the interviews would be conducted. At interview, participants were invited to sign an informed-consent form, following best-practice advised by the British Oral History Society, to ensure that they were clear about process, intellectual property and outcomes. Participants were invited to choose whether they wished to be named or anonymous in any follow-up work from the interviews. The majority of participants elected to be named and, indeed, were quite forthright in their wish to be named and formally associated with the research, with only five preferring to be anonymous. For the most part, real names have been used in the presentation of the data – but where pseudonyms are used this is indicated by a 'p' in brackets after the fictional name. Following the interview, participants were sent regular updates of project development, including a participants' newsletter and were offered a digital copy of their recorded interview. Interviews took place between November 2010 and November 2011.

In planning the oral history interviews, a series of broad key themes was identified to guide and prompt the discussion and presented as a mind map on one sheet of paper, with some questions identified against each theme. The themes included: a general overview of career history; professional development experience, identification of different models; motivation to engage in professional development; access to, funding and resourcing of professional development activity; impact and evaluation of professional development on practice; understanding of wider policy. This guide was used in a pilot interview and the first two full interviews. Following feedback from these participants, it was decided that the guide would only be used as an aide-memoire by the interviewer and not to be given to participants. Participant feedback suggested that providing this set of themes in advance worried or impeded them as they were concerned to try to respond to every single theme and question suggested. In reality the interviews were fairly open-ended and participants were invited to begin by recalling their own initial teacher training and their early career and to reflect on early career professional development opportunities. Each interview then followed its own particular path, led very much by the participant and by what the participant wanted to raise. The duration of the interviews varied from one to six hours, with the average interview lasting two hours. Once warmed to the process participants clearly valued the experience to reflect upon their professional development careers, and to have the stories of their professional practice, values and experiences listened to and deemed important for this research. For the majority, this was the first time that they had consciously reflected upon these professional experiences in a focussed way and in an interview context. The interview experience evoked memories of classrooms, colleagues, children, curriculum developments, courses, conferences, ambitions, opportunities, disappointments and career-long histories that for many had long been buried away in the recesses of the mind. It also enabled participants to make some important connections that they had not previously considered, between different stages of their careers, the role of significant professional colleagues in shaping professional development, relationships between personal and professional development and how all of this combined to reinforce their professional identities and values. Though the majority of participants were formally retired from their professional jobs, a surprising aspect of the study was to discover how many of them in retirement were still using their professional teaching skills and expertise in voluntary capacities and also engaging with professional learning in new and different forms, supporting the notion of life-long professional learning. Participants were generous with their time and with their memory. A number prepared for their interviews in advance by hunting out miscellaneous personal memorabilia from their career lives. These included personal Curriculum Vitaes; employment references; letters of application for jobs, which listed professional experience, job descriptions, certificates of attendance at courses; course programmes and materials; conference brochures. As artefacts to stimulate memory as well as provide a focus for discussion these memorabilia were important. Together with the oral history testimony and the plethora of documentary material accessed for the wider project these artefacts have contributed to a substantive archive of material related to the twentieth-century history of teacher professional development.

Moving from collecting the interview data to analysing and making sense of such a rich, detailed and complex set of individual oral histories posed some interesting methodological challenges. In particular, striking a balance between honouring and capturing the uniqueness of each participant's personal career story and a concern to make sense of inevitable similarities, patterns of experience and shared descriptions as they emerged not just from the oral history testimony but also to be contextualised against the wider historical record developed in the earlier stages of the project, required some careful consideration. A decision was taken to use a basic content analysis of the interviews to identify key themes and to use these to analyse all of the interviews as a complete data set. Recorded interviews were transcribed verbatim and a detailed coding framework based on a triangulated analysis of a sample of interview transcripts. Key themes and sub-themes were identified and through an iterative approach this coding framework was modified and refined so that it could be used to code the whole data set. In total 35 major themes, many of which are further sub-divided, were identified. This oral history study gave voice to a range of teachers and educational professionals who 'lived' the complex, diverse and constantly shifting world of teacher professional development as it developed in the second half of the twentieth century. In presenting the voice and experience of teachers engaged in professional development the work contributes to the growing field of oral history work with the teaching profession and the methodological development of using teachers' testimony as history and method.

ORGANISATIONAL STRUCTURE OF THE BOOK

The book is conceived in three main parts with nine chapters overall. Part One of the book, *Setting the Scene*, is concerned with providing an historical overview of the twentieth century development of teacher professional development. Following this chapter's brief rationale and methodology for the study, Chapter Two maps and reviews the national policy terrain of teacher professional development 1900–2000. Based on new documentary analysis and the consultation of key legislation, research studies, reports and central government policy, it will identify critical dates, phases and patterns of policy making and the ways in which central policy was disseminated and managed. It provides a broad framework of the development of different models of teacher professional development onto which greater detail are mapped in subsequent chapters.

Part Two of the book, *Chronological Case Studies*, offers three in-depth case studies to illustrate and evaluate different models of professional development provision across the century. In Chapter Three there is an examination of the vacation course model of professional development 1920–1940. By the end of the interwar years, there were a variety of models of in-service training being developed nationally, with residential summer vacation courses being a popular way of bringing groups of teachers together for professional, intellectual and personal 'refreshment' in the school holidays. This chapter examines and compares three types of vacation course: a Board of Education sponsored summer school at Derby Teacher Training College; A Welsh Education Office vacation course at the University of Oxford; and the City of London Vacation Course, an independent commercial venture organised by a leading educational publisher, Robert Evans. At a time when the nature of teacher professionalism was undergoing transformation, the vacation course model offered a new way of conceptualising the wider question of teacher status and identity and tensions between ideas of personal and professional improvement. In Chapter Four there is an analysis of the special advanced course for teachers 1945–60, which focussed on the idea of teacher secondment. In the post-war period, programmes of continued professional development became increasingly well-established. From 1948, the Ministry of Education began to fund 'special courses for experienced serving teachers', which allowed a relatively small, but selected group of teachers to take advanced courses in particular fields of education. This development coincided with the expansion of professional development programmes in university departments of education, with a focus on award-bearing Diplomas in Child Psychology, Infant Education, Special Needs Education and Special Subjects. These courses were aimed at teachers who were expected to take on positions of greater responsibility, either in schools as head teachers or as teacher trainers. This chapter examines the aims, objectives and content of special advanced courses for teachers at two leading institutions: The University of London, Institute of Education and the University of Bristol. It is also a model which embodies a number of perennial issues which have characterised the history of teacher professional development – namely the role and function of the universities; debates over the appropriate balance of academic theory and professional practice in teacher education and the relationship between the status of the teaching profession, the academic study of education and accredited higher qualifications for teachers. In Chapter Five there is a re-examination of the teachers' centre phenomenon. From the late 1960s to the late 1980s teachers' centres emerged as a popular focus for teacher professional development, bringing groups of teachers together from across a local area and offering a central forum and physical space in which teachers could access resources, meet together and engage in various professional courses. Energised by new directions in curriculum development, particularly through the work of the Schools Council, and responsive to ambitions of the 1972 James Report, the teachers' centre appeared to offer a promising new conceptualisation of professional learning. Regarded by some educationists as a distinctive 'movement' for democratic, practical and genuinely teacher-led professional development, but by others as incoherent, divisive and highly differentiated in terms of quality of provision, the teachers' centre phenomenon divided professional opinion. This chapter revisits the teachers' centre model and critically evaluates its contribution.

Part Three of the book, *Teachers' Reflections on Professional Development 1950–2000*, is devoted to oral history testimony from teachers and professional educators engaged in professional development from the 1960s to the present. Aside from the intrinsic novelty of presenting previously unheard stories and experiences of professional development from the perspective of participants in the process, this part of the book will draw together emerging themes already identified in earlier sections. These turn on those fundamental questions of teacher professional identity, notions of professional autonomy and regulation as well as the interplay between external demands and internal professional agency that lie at the very heart of the problem of teacher professional development today.

Chapter Six examines participants' experience of professional development in terms of their access to different types of provision throughout their careers. It considers how decisions were made about professional development, how professional development was funded and where and when it took place. It explores whether certain forms of professional development were favoured over others for different teachers at different stages. It also reflects on obstacles to teacher engagement with professional development as well as ways in which professional development was promoted. It identifies different models of provision as well as changing ideas about professional learning. Chapter Seven explores how the oral history participants viewed the impact of their professional development experiences. Currently, impact measures on pupil learning are seen as critical to successful teacher professional development, however difficult these are to evaluate and whether or not they are about enhanced teacher professional identity, capacity and expertise. This chapter seeks to evaluate the wider impact of professional development on individuals, in terms how they believed their professional behaviours and practices were changed as a result of their professional development experiences. It also looks at how teachers assessed their experiences of professional development and what purpose it served. Chapter Eight considers the relationship between the experience of professional development and ideas of professional identity, status and community. Chapter Nine draws together the main themes examined in the book and considers how these might inform current frameworks for teacher professional development as well as more general ideas about professional lifelong learning.

NOTES

[1] See for example: Bocko, H. (2004). 'Professional development and teacher learning: mapping the terrain', *Educational Researcher*, 33(8), 3–15, for a discussion of the United States context; Opfer, V., Pedder, D., & Lavicza, Z. (2008). *Schools and Continuing Professional Development (CPD) in England - State of the nation research project: A report for the Training and Dvelopment Agency for Schools.* London, UK: Training and Development Agency for Schools, for a recent English perspective; Timperley, H. (2008). *Teacher Professional Learning and Development: Best Evidence Synthesis Iteration.* Brussels: UNESCO/International Bureau of Education, for a comprehensive review of practice in the United States, New Zealand, Australia, The Netherlands and Israel; Musset, P. (2010). *Initial teacher education and continuing training policies in a comparative perspective: Current practices in OECD countries and a literature review on potential effects.* Paris: Organisation for Economic Co-operation and Development (hereafter, OECD).

[2] Neufeld, J. (2009). *Redefining teacher development.* London, UK: Routledge, preface.

[3] See for example: Hargreaves, A., & Fullan, M. (1992). *Understanding teacher development.* London, UK: Cassell; Hoyle, E., & John, P. (1995). *Professional knowledge and professional practice.* London, UK: Cassell; Day, C. (1999). *Developing teachers: The challenges of lifelong learning.* London, UK: Routledge Falmer; Evans, L. (2002). 'What is teacher development?', *Oxford Review of Education*, 28(1),123–137; Darling-Hammond, L., & Sykes, G. (Eds.). (2005). *Teaching as the learning profession: A handbook of policy and practice.* San Francisco, CA: Jossey-Boss; Day, C., & Sachs, J. (2005). *International handbook on the continuing professional development for teachers.* Milton Keynes: Open University Press.

[4] OECD, *Staying ahead: In-service training and teacher professional development* (Paris: OECD, 1998); OECD, *Teachers matter: Attracting, developing and retaining effective teachers* (Paris: OECD, 2005); OECD, (2009), *Teaching and learning international study* (Paris: OECD, 2009); OECD, *Building a High-quality teaching profession: Lessons from around the world, (Paris, OECD, 2011).*

[5] Department for Education and Science (hereafter DES), (1972). *Teacher education and training: A report by a committee of inquiry appointed by the secretary of state for education and science, under the chairmanship of Lord James of Rusholme.* London, UK: HMSO.

[6] For general historical studies of teaching, see for example: Jones, L. (1924). *The training of teachers in England and Wales: A critical survey.* Oxford, Oxford University Press; Rich, R. (1933). *The training of teachers in England and Wales during the nineteenth century.* Cambridge, Cambridge University Press; Tropp, A. (1957). *The school teachers* (London: William Heinmann Ltd; Gosden, P. (1972). *The evolution of a profession.* Oxford: Basil Blackwell; Dent, H. (1977). *The training of teachers in England and Wales 1800–1975* (London: Hodder and Stoughton; de Vroede, M. (1981). 'The History of Teacher Training', *History of education society bulletin*, 10(1), 1–8; Lawn, M. (1987). *Servants of the state: The contested control of teaching 1900–1930*, London, UK: The Falmer Press; Robinson, W. (2003). *Pupil teachers and their professional training in pupil teacher centres in England and Wales, 1870–1914.* New York, NY: Edwin Mellen Press; Robinson, W. (2004). *Power to teach: Learning through practice.* London, UK: RoutledgeFalmer; Gardner, P., & Cunningham, P. (2004).

Becoming Teachers: texts and testimonies 1907–1950. London, UK: Woburn Press; Robinson, W. (2008). 'Teacher education in England and Wales', in T. O'Donoghue & C. Whitehead (eds.) *Teacher education in the English speaking world: Past, present and future*. Charlotte, NC: Information Age, 45–61.

7   Recent exceptions include: Robinson, W. (2010). 'Revisiting teacher professional development: past and present models 1920–2008', *History of Education Researcher*, *85*, 28–34; Robinson, W. (2011). "That great educational experiment' the city of London vacation course in education 1922–1938: A forgotten story in the history of teacher professional development', *History of Education*, *40*(5), 557–575; Crook, D. (2011). 'In-service education and professional development for teachers in England: historical perspectives from the late twentieth century', *History of Education Researcher*, *87*, 4–12; Robinson, W., & Bryce, M. (2013). 'Capturing the 'Willing Enthusiasts' and 'Lame Ducks': Central government and the history of teacher professional development in England and Wales 1920–1975', *Paedagogica Historica*, *49*(3), 345–360.

8   British Academy Research Development Award 53026, 'Revisiting Teacher Professional Development: Past and Present Models, 1920–2008', February 2010- December 2012.

9   For a fuller discussion of the historical method in educational research see McCulloch, G., & Richardson, W. (2000). *Historical research in educational settings*. Buckingham: Open University Press.

10   Altenbaugh, R. (1992). *The teacher's voice: A social history of teaching in twentieth century America*. Lewes: Falmer Press; Rousmaniere, K. (1997). *City teachers: Teaching and school reform in historical perspective*. New York, NY: Teachers College Press; Gardner, P. (2003). 'Oral history in education : teacher's memory and teachers' history', *History of Education*, *32*(2), 175–188; Cunningham, P., & Gardner, P. *Becoming teachers: Texts and testimonies 1907–1950*; Robinson, W. *Power to teach*.

11   McCulloch, G., & Richardson, W. (2004). *Historical research in educational settings*; G. McCulloch, *Documentary research in Education, History and the Social Sciences*. London, UK: RoutledgeFalmer.

12   Humphries, S. (1984). *The handbook of oral history: Recording life stories*. London, UK: Inter-Action; Perks, R. (1998). *Oral history: Talking about the past*. London, UK: Historical Association and Oral History Society; Perks R., & Thomson, A. (Eds.). (1998). *The oral history reader*. London, UK: Routledge; Plummer, K. (2001). *Documents of life 2: An invitation to critical humanism*. London, UK: Sage; Thomson, P. (1988). *The voice of the past: Oral history*. Oxford: Oxford University Press.

13   Tonkin, E. (1992). *Narrating our pasts: The social construction of oral history*. Cambridge: Cambridge University Press.

NATIONAL POLICY MAPPING

INTRODUCTION

This chapter outlines the chronology of the national policy map of teacher professional development in England and Wales 1920–2000. It identifies the range of opportunities offered to serving teachers, largely through formal courses of various types and considers issues of funding, organisation, access and control. It also discusses the roles played by various stakeholders involved in the development of in-service provision for teachers, namely the Board of Education and its successor departments in government, His/Her Majesty's Inspectorate of Schools (HMI), Local Education Authorities (LEAs), and Area Training Organisations (ATOs). Based on new documentary analysis and the consultation of key legislation, research studies, reports and central government policy, the chapter will identify critical dates, phases and patterns of policy making and the ways in which central policy was disseminated and managed. As well as identifying and describing the various models available to teachers during the twentieth century, the chapter also aims to evaluate their broader significance, and to establish where there have been elements of continuity or change. The chapter will also focus on three milestone reports which shed further light on the changing nature of professional development opportunities training during this period: the Departmental Committee Report of 1924–5; the McNair Report of 1944; and the James Report of 1972. These three reports all resulted from committees set up by government to analyse various aspects of teacher education and to suggest improvements, and though all mainly concentrate on initial training, they also make important observations on and recommendations for the future development of in-service education.

Though precise periodization for this historical mapping is not realistic, given that so many of the models introduced in the early part of the century went on to shape future developments, albeit in different ways, four broad chronological phases have been identified, which form the shape of this chapter: initial development (1910–1945); consolidation (1945–60); challenge and expansion (1960–1979); privatisation and central control (1980–2000). Undoubtedly, by virtue of its evidence-base and its concern to map out a general overview of key developments from a central government perspective, this chapter presents a largely 'top-down' history. Whilst this is not, of course, the complete story of teacher professional development, which involved many other bodies including universities, training colleges, voluntary organisations, and special interest groups, the purpose of this broad policy overview is intended to act as a framework around which other, more detailed aspects of teacher professional development will be examined, either as case-studies in their own right, or as part of the experience and testimony of teachers, in the remainder of the book.

PHASE ONE: INITIAL DEVELOPMENT 1914–1945

This earliest phase saw the preliminary development of what was then known as in-service provision, organised and funded by central government and complementing other embryonic, though very ad hoc, forms of activity organised by voluntary bodies, professional associations, teacher unions and LEAs. The Board of Education began its interest in providing in-service training to teachers just before the First World War, though Dent has alluded to even earlier in-service opportunities in his brief historical overview of the period.[1] Initially the Board sought to limit its involvement to providing courses in areas where it considered the training opportunities provided by LEAs to be insufficient, and therefore particularly targeted its courses at teachers in isolated rural schools. What clearly emerged during this early phase was the idea of the short course, full-time and part-time for serving teachers, the vacation course and a modest scheme of funded studentships.

1914–1925

During the First World War the Board began to organise courses for teachers in technical schools aimed at improving their subject knowledge or craft skills. These courses were dropped for a time during the conflict, but were partially re-instated in 1915, and were supplemented in 1916 by a course in Modern Languages for secondary school teachers.[2] During the next few years, provision grew considerably. In 1918, for example, two courses were held, one in Advanced Dressmaking at Bournemouth Technical College, and the other in Needlework at St Anne's-on-the-Sea, on a full-time, short course basis during the summer vacation period.[3] This 'vacation school' model was typical of much of the Board's provision during the 1920s and 1930s, with teachers gathering for intensive residential summer schools for two or sometimes three weeks, and will be discussed in further detail in Chapter Three. As well as these full-time courses, the Board also organised some part-time courses from 1918, again in Needlework and Dressmaking, held in five cities across the country at the beginning of the year.[4] In 1918, 70 teachers attended the full-time courses and 96 their equivalent part-time versions. From the outset these courses assumed co-operation between the Board and the LEAs, which were relied upon to provide facilities and accommodation. In the summer of 1919, fifteen vacation courses were held for teachers in secondary schools.[5] These courses each focused on a particular subject and were held in grammar and public schools, including Eton, Rugby and Cheltenham, as well as at various teacher training colleges. A total of 684 teachers were selected to attend these courses, from 1,550 applicants – figures which suggest that such courses were oversubscribed and popular with some teachers.

New courses were offered in 1919 for elementary school teachers, but differed from those provided for their secondary school counterparts as they were held for a fortnight in term-time, and required teachers to be selected for attendance in consultation with LEAs. Three of these courses were held, with one at Stratford-on-Avon focused on History, and two focused on Geography held at Matlock and Saffron Walden, with a total of 121 participants. In a later review of the development of in-service training, the Board identified these courses as having been aimed specifically at teachers in isolated rural elementary schools *'who would find it difficult to keep in touch with modern developments or to exchange ideas with other members of their profession.'*[6] The Board seemed keen to stress the success of these courses, and noted that in one (unspecified) LEA teachers who had attended the courses later arranged meetings at which they would pass on information about new teaching methods, again suggesting an appetite amongst teachers for further training and discussion about their work.[7] This might be seen as an early example of what came to be known and widely accepted as the 'cascade' model of professional development in which selected teachers in receipt of any formal training would be responsible for sharing and disseminating their new knowledge to fellow teachers.[8] Generally, these courses focussed either on specific subject knowledge for secondary teachers or particular craft skills for elementary school teachers, with Physical Training, Arts and Crafts, Music, Rural Subjects and the teaching of 'mentally deficient' children being popular. For this period teaching methods appear to have been of secondary importance, thought these were sometimes examined as part of wider subject knowledge. Courses were staffed with a combination of HMI, teacher training college lecturers and other specialists. The dominant mode of delivery was the lecture, followed by some informal discussion between teachers and there was strong support for the idea that teacher from different schools and possibly different areas would benefit from networking with each other.

By 1924 the Board of Education claimed that the reason why it wished to expand its programme of in-service training was their popularity with teachers and a firm impression that there was a strong professional need and interest.[9] However, this period in the mid-1920s also corresponded with the wider challenging economic crisis of the time. Financial stringency which characterised government spending on education following the recommendations of the Geddes Committee on National Expenditure, aimed at limiting public spending, slowed down any planned expansion of courses.[10] By 1925 though, six courses were held at Oxford and Cambridge Universities for elementary school teachers with 256 attendees; nineteen courses were held for secondary school teachers, with 767 attendees from over 2,000 applicants; and eight full-time courses, five weekend courses and nine part-time courses were held for teachers in technical and evening schools, with nearly 800 attendees in all for these.[11]

Courses were open to teachers from across England and Wales, but there also existed a separate category of courses open only to teachers in Wales and aimed at specific issues in Welsh education. These were organised by the Welsh Department of the Board of Education, which had been established in 1907, and came to focus on issues surrounding Welsh Language teaching and Welsh History, Literature and Rural Lore.[12] The first of these courses, organised in 1922, was a Welsh Literature course held first at Bangor, and later at Swansea, and was attended there by 36 teachers in 1924, whilst the Welsh Rural Lore courses were held at Jesus College, Oxford, and attended by 42 teachers in the same year.[13] These will also be discussed in greater detail in Chapter Three.

These figures, however, only show the numbers of teachers attending courses organised by the Board of Education and do not include the other strata of provision organised by LEAs and voluntary associations and interest groups. By 1925 the Board recognised that provision of in-service training was complex and multi-stranded in nature with LEAs and other providers, running various part-time classes held in the evenings or on Saturday mornings, as well as organising short full-time courses during the summer vacation period.[14] The numbers of teachers recorded as having attended courses organised by LEAs and others are, not surprisingly perhaps, significantly larger than those who attended centrally organised Board of Education courses, with 30,000 teachers in England and 1,600 in Wales said to have attended part-time courses in the 1924–5 academic year, whilst the numbers for full-time courses were 1,900 and 450 respectively. Evidently the courses organised at a local level were largely provided to meet local needs, and the Board itself identified them as being aimed at the majority of teachers, in public elementary schools. The Board's own courses, therefore, were supposed to be aimed at meeting the needs of other groups of teachers, such as those in secondary or technical schools, or those teachers in isolated rural schools where provision of training from other sources was bound to be more limited.[15]

During the 1920s, the Board of Education also funded a programme of Studentships which allowed serving teachers to undertake either full- or part-time study. Initially, this programme was open solely to science teachers and the full-time awards were tenable only at the Imperial College of Science and Technology, London, whilst part-time awards could be held at other Universities or University Colleges and was the continuation of a scheme which had originated under the Science and Art Department in the nineteenth century.[16] However, from 1921 onwards, the programme was extended to teachers of any subject.[17] Awards were normally for one year only, but were in some cases renewed for another year.[18] Teachers arranged their own application to the university of their choice and had to have been accepted before submitting their application for a Studentship to the Board of Education.[19]

From 1921, full-time awards were available for teachers wishing to undertake a year of study or research at a university or other institutions of university rank, either in the UK or abroad.[20] Full-time awards were aimed at teachers '...*of some experience, normally not less than seven years...*', and that they were intended to allow teachers to pursue post-graduate study or research.[21] Training College Inspectors were specifically targeted to draw the attention of training college lecturers to apply, and the restriction of the awards to those following post-graduate courses of study, suggests that full-time Studentships of this type would have been largely restricted to graduate training college staff or those teaching in secondary schools, as the number of graduates working in elementary schools was very limited in the 1920s, though this began to change during the 1930s.[22] Information about what types of schools successful applicants for Studentships came from is not available for every year during the period, but the Annual Reports of the Board of Education for 1928 and 1929 do contain this information, and show that of twelve full-time awards made in the first of those years, ten were to teachers in secondary schools, one to a training college lecturer and one to an elementary school teacher; in 1929, seventeen awards were made, of which eleven went to secondary school teachers, four to elementary school teachers and two to teachers in technical schools.[23]

Those awarded a full-time Studentship by the Board of Education were eligible for funding of up to £100, with the exact amount dependent upon an assessment of the individual teacher's circumstances, as well as the length and nature of their course of study.[24] The maximum amount of funding was increased to £200 in 1937/1938.[25] Even when aided by Studentship funding from the Board of Education, undertaking a full-time course of study could necessitate considerable personal sacrifice by a teacher. The Board of Education did not recognise for grant any salary for these teachers during their sabbatical period, and it was left to the LEA to decide if any payment would be made to the teacher under such conditions – therefore, teachers applying for Studentships could be giving up their salaries and pensionable service for the period.[26]

There were, however, also advantages to the scheme for those teachers awarded Studentships. The course of study was their own choice, and so represented an opportunity to pursue subjects of personal academic interest, and the chance to study abroad was a significant aspect of the Studentship programme, of which many of those awarded took advantage. Amongst the countries where teachers studied during the interwar years were France, Germany, Italy, and the United States.[27] Topics included a study of 'the working of the United States Federal Vocational Law', and a study of 'Psychiatric Education' at Columbia University New York.[28] In some instances, the 'investigations' or research carried out by teachers was deemed by the Board to be of wider interest, with a joint report produced by two secondary school teachers who had investigated Physical Education in Denmark and Sweden having been published by the Board as Number 104 in its series of Educational Pamphlets.[29] The focus on the importance of Physical Education during this period perhaps also impacted upon this decision, and saw funding given to another teacher in 1937 to enable them to travel to Czechoslovakia, Denmark and Finland to study Physical Training there.[30] The Board also requested reports be written in other 'appropriate cases', including those where the subjects of study had been '... *Vocational Training in the United States of America, the teaching of Domestic Subjects in Denmark and the Netherlands, and Industrial Administration and Works Management in England.*'[31]

As well as offering funding to some teachers who selected their own subjects of study, the Board of Education also sometimes used the Studentship scheme to pursue its own agenda. In 1933, for instance, from a total of fifteen new awards made, eight were for teachers of building subjects in technical schools and colleges in order to enable to attend a specific course at Imperial College, which had been arranged there in co-operation with the Board itself '*for the purpose of disseminating among teachers and others a knowledge of the results of modern scientific research in building...*'.[32] There was also a very small scheme of part-time Studentships which allowed teachers to continue to work in their schools on a day release model.[33] The conditions for part-time awards were different to those for full-time Studentships, as teachers were allowed to use this funding to pursue undergraduate courses, and were not required to have as much experience in teaching, and the funding would pay up to three-quarters of the cost of the course they were to study, rather than being limited to a set amount.[34] This type of award still necessitated some financial contribution from the teacher themselves. It was expected by the Board that these awards would be made to teachers who would need to spend no more than a day or half a day per week out of school in order to attend university.[35] Although the part-time Studentships were awarded to increasing numbers of teachers throughout the 1920s, in 1927 funding for new part-time awards was halted, and never resumed. The explanation given for this by the Board of Education was that its priority was to increase the numbers of full-time awards and that, as the amount of funding for the whole Studentship programme was strictly limited, focusing on full-time awards necessarily meant decreasing spending on the part-time aspect of the programme.[36] In 1927, the Board also set out to publicise the full-time awards more widely in order to attract more applicants, an approach which the Annual Reports for 1928 and 1929 suggested had had the desired effect.[37] As well as bringing an end to the part-time awards, the limited amount of money available for Studentships meant that some process of selection was in place as the Board of Education had to decide which teachers would receive funding, however it is not known how the Board decided between candidates who met all the criteria set out in the regulations.[38] That the Board of Education set out to attract more applicants to the Studentship programme suggests that the scheme was considered to have some merit and significance. The full-time awards represented the pinnacle of continued professional development efforts for teachers during this period in the 1920s and 1930s, particularly as they offered teachers the opportunity to spend a lengthy period abroad and also gave some the chance to pursue independent research. The subjects of study suggest a mixed focus, with some aimed at acquiring further subject knowledge and others – perhaps the majority – addressing some aspect of teaching practice or theory.

By the early 1920s there were a number of models of in-service training in operation, including the full-time short courses normally held in the summer vacation period, and part-time courses held in evenings and weekends. Whilst in some cases teachers were released from their duties for courses during term-time, the vast majority of opportunities required the teacher to give up some of his or her free time to attend. Access to courses seems also to have been decided by selection either by the Board or by an LEA, and the Board's figures suggest that demand for its courses outweighed supply. In all, the picture by 1925 is one of increasing provision, but still on a somewhat ad-hoc basis, with courses and locations changing from year to year. It was at this point that a Departmental Committee on the training of teachers was set up to consider the entire system of teacher recruitment, supply and training. For the first time, in-service training for teachers was exposed to public policy scrutiny and it is worth considering its recommendation for in-service training as a significant moment in the history of teacher professional development.

The 1924–5 Departmental Report

In 1923, Edward Wood, then President of the Board of Education, established a Departmental Committee under the leadership of Lord Burnham, by then already famed for the new pay scales for teachers which came to bear his name, and gave its members the task of reviewing the existing arrangements for the training of teachers for Public Elementary Schools and considering what changes might be made to this system in order to secure an adequate supply of well-qualified teachers for these schools in the future.[39] The Committee took submissions of evidence and interviewed witnesses from a wide range of backgrounds, including representatives from LEAs, training colleges, universities, teachers' associations, as well as staff from the Board itself.[40] The Committee delivered its report in 1925 to Wood's successor at the Board, Lord Eustace Percy and, though it focused mainly on securing a supply of entrants to the teaching profession and their initial training, it did make some notable statements about the desirability and possible future direction of in-service training.

The report's major concern was to secure an adequate supply of entrants to the teaching profession. It traced the history of teaching in elementary schools and noted that until the early years of the twentieth century it remained common – indeed expected – that most entrants to elementary school teaching would come through the pupil-teacher or student-teacher systems and would themselves have little, if any, education beyond that offered in the elementary schools prior to entry to a training college.[41] These teachers were also drawn from what was termed by the Report as the 'less well-to-do' social classes. The complex history of initial teacher education in England and Wales has been developed in the author's own earlier work and that of Phil Gardner and Peter Cunningham.[42] In essence, the 1925 Departmental Committee Report wanted teachers to have experienced a fuller secondary education before initial training and favoured the expansion of the profession through more middle-class, educated recruits. Regarding in-service training specifically, it stated that all the witnesses consulted favoured the provision of facilities for teachers which would help to '...*maintain and supplement their interests and efficiency...*'[43] Recommendations from the Report identified two major needs which in-service training should seek to meet: firstly, to refresh subject knowledge and learn new developments, and to improve teaching techniques and introduce new methods; secondly, to have a generally positive effect '*upon the teacher's mind and outlook*'.[44] Enshrined within the first of these two purposes for in-service training is the relationship between subject knowledge acquisition and professional skills training which has been identified as being at the heart of much dispute about the purpose of initial teacher training during the late nineteenth and early twentieth centuries. The Committee had already suggested that initial training courses should shift towards a greater emphasis on professional skills, so it is interesting that it advocated in-service provision which contained both of the elements. This was probably due to recognition of the fact that many practicing elementary teachers at this time would have come through the pupil-teacher system and would therefore not have had a high level of personal education before entering the profession.

The second purpose foreseen for in-service training is somewhat more abstract, and idealistic, and arose from a view of teaching which believed that repeating the same work year after year could '...*dull the teacher with it monotony and narrow his interests.*'[45] Here, the Departmental Committee touched upon another strand of thought about teaching which held that the very repetitious nature of the job was bound to lead to some deterioration in the teacher's enthusiasm over time, perhaps exacerbated by the isolated locales and rural communities in which some teachers found themselves. Supplementary courses of training could, therefore, represent an opportunity for teachers to refresh their interest in their craft by acquiring new knowledge, studying new methods, and by exchanging ideas and experiences with their peers.

In a survey of existing in-service provision, the Departmental Committee identified short courses organised by the Board of Education, as well as short summer courses organised by universities, LEAs, and other bodies, and also noted that some LEAs ran part-time courses, and mentioned private lecture courses in London and other large cities.[46] Notably, the report stated that large numbers of teachers applied to practically all holiday courses showing that these were very popular, but went on to argue that supplementary courses should not only be offered during teachers' holidays, and but that those that were should not take up too much of the teachers' free time.[47] In suggesting an extension of term-time courses, the Committee wrote that LEAs, universities and training colleges should organise as many such courses as possible on any subjects relating to elementary school teaching and that attendees at such courses, provided it was approved by the Board, should receive their full pay and pension entitlements for the duration of the training.[48] Such courses, it went on, might extend over a term, or for a period of for three to six weeks, and that in some cases individual teachers might even be granted a leave of absence for a year.

The Departmental Committee also made particular recommendations for the in-service training of teachers in rural schools who were already the focus of special attention from the Board of Education.[49] Referring to a suggestion made by witnesses from the Ministry of Agriculture, the report suggests that LEAs should organise 'progressive' supplementary courses over two or three years, or individual teachers should be given the opportunity to undertake advanced study of the science of horticulture or agriculture.

Interestingly, the Departmental Committee report looked forward to a time when attendance at supplementary courses for teachers might become compulsory and when '*arrangements for all teachers to attend them at regular intervals of a few years will have become part of the national system of education.*'[50] Considering the limited extent of in-service provision in 1925, and the variety of provision from one LEA to the next, this statement of intent seems quite radical. The idea of teachers undertaking a period of in-service training periodically throughout their careers is one which would recur later, as would some other issues raised in this report, such as the balance between professional skills and subject study within training. Though the report's discussion of in-service training is only a few pages long, it is clear that it was a matter which had been given serious consideration by the Committee and which it was felt should play a role in future in the long-term development of the teaching profession.

Post-1925 Developments

Following the publication of the 1925 Report, the Board continued to add new courses to those it already provided, including in 1926 a full-time course for teachers in Schools of Art and Art classes, which was attended by 57 teachers, drawn from 92 applicants, and a course for teachers of 'physically deficient' children. The latter course was during the autumn term in order to enable visits to special schools, and was run in conjunction with the Central Committee for the Care of Cripples.[51] Another course was held in London for teachers of 'mentally deficient' children, and was attended by 40 teachers, drawn from 128 applicants.[52] The Central Committee for the Care of Cripples was not the only special interest group to interest itself in the provision of in-service training to teachers during this period. A number of other such groups offered courses for teachers, either in conjunction with the Board of Education or of their own accord. More examples of those working with the Board included the National Association for the Prevention of Infant Mortality, which offered a course in 1929 for 'women teachers of older girls', specifically aimed at those who taught in elementary schools in urban areas, and the Central Association for Mental Welfare, which offered three courses for teachers of 'mentally retarded' children in the same year.[53] Significantly, employers and employers' associations were also sometimes involved in providing training or training facilities for teachers, particularly those in technical schools, suggesting a desire on their behalf to ensure that particular skills were transmitted to school children via their teachers, and perhaps in the hope that particular occupations would also be promoted. In 1933, for instance, a 'refresher' course was held over three or four days for teachers of boot and shoe manufacture, for which facilities were provided by a firm of manufacturers.[54] This course was seemingly repeated in 1934, when a more detailed report by the Board located it at Mansfield, in Nottinghamshire, traditionally a centre of shoe manufacture, and again noted the involvement of a local firm, though it also states the course was attended by teachers from around the country.[55] In 1937, a course for teachers in technical schools and evening institutes, focusing on radio-servicing, was organised in conjunction with the Radio Manufacturers' Association.[56]

Throughout the 1920s and 1930s, a number of different models of course continued to be offered by the Board of Education – and by LEAs and other providers – and there is evidence that different types of course served to meet different needs. Weekend 'refresher courses' for elementary teachers became popular, with 26 organised during 1929 as a result of co-operation between LEAs, which made the arrangements for them, and HMI, who directed the lectures and discussions during the courses.[57] These courses were aimed at '...*widening the teachers' interest in one or more aspects of their work*', through lectures from experts, with teachers travelling some distance to attend, for example from Middlesex to Oxford, and from Birmingham to Llandudno.[58] These particular courses, therefore, do seem to have been intended to fulfil one of the aims set out for in-service training by the Departmental Committee Report of 1925, by removing teachers from their normal school routines and presenting them with an opportunity to re-engage with their subjects on a different level than day-to-day teaching might allow, and to meet their peers. Indeed, the Board also stressed that the opportunity for discussion amongst teachers and inspectors offered by such courses was '*becoming an important element in the general educational life of the country.*'[59] Of course, it is very likely that many of these courses for teachers would have offered invigorating opportunities for discussions and exchange of ideas, as recognised by Lord Eustace Percy, President of the board of Education between 1924–1929, in his memoirs in which he referred to 'the freedom of discussion' which he had encountered both at local conferences and at the Board's summer courses held at Oxford and Cambridge.[60]

In 1937, particular consideration was given to the provision of additional full-time, longer courses to meet the needs of teachers of older children in reorganised infant/junior schools.[61] The Board's desire that such longer courses should be organised was issued in Circular 1453, in March 1937, which invited LEAs to indicate to what extent they would support such courses by releasing teachers to attend them, and proposed that where teachers were released from their duties for this purpose, the Board would recognise their salaries for grant purposes for up to three months.[62] Furthermore, teachers taking part in such courses would be treated as having worked normally for pension purposes. The Board reported a positive response to this appeal to LEAs and, despite the limited time available to organise them, ten courses were started for the 1937 autumn term: four in Physical Training, two each for men and women, held at training colleges; four in Arts and Crafts, one held at an art school for both men and women, and the rest at training colleges for women; and two in Music at training colleges for women.[63] Such courses were to run for one term or three months and in 1938 over 700 teachers were released by 150 LEAs to attend them.[64]

By the end of the interwar years then, there were a variety of models of in-service training being offered by the Board of Education and LEAs, with fortnight-long summer schools remaining popular, alongside part-time and weekend courses, and the newer model of term-long courses being introduced. In total, in 1938, there were 270 full-time short courses of which 51 were organised by the Board itself, 136 by LEAs, and 83 by other bodies.[65] These courses were attended by a total of 7,487 teachers, of whom 3,362 were men and the remainder women. There were more of these courses focused on practical subjects, such as Domestic Subjects (21 courses), Handwork (52), and forms of Physical Training (77), than there were for 'academic' subjects such as English (2), History and Geography (7), or Mathematics (2). There were also 1,438 part-time courses organised, of which three were organised by other bodies and the remainder by LEAs, which were attended by 46,618 teachers, just over 12,000 of whom were men. As already mentioned, just over 700 teachers attended the new term-long courses, of which there were 42 organised in 1938 in Physical Training, Arts and Crafts, Music, Rural Subjects, and 'the teaching of retarded children.' These figures clearly show that by the end of the interwar period, the Board of Education was limiting its direct involvement in the organisation of training for serving teachers to providing full-time short courses, in keeping with its longstanding policy of only offering courses where it felt shortages or particular need existed, whilst LEAs and others provided more varied opportunities. The Second World War represented a period of considerable disruption for all educational provision, as for other areas of civilian life, as many male teachers joined the armed forces and many schoolchildren and their teachers found themselves evacuated to rural areas. In such circumstances, it is no surprise that the organisation of in-service teacher training also suffered as the normal programme of courses was suspended for the duration of the conflict.[66] It is interesting to note, however, that where there were very modest new initiatives in in-service training, these reflected some of the contemporary political concerns highlighted by the War – such as in a programme of special short courses for teachers focusing on American History, aimed at promoting a positive view of the United States, along with others focusing on the USSR and the British Empire, all held during 1942 and 1943.[67]

PHASE TWO: MCNAIR AND THE CONSOLIDATION OF EXISTING MODELS 1945–1960

The second main phase in the development of teacher professional development, following World War Two, represented a modest expansion and consolidation of earlier models of provision – but broadly followed a similar pattern. The normal programme of in-service training was re-instated on a limited scale in 1945 and grew steadily in subsequent years.[68] Foregrounding this period of expansion was the second of the key milestone government reports which addressed the general issue of teaching and teacher education – the McNair Report of 1944. This Report was part of a suite of significant policy developments which emerged in the post-war period and which went on to shape the education system for much of the rest of the century. The 1944 Education (Butler) Act had replaced the old Board of Education with a Ministry, divided education between primary (ages 5–11) and secondary

(11–15) phases, and created a free system of differentiated secondary education for all children, based on ability and aptitude. In the context of these radical policy developments came the recommendations of the 1944 McNair Report, 'Teachers and Youth Leaders'.[69] Broader in scope than the earlier 1925 Departmental Committee report, it looked at issues surrounding the supply and training of teachers for all types of maintained schools, including elementary (which it shifted to describing as primary schools, in keeping with the incoming system), secondary schools, as well as technical and arts schools. A detailed history of McNair and teacher education during the post-war period can be found in the work of David Crook.[70]

The most significant proposal from this report in relation to teacher professional development was the idea of setting up Area Training Authorities, which would eventually come into being as ATOs. McNair recommended that the organisation of teacher education be reformed in order to cope with the training of the greater number of teachers it predicted would be necessary once the education system changed.[71] It also advocated '...*the integration, on an area basis, of the institutions which are to be responsible for the education and training of teachers*', though opinion amongst its members was divided as to the best way to organize this, and so two schemes were proposed.[72] The major aim of both schemes was to promote closer co-operation between the various providers of training for teachers, particularly training colleges and universities, in a way which the existing Joint Examination Board system was felt to have failed to do.[73] The first proposal, known as the 'University Schools of Education scheme', sought to place greater responsibility for teacher education in the hands of the universities through the organisation of schools of education which would bring together the various training institutions in an area under the supervision of a named university.[74] The second scheme proposed by members of the McNair Committee was for an enhanced 'Joint Board Scheme', under which universities and other institutions would also work in co-operation with each other to provide training services, but within which training colleges would maintain their separate identities and would not become subject to university authority.[75] The major difference between the two proposals, therefore, centred on the exact level of integration and the question of training colleges' independence, but there were also significant similarities. Both schemes aimed to enhance the role played by the universities, and both sought to avoid any centralised control of teacher education and training, arguing that whilst there should be a central body to oversee the implementation of the new system, its actual operation and administration should be carried out on an area basis. Eventually, the ATOs organised between 1947 and 1951 were a modified version of the 'schools of education scheme', and saw universities establishing new institutes of education.[76]

Though its overall scope is broader, and its proposals for reorganising the provision of teacher education obviously significant, the McNair Report contained fewer direct references to in-service training than had the earlier Departmental Committee Report. In describing the state of in-service training provision at the time, the McNair Report stated that it was not organised on a '*systematic*' basis, and that the availability of courses was '*by no means equal to the demand.*'[77] Some of its recommendations were direct echoes of those made by the earlier committee – for example the idea that teachers should be able to take sabbatical periods in order that they might undertake further study, which the McNair Report states had not been introduced in any systematic way despite much discussion, and argues that they should be so as to allow the possibility for teachers to take a term or more as sabbatical leave on full pay once they had taught for five years.[78] The existence of the studentships offered by the Board, which offered something of an opportunity for further study to teachers, was noted by the Committee, but their report states that the money available to fund these awards had never been more than £1,500 per year, with each award being worth up to £200 by this stage.[79]

Also in common with the earlier report, McNair expressed real concerns about the '*narrow life*' of teachers, arguing that the institutional nature of life in school could be repetitive and limiting.[80] In recommending sabbatical terms, it argued that it was necessary to make the life of the teacher more '*attractive*', and though it also states that '*not all teachers or perhaps even most teachers wholly lose their freshness*' after long service, it endorsed a view that there was a danger that teachers would cease to work at '*maximum capacity*' after a number of years of continuous teaching.[81]

Regarding the organisation of in-service training, McNair suggested that courses should not be limited to vacation periods, again echoing the earlier report. It was also critical of the fact that the situation had not much changed since 1925, as many courses were still held in the school vacations, particularly during the summer, in spite of the development of a few longer term-time courses.[82] McNair also offered an intriguing suggestion that teacher education should come to be seen as consisting of two parts – one being initial training, and other made up of training undertaken after a period spent working as a practising teacher. It was suggested that a person would not become fully qualified as a teacher until they had undertaken both stages of this training. This was deemed to be '*an ideal to be kept in mind*', and could be argued to be a basis for future discussions about the role of an induction period for newly qualified teachers which was introduced much later on, following the James Report of 1972.[83] McNair also noted that the recruitment of a large number of extra teachers via emergency training schemes, just then being introduced in 1944, would mean that those entering the profession in this way would certainly need further training.[84] However, in terms of specific proposals regarding in-service training, McNair Report had little to say beyond its recommendation of sabbatical terms after five years' service, other than a rather general appeal to the Board of Education to ensure that staffing and funding would allow HMI to take part in more short courses, and that generous grants-in-aid were available for courses run by area training authorities and other approved bodies.[85]

Developments Following McNair

The new Ministry of Education began to offer a limited version of the pre-war programme of in-service training courses in 1945 and, in 1946, operated a full programme which considerably expanded on that offered in 1938, with 77 full-time short courses.[86] The programme was developed even further in 1947 with 119 courses being offered for which 14,000 applications were received and which 7,000 teachers then attended.[87] Courses were held in most curriculum subjects, though one course – held for teachers of French in Paris – was reported to have attracted the most enthusiastic response from teachers.[88] In 1948, three courses were held in Paris, with one again being for French teachers whilst the other two catered for teachers of Science and History, and in total 192 successful applicants attended them, from a pool of nearly 900.[89] The number of courses which the Ministry organised abroad gradually increased during the early 1950s, with the addition of a course for Spanish teachers held in Madrid for the first time in 1953 and a course focused on the language, history and culture of Austria held in Vienna in 1954.[90]

As in the interwar years, full-time short courses were not the only model of in-service training which the Ministry supported. In 1947, it also introduced a special one-year course for uncertificated teachers with at least five years' service, the successful completion of which would lead to them becoming recognised as fully qualified teachers.[91] Applications for these courses were received from 1,994 teachers, of whom just 131 were men, with 444 being accepted, of whom 58 were men. The successful applicants, who were apparently selected according to the length of their service with places given in this first year to men with at least fourteen years' experience and women with thirteen and a half years or more experience, would follow courses in training colleges. One former emergency training college was entirely given over to this type of course, accepting around 200 of the enrolled teachers, whilst the remainder were spread amongst permanent training colleges in groups of around twenty, where they were expected to take a full part in the general life of the college whilst following a course specially devised for their circumstances.[92]

From 1948, the Ministry also began to offer what it termed 'special courses for experienced serving teachers', which allowed a small number of teachers to take advanced courses in particular fields of education, and for which only teachers who were deemed likely to achieve 'more responsible posts', such as training college lectureships, were eligible.[93] These courses were to last for a year, and those taking them were granted unspecified financial assistance towards tuition and maintenance costs. These courses in some way replaced the studentships which the Board of Education had awarded to serving teachers in the 1920s and 1930s to allow them to undertake further studies, and which had not been revived after the Second World War and are discussed in detail in Chapter Four. The Welsh Department also continued to organise separate courses for teachers in Wales and, by 1954, was offering a programme of one year supplementary courses as well as its course in Welsh language and literature, though this was now held in Aberystwyth rather than Oxford.[94] Other short courses and non-residential one day courses were also held, organised through collaboration between HMI and LEAs.[95]

PHASE THREE: CHALLENGE AND EXPANSION 1960–1980

The third phase, which gathered momentum during the 1960s and 1970s, represented a somewhat tumultuous period, when significantly increased demand for new forms of teacher professional development exposed serious deficiencies in existing provision. The 1960s witnessed substantial change in education generally. New developments in Science teaching, as well as an overhaul of other curriculum areas, the development of the Nuffield Science Project, the establishment of the Schools Council, revised General Certificate of Education (GCE) and Certificate of Secondary Education (CSE) examinations, planning for the raising of the school leaving age to sixteen years, as well as comprehensive school reorganisation, combined to create a real need for the modernisation of teacher professional development. The existing model of short courses with a restricted advanced level programme was found wanting – it simply did not cater for enough teachers and was not sufficiently geared to the immediate updating required. Behind the scenes the Department set up special advisory groups and commissioned numerous surveys to try to get a clear sense of what was already going on and what needed to be done – to rethink a national strategy for provision.

Circular 7/64, issued in May 1964, outlined the government's intention to significantly expand teacher professional development through a massive increase in short courses and a new programme of long and short advanced level courses.[96] Science-based training was prioritised.[97] It also envisaged that all local and regional providers of short courses for teachers would review their provision in order to ensure that they would meet future demand. The Department, meanwhile, had introduced into its own programme of short courses in 1964 five higher level courses which were intended to focus on teaching techniques and new subject matter. These courses were attended by 260 teachers and addressed Mathematics in the context of the CSE, the teaching of Modern Physics, English in secondary modern schools, Religious and Moral education for older secondary pupils, and contemporary trends in thought and practice in primary schools.[98] This year also saw a conference being held for science teachers taking part in the Nuffield Foundation's science teaching project, which dealt with the new materials to be used in Biology, Physics and Chemistry classes.[99] Short courses also continued to be held abroad, with courses in Paris, Madrid, Rome, and Oslo.[100]

In 1965, the expansion of in-service training provision by the Department heralded by Circular 7/64 the previous year began to take effect, with the number of one-year courses increasing from 156 in 1964–65 to 185 in 1965–66, attended by 1,685 teachers.[101] There were also 42 term-time courses, up from seventeen the previous year, attended by 333 teachers. By 1967, the Department was keen to ascertain more facts about the provision and extent of in-service training and two national surveys were commissioned.[102] The first, conducted internally by the Statistics Division of the Department's Planning Branch, compiled information on all courses offered to serving teachers in England and Wales during the period 1/09/1966 – 31/08/1967.

The second, carried out by the University of Manchester's School of Education involved the distribution and analysis of detailed questionnaires to ten thousand teachers.[103]

The Department continued to expand its programme of training for serving teachers throughout the later years of the 1960s, and also continued to offer a range of different types of courses. In 1968, in addition to the one year courses for experienced serving teachers discussed already, there were also one year courses designated as 'special educational treatment', (38 courses, 562 students), one year supplementary courses (39 courses, 321 students), and one year courses in Russian (2 courses, 26 students).[104] However, the Department's Annual Report gives no further information about these courses, though we might assume that the provision of courses in Russian reflects the importance of that language during the Cold War. For the next decade the question of teacher professional development exercised government and issues of access, reach, timing, availability, control and entitlement, all of which had been raised in earlier phases, came under intense scrutiny. This culminated in the James Report of 1972 which represented a significant landmark in this history, recommending that ongoing in-service training should form an integral part of every teacher's career and proposing, like McNair, paid sabbaticals for teachers.

In common with the previous two milestone reports, the members of the James Committee – who included head teachers, a Chief Education Officer, a training college principal, and the Dean of a University Faculty of Education – took submissions of evidence from a variety of interested parties, including ATOs, training colleges, universities, and teachers' associations.[105] The report recommended that significant changes should be made to the way in which teachers were educated and trained, not just before their employment but also throughout their careers. The system envisaged by James consisted of three 'cycles' in a teaching career: cycle one was to be the intending teacher's higher education; cycle two was to encompass their initial teacher training and their induction into teaching; and cycle three was to be in-service training. James recommended that in future, intending teachers '...should have already achieved a good standard in higher education' before embarking upon a course of teacher training.[106] This did not, however, mean that the Committee was pushing for a move to an all graduate teaching profession, though it was expected and intended that some – particularly those aiming to become subject specialists – would hold degrees, as the Committee also advocated other forms of higher education as being appropriate for entrants to the profession.[107] In particular, the James Committee advocated the development of a Diploma in Higher Education, which would take the form of a two year course, combining some general and some more specialist studies, which intending teachers could take instead of a degree.[108] The Report proposed that having taken either a Diploma or a degree course, all prospective teachers would then move on the second cycle of their training, a dedicated teacher training course.[109] This second cycle would last for two years, of which the first would be spent in a training college or a university department of education, and would involve an '*unashamedly specialised and functional*' training, aimed at equipping each individual teacher to work with a clearly defined area – according to age of pupil or subject area, for example.[110] Though the first year of the second cycle was expected to include some periods of teaching practice, the prospective teacher remained a student of the college or university. In the second year, however, they would begin working in a school and receiving a salary, but as a 'licensed' or probationary teacher, and it was intended that during this period, they would receive further advice from their senior colleagues and that they would spend one-fifth of their time on further training in a 'professional centre'.[111] These professional centres were intended to be an important part of the James Committee's vision of in-service training, and represented an extension of the idea of the local teachers' centre – an expanding new phenomenon in the landscape of teacher education which will be discussed in detail in Chapter Five.

Though both the Departmental Committee Report of 1924–5 and the McNair Report of 1944 had paid some attention to in-service training provision and had favoured its expansion, the prominence given to it by the James Report was unprecedented. Where previously in-service training had been presented as being of secondary importance to recruitment and initial training, the James Committee privileged it and placed discussion of it first in its report suggested that:

> Much of the argument of this report depends upon the proposals made for the third cycle. To none of our recommendations do we attach greater importance than to these for they determine a great deal of the thinking which underlies the report as a whole.[112]

The vision for the third cycle was that it would include a whole range of activities through which teachers would be able to '*extend their personal education, develop their professional competence and improve their understanding of educational principles and techniques.*'[113] The cycle was, therefore, intended to include a balance between subject knowledge, intellectual stimulus and professional skills – all elements which we have seen have played an historical role in in-service training, though sometimes at the expense of one another.[114] Practically speaking, the third cycle was to encompass a variety of models of training including evening meetings and discussions, weekend conferences and other short-term activities, as well as longer term courses requiring teachers to be released from their work duties.[115] Here, in fact, the James Report directly echoed the earlier McNair Report by advocating that teachers should be eligible for release from their duties for a period of up to twelve weeks on full pay in order to undertake training courses after a to-be-determined period of service.[116] The shorter courses and activities were expected to focus on specific and limited objectives, whilst the longer courses were intended to allow teachers to study for higher degrees or advanced qualifications, and it was suggested that this could also include the secondment of teachers to other fields in order to widen their personal experiences.[117]

The report acknowledged that there had already been a significant expansion of provision in the years before its publication, but argued that this had been uncoordinated and that there had been frequent duplication of effort or inadequate facilities.[118] At the time, the report noted that in-service training was offered by a wide range of providers including LEAs, universities, training colleges, polytechnics, Institutes of Education, as well as government. James suggested that, in future, third cycle activities should begin in schools themselves, stating that they should organise discussions and seminars for their staffs, and that other activities should take place in a network of 'professional centres', among which might be counted training colleges and university departments of education, and which would be the main providers of full-time courses.[119] In addition, further professional centres – of which a considerable number would be needed so that all schools might have reasonable access to one – should be maintained by LEAs and could be developed out of existing teaching centres.[120]

The James Report did not advocate that in-service training should be made compulsory, but its determination to enhance its importance was made very clear, and it did argue that all teachers ought *'to have the opportunity to extend and deepen their knowledge of teaching methods and educational theory.'[121]* Furthermore, it recognised that in-service training could fulfil a variety of functions and meet various needs, making reference to the need of subject specialists to refresh and update their subject knowledge, whilst shortages in certain areas might necessitate training for non-specialists required to teach an unfamiliar topic.[122] Moreover, the report identified that there might be a need for teachers in some areas to receive training focused on teaching in a multi-cultural society, highlighting the impact of contemporary social change, whilst those teachers who were promoted to head, deputy head or head of department might benefit from professional training focused on management skills.[123] The James Committee, therefore, proposed that there should be a significant and systematic reorganisation and expansion of the provision of in-service training for teachers, though it should be noted that the Committee's report stated that the term 'in-service training' was an inadequate descriptor for what it proposed.[124]

Like the previous reports, recommendations did not necessarily convert into policy or practice and were not always able to deliver the resource or logistical organisation to enable their proper fruition. Harold Dent reports that the ideas for in-service training espoused by the James' Report were 'widely accepted' and they were for the most part incorporated into the White Paper, 'Education: A Framework for Expansion', presented to parliament later in 1972, which set out a national framework for teacher professional development.[125] Arguably, the years immediately following the optimism of James might be heralded as a heyday for teachers when in-service education and training was expanded, consolidated and, according to David Crook, increasingly professionalised, with improved funding, and more diversified provision through accredited degree and higher degree courses in universities and colleges of education, generously resourced government-organised courses, LEA programmes as well as more informal activity in the teachers' centres.[126] However, it was also during this phase that particular questions were raised about the reach of professional development to a much wider constituency of teachers than had previously been possible, though as it turned out the challenge was not just about increasing resource – but was also one of persuading this wider group of teachers to engage. Questions of quality, not just quantity of provision, as well as that of impact and value for money also began to emerge and these were to become more pressing as the financial pressures of the late 1970s gave impetus to the neo-liberal political reform agenda which shaped educational policy and reform in the following decades.

PHASE FOUR: PRIVATISATION AND CENTRAL CONTROL 1980–2000

The new archival data uncovered for this study of teacher professional development focussed mainly on the years up to 1980, dictated very much by rules in England and Wales governing restricted access to historical documents in public archives within the confines of the '30 year rule'. The project was, however, interested in more recent developments in teacher professional development in as much as they informed and shaped some of the lived experiences of teachers consulted as part of the oral history study, discussed in detail in Part Three of this book. For this reason, the fourth phase in the twentieth-century history of teacher professional development is only briefly outlined here to complete the picture drawn so far in this chapter and will later be considered through a different type of historical lens – that of the oral history testimony of teachers who participated in the research project. This highly complex recent phase in the history of teacher professional development has been comprehensively critiqued and analysed elsewhere by experts working in the contemporary field of teacher development research, which in itself has grown as a distinctive area of international educational inquiry during the last two decades.[127] It is a phase which is firmly rooted in the much wider context of systemic educational reform and policy-making in the last 25 years, characterised by dominant neo-liberal discourses of control, accountability and performativity – all of which have had a profound collective and individual impact on the nature of teachers' initial training, professional development, lives and work.

In brief, from the 1980s there was an increasingly centralised approach to teacher professional development, just as there was to initial teacher training, the school curriculum and all other aspects of the education service. The funding, management and focus of in-service training and education became part of the whole movement for educational reform. Direct dedicated funding from government to LEAS for in-service education and training was subjected to steady attrition throughout the 1980s and 1990s until eventually it was devolved entirely to schools to do with as they so wished. Radical changes to teachers' conditions of service saw the introduction of a new working contract in the mid-1980s, which mandated that five out of the 196 designated working days per year should be formally spent on professional training

– days which were commonly known as 'Baker Days', after Kenneth Baker, the Secretary of State for Education responsible for their introduction, and which were not always held in high regard by many teachers who resented being forced into this type of activity. The introduction of the National Curriculum as part of the 1988 Education Reform Act, as well as the identification of subsequent national priorities and strategies for school reform shaped the content and focus of funded professional training for serving teachers, monitored and scrutinised by various new government agencies, including the Teacher Training Agency, later to be re-designated as the Teacher Development Agency to reflect its wider remit for professional development, and the Office for Standards in Education. Central funding was distributed through various complex and strictly controlled grant initiatives, designed to incentivise development of certain types of programmes for teachers which concentrated on national priorities, including the Technical Vocational Educational Initiative (TVEI) for secondary and further education colleges in the early 1980s followed closely by TVEI- related in-service training (TRIST), then Grant Related In-Service Training (GRIST) for the primary as well as secondary and FE sector and the Grants for Education Support and Training Scheme (GEST) in the 1990s.[128]

There was certainly no shortage of professional development activity and opportunity, but this was very much geared to core government priorities around curriculum, assessment and school management. Increasingly there was preference for school-based and school-led models of training with a strong practical, skills-based focus and a lesser emphasis on the traditional role of universities and higher degree programmes with their perceived theoretical and academic approaches, removed from the realities of classroom life. Effective teaching, pedagogy and a sharp emphasis on the impact of professional development on improved pupil learning characterised this period and was heavily influenced by the whole school reform agenda and the increasing emphasis on individual school performance and development planning. A diverse and competitive private market for professional development provision emerged, outside of the traditional routes and assisted by a proliferation of private consultancies and training companies whose wares were brokered to schools by government agencies. By 2000 a National College for School Leadership had been established to train new headteachers and to deliver professional training for school management. If the broad pattern of teacher professional development as it emerged during the early years of the twentieth century and continued until the early 1980s recognised a dual function and purpose, which variously embraced both the practical/professional needs of teachers and the wider education system, as well as those less tangible opportunities for individual personal growth and development, that which characterised the latter years of the twentieth century was quite different. Here the emphasis was less on the individual teacher and their local context and more on whole school improvement against national priorities.

In this chapter key phases in the twentieth century history of teacher professional development in England and Wales have been identified and outlined, with a particular focus on the role and contribution of central government. Emerging and continuing models included short and longer courses for teachers, vacation courses, paid secondments, accredited higher degree study at universities, as well as more localised, informal opportunities. Though a developmental history, with dominant elements of continuity as well as change over time, it is possible to identify a number of perennial themes which appeared to characterise the whole endeavour. These include: the inability of government and other providers to adequately quantify or capture the range of opportunities available to teachers and their take-up nationally; an overall lack of national coherence; the relatively restricted engagement of teachers relative to the whole teacher population until mandatory requirements in the mid-1980s; and high levels of central control over content, focus and access of teachers. These raise important generic questions for the field of teacher professional development more widely as well as framing some of the discussions subsequently developed in this book.

NOTES

[1] Dent, H. (1977). *The training of teachers in England and Wales 1800–1975*. London, UK: Hodder and Stoughton, pp.44–46.

[2] Board of Education, *Report of the board of education for the Year 1924–25*, pp.153–4. (hereafter cited as BoE, Annual Report with date)

[3] BoE, Annual Report, 1917–1918, p.35.

[4] Ibid., p.36.

[5] BoE, Annual Report, 1918–1919, p.79.

[6] BoE, Annual Report, 1924–25, p.154.

[7] BoE, Annual Report, 1918–1919, p.79.

[8] For contemporary discussions of the idea of the 'cascade model' see: Bax, S. (2002). 'The social and cultural dimensions of trainer training', *Journal of Education for Teaching*, 28(2), 165–178; Gilpin, A. (1997). 'Cascade training: sustainability or dilution?', in I. McGrath (Ed.), *Learning to train: Perspectives on the development of language teacher trainers*. Hemel Hempstead: Prentice Hall; Hayes, D. (2000). 'Cascade training and teachers' professional development', *English Language Teaching Journal*, 54(2), 135–145.

[9] BoE, Annual Report, 1924–25, p.154.

[10] See Aldrich, R. Crook, D., & Watson, D. (2000). *Education and employment: The DfEE and its place in history*. London, UK: Institute of Education, University of London, p. 59 which states that the Board of Education was required to cut £6.5 million from its budget of £50 million.

[11] BoE, Annual Report, 1924–25, pp.155–6.

[12] On the Welsh Department, see Jones, G., & Roderick, G. (2003). *A history of education in Wales*. Cardiff: University of Wales Press, pp.111–113.

[13] BoE, Annual Report, 1924–25, p.155.

[14] Ibid., p.153.

[15] Ibid.

[16] BoE, Annual Report, 1919–1920, p. 80; The UK National Archives (hereafter TNA), ED/86/222, Memo to Inspectors TC No. 65, dated 23/7/1923, which gives two years as absolute limit.

[17] BoE, Annual Report, 1919–1920, p. 80; BoE, Annual Report, 1920–1921, p. 58. See also TNA, ED/86/222.

[18] TNA, ED/22/129, Memo to Inspectors TC No. 65, dated 23/7/1923.

[19] Ibid.

[20] BoE, Annual Report, 1920–1921, p.58.

[21] TNA, ED/22/129, Memo to Inspectors TC No. 65, dated 23/7/1923.

22 On the division between secondary and elementary teachers see Dent, *The training of teachers in England and Wales 1800–1975*, pp.70–72. On the shift to more graduates in elementary schools see Tropp, A. (1957). *The school teachers: The growth of the teaching profession in England and Wales from 1800 to the present day*. London, UK: William Heinemann Ltd, p.228.

23 BoE, Annual Report, 1928, p. 60; BoE, Annual Report, 1929, p.77.

24 BoE, Annual Report, 1925–26, p.102.

25 BoE, Annual Report, 1937, p. 49.

26 TNA, ED 22/129, Memo to Inspectors TC No. 65, dated 23/7/1923.

27 See various Board of Education Annual Reports (1922–23 (p. 141); 1923–24 (p. 122); 1924–25 (p.157); 1926–27 (p.58)).

28 BoE, Annual Report, 1931, p.50.

29 BoE, Annual Report, 1935, p.70.

30 BoE, Annual Report, 1937, p.49.

31 Ibid.

32 BoE, Annual Report, 1933, p.60.

33 TNA, ED 22/129, Memo to Inspectors TC No. 65, dated 23/7/1923.

34 Ibid.

35 Ibid.

36 BoE, Annual Report, 1927, p.58.

37 BoE, Annual Report, 1928, p.60; BoE, Annual Report, 1929, p.77.

38 TNA, ED 22/129, Memo to Inspectors TC No. 65, dated 23/7/1923.

39 BoE, Annual Report, 1924–25, p.9.

40 Ibid.

41 BoE, Annual Report, 1924–25, p.2.

42 Ibid., pp. 33–34. See also: Gardner, P., & Cunningham, P. (2004). *Becoming teachers: Texts and testimonies 1907–1950*. London, UK: Woburn Press.; Robinson, W. (1993). 'Pupil teachers: the Achilles heel of higher grade schools 1882–104', *History of Education*, *22*(3), 241–53; Robinson, W. (1996). "Expert and novice' in the pupil teacher system of the later nineteenth century', *Journal of Educational Administration and History*, *28*(2), 129–141; Robinson, W. (1999). "In search of a plain tale": rediscovering the champions of the pupil-teacher centres 1900–1010', *History of Education*, *28*(1), 53–72; Robinson, W. (2002). 'Towards a bi-centenary review? Historiographical reflections on the 1902 Education Act', *Oxford Review of Education*, *28*(2), 159–172; Robinson, W. (2003). *Pupil teachers and their professional training in pupil teachers centres in England and Wales, 1870–1914*. New York, NY: Edwin Mellen Press.

43 BoE, Annual Report, 1924–25, pp.118.

44 Ibid., p.119.

45 Ibid.

46 BoE, Annual Report, 1924–25, pp.119–120.

47 Ibid., p.120.

48 Ibid.

49 BoE, Annual Report, 1924–25, pp.120–121.

50 Ibid., p.121.

51 BoE, Annual Report, 1925–26, p.101.

52 Ibid., p.102.

53 BoE, Annual Report, 1929–30, p. 56.

54 BoE, Annual Report, 1933–34, p. 60.

55 BoE, Annual Report, 1934–35, p. 65.

56 BoE, Annual Report, 1937–38, p. 48.

57 BoE, Annual Report, 1929–30, p. 57.

58 Ibid., p.57.

59 Ibid.

60 Lord Eustace Percy, *Some Memories* (London: Eyre and Spottis, 1958), p.123.

61 BoE, Annual Report, 1937–38, p.48.

62 Ibid.
63 Ibid.
64 BoE, Annual Report, 1938–39, p.53.
65 Ibid., p.203.
66 Ministry of Education (hereafter MoE), Annual Report, 1947, p. 45.
67 Ibid.
68 Ibid.
69 Board of Education. (1944). *Teachers and youth leaders: Report of the committee appointed by the president of the board of education to consider the supply, recruitment and training of teachers and youth leaders.* London, UK: HMSO (hereafter McNair Report).
70 See Crook, D. (1995). 'Universities, teacher training, and the legacy of McNair 1944–94', *History of Education, 24*(3), 231–245.
71 McNair Report, pp.45-.47.
72 Ibid, pp.48–62.
73 Ibid., p.49.
74 Ibid., pp.48–53.
75 McNair Report, pp.54–62.
76 Dent, *The training of teachers in England and Wales 1800–1975*, p.114.
77 McNair Report, pp.16–17.
78 Ibid., p.28.
79 Ibid., p.17.
80 Ibid., p.25.
81 Ibid., p.28.
82 Ibid., p.137.
83 Ibid.,
84 Ibid,.
85 Ibid., p.137.
86 MoE, Annual Report, 1947, p.45.
87 Ibid.
88 Ibid.
89 MoE, Annual Report, 1948, p.64.
90 MoE, Annual Report, 1954, p.39.
91 MoE, Annual Report, 1947, p.45.
92 Ibid; MoE, Annual Report, 1948, p.63.
93 Ibid., pp.60–61.
94 MoE, Annual Report, 1954, p.56.
95 Ibid.
96 Department of Education and Science (hereafter DES). (1964). *Course of further training for teachers,* Circular 7/64. London, UK: DES.
97 DES, Annual Report, 1964, p.70.
98 Ibid., pp.70–71.
99 Ibid., p.71.
100 Ibid.
101 DES, Annual Report, 1965, p.67.
102 DES, Annual Report, 1967, p.66.
103 DES, (1967). *Statistics of education, survey of in-service training for teachers.* London: HMSO.
104 DES, Annual Report, 1968, p.69.
105 DES, (1972). *Teacher education and training: A report by a committee of inquiry appointed by the secretary of state for education and science, under the chairmanship of Lord James of Rusholme.* London: HMSO (hereafter James Report), p.vi; for a list of those who submitted evidence see James Report, Appendices 1–3, pp.80–94.
106 James Report, p.40.
107 Ibid., pp.40–41.

[108] Ibid., pp.41–48.
[109] Ibid., p.41.
[110] Ibid., pp.22–24.
[111] Ibid., pp.26–27.
[112] Ibid., p.5.
[113] Ibid., p.5.
[114] Ibid., p.7.
[115] Ibid., p.5.
[116] Ibid., p.12.
[117] Ibid., p.12.
[118] Ibid., p.6.
[119] Ibid., pp.11, 14–16.
[120] Ibid., p.16.
[121] Ibid., p.7.
[122] Ibid., p.9.
[123] Ibid.
[124] Ibid., p.5.
[125] Dent, *The training of teachers in England and Wales 1800–1975*, p.151; DES, (1972). *Education: A framework for expansion*. London: HMSO.
[126] Crook, 'Universities, teacher training, and the legacy of McNair 1944–94'.
[127] See an overview of this international field, for example, in Day, C. & Sachs, J. (2004). *International handbook on the continuing professional development of teachers*. Maidenhead: Open University Press.
[128] For further discussion of these schemes see for example: Moreland, N. (1988). 'Grist to the mill: emergent practices and problems in the grant-related in-service training system – a perspective from a providing institution', *Innovation in Education and Training International*, 25(2), 129–135; Burgess, R. (1993). *Implementing in-service education and training*. London, UK: Routledge; Bridgwood, A. (1996). 'Consortium collaboration: the experience of TVEI', in D. Bridges & C. Husbands (Eds.), *Consorting and collaborating in the education market place*. London, UK: Falmer Press; Gleeson, D. & McLean, M. (2004). 'Whatever happened to TVEI?: TVEI, curriculum and schooling', *Journal of Education Policy*, 9(3), 233–244.

PART 2

CHRONOLOGICAL CASE STUDIES

THE VACATION COURSE 1920–1940

INTRODUCTION

In the period 1920–40 a variety of models of in-service training was developed nationally, with residential summer vacation courses being a popular way of bringing groups of teachers together for professional, intellectual and personal refreshment in the school holidays. Vacation courses were organised by a variety of providers, including the Board of Education, LEAs as well as private and voluntary organisations. Some vacation courses catered for teachers of a particular subject or for those with a particular specialism. Other courses were more broadly based and catered for a range of different teachers with various interests. This chapter examines and compares three types of vacation course: a Board of Education sponsored summer school at Derby Teacher Training College; A Welsh Education Office vacation course at the University of Oxford; and the City of London Vacation Course (CLVC), an independent commercial venture organised by a leading educational publisher, Robert Evans. At a time when the nature of teacher professionalism was undergoing significant transformation, the vacation course model offers a new way of conceptualising the wider question of teacher status and identity and tensions between ideas of personal and professional improvement.

Though each of these three cases of vacation course had distinctive characteristics and styles there were clearly shared features which defined this model of teacher professional development. Following a brief contextual outline of each of the three cases, four core themes emerging from this model will be examined. These include: organisation, location and funding; educational content and pedagogy; opportunities for social networking and cultural development; and conceptions of teacher professionalism.

HISTORICAL CONTEXT AND VACATION COURSE OUTLINES

Before discussing the vacation course model it will be instructive to consider briefly the wider political and economic context of this period 1920–40, which had profound effects on teachers and teaching. This was a time of national crisis, politically and economically, as well as a period of attrition, change and financial uncertainty in education.[1] National recession in the 1920s gave way to a hugely damaging international recession in the early 1930s, which led to large-scale unemployment, poverty, social and political unrest. In spite of the laudable ambitions for public education heralded by the 1918 Fisher Education Act, which looked forward to the raising of the school leaving age to 14 and the expansion of secondary education, the reality of the inter-war years fell far short of the mark. Indeed, the evolution of these vacation courses in the early 1920s coincided with the infamous scourge of the notorious 'Geddes Axe', which tried to slash public spending on education by 30% and threatened the salaries and conditions of service for teachers working in publicly funded schools across the country. Financial cuts and constant political wrangling over the nationally agreed Burnham pay scales and superannuation for teachers, between the government, LEAs and teacher unions dominated the 1920s and 1930s, as has been well documented elsewhere by Tropp and Simon.[2] Attempts to raise the school starting age to six years and to significantly increase class sizes, allow school buildings to fall into disrepair, as well as blocking any expansion of secondary education were proposed by both political parties in the interests of educational economy and fiercely resisted by teachers themselves. There were losses and gains on both sides and the whole period has been characterised as a constant battleground over scarce resources, with a dampening down of any real innovation or improvement in the system as a whole.[3] Ironically, at this time of national crisis and seemingly bleak times for education, the prospect of the elementary teacher was, for the first time in the history of the profession, relatively bright. However hard won, it was during this difficult period those teachers' salaries, pensions; conditions of service and security of tenure were properly secured. Tropp has argued that these were 'golden years' for teachers, both in terms of rising status and in terms of remuneration, especially as salaries were preserved during severe economic recession, and teachers had more disposable income than ever before at a time of low inflation and falling prices.[4] Against this context, the vacation model of teacher professional development emerged.

The Derby Summer School

The Derby Summer School, organised by the Derby Diocesan Training College, was offered annually to teachers from 1918 until the outbreak of the Second World War in 1938. Derby Training College, which delivered initial training for women teachers, was an early provider of in-service training, offering model lessons and weekend courses for teachers from the early 1900s.[5] These developed into two-week long vacation courses sometime between 1914–18, endorsed and supported by the Board of Education.[6] Usually held in the last week of July and first week of August, the Derby Course was attended by over 250 teachers in 1921 and by over 500 in 1926, from across England, Wales, Scotland and Ireland.[7] It was open to men and women teachers, and to those teaching in nursery, elementary and secondary schools. Teachers could apply to attend for either one or two weeks, with those staying for the whole fortnight able to dedicate the second week either to continued study of the subject of their first week or to another subject entirely.[8] A range of subject courses were offered, including Music, Art, English Literature, and a variety of craft subjects, as well Geography.[9] In addition, there was a series of daily general education lectures. Teachers, either themselves or subsidised by their LEA, paid £1 per week for lectures and tuition, with an additional fee of £2 for men and £1.15s for women for board and lodgings at the College, though they were also welcome to make their own accommodation arrangements elsewhere.[10] The 1935 course prospectus neatly summarises the purpose and objectives of this particular example of a vacation course, organised by a training college with the full support of the Board of Education:

> A vacation course is not intended to be a substitute for fuller training. It is intended to stimulate interest in educational ideas and new methods; to encourage discussion and the exchange of thought; to give opportunities for teachers to come into close contact with lecturers who may claim to have travelled a little further on the paths of learning and skill; to provide instruction and practice in handicrafts and other practical subjects where teachers find their lack of personal skill a handicap in school work.[11]

Vacation Courses for Welsh Teachers

During the 1920s, the Welsh Department of the Board of Education organised a series of funded short courses for fairly small groups of selected teachers, typically lasting for two weeks during the summer vacation period. The programme began in July 1922 with a course focused on 'Rural Lore as an Aid to Education' held annually at Jesus College, Oxford until 1935, with between 35–50 teachers attending each year.[12] In addition, a two-week course on Welsh Language, Literature and History, which was aimed at teachers working in secondary schools or those who taught older pupils in elementary schools was first held in 1922 at the University College of Wales in Aberystwyth.[13] In 1923, this literature course was held at the University College, Bangor, and focused specifically on the topic of 'Welsh Literature and thought in the eighteenth and nineteenth centuries in relation to the social life of the period.'[14] In 1925 it was transferred to Jesus College, Oxford, where the course on Rural Lore as an Aid to Education was already held annually.[15] From 1930, the course was held at St Peter's Hall, Oxford, where it continued as an annual fixture, attended by around fifty teachers each year - although with some alterations as it became aimed at elementary school teachers as a result of the Departmental Committee report on the use of Welsh in schools - until 1935 after which it was replaced by a course for elementary school teachers focused on the teaching of Welsh and English.[16]

The City of London Vacation Course

The City of London Vacation Course in Education (CLVC) was different in scope and organisation than the two government endorsed courses outlined above. Each summer between 1922 and 1938, up to 500 elementary school teachers from across Britain and some from overseas, joined together in London for a two-week residential vacation course, designed to refresh them professionally and to invigorate them socially and culturally. The CLVC was hosted at hotels, rooms and restaurants in central London, with sophisticated social and cultural programmes of recreational activities, educational visits, receptions, exhibitions and courses of professional lectures directed by leading educationists and practitioners of the day. The brainchild of the educational publisher Sir Robert Evans, the CLVC was a private not-for-profit enterprise, funded by the teachers themselves and operated outside of the official control and endorsement of the Board of Education. During its lifetime it received increasing publicity in the educational and broadsheet press and became notable for its patronage by the 'great and the good', including the Prince of Wales and the Prime Minister, its President, Viscount Burnham, its Principal H. A. L. Fisher, various Presidents and Permanent Secretaries of the Board of Education, politicians, ministers, members of the aristocracy, artists, musicians, writers and explorers. There was a full lecture programme, with a general course covering various curriculum subjects and new methods in education, and a course for 'teachers of little children' which ran every morning across the weekdays of the fortnight. Lectures concluded with a course luncheon which would be followed by an informal after-luncheon speech, presented by a guest speaker. Afternoons were devoted to visits to places and buildings of interests around London and evenings to dinners, concerts, theatres, dances and other recreations. At the first course in 1922, there were 450 teachers from the United Kingdom, including 75 teachers from overseas. This number remained more or less constant throughout its duration. The international appeal of the course seemed to increase over the years with representation from the British Colonies but also other countries in Europe and North America. By 1929 it was suggested that 21 different nations were represented on the course. Informal cultural exchange between teachers, particularly at impromptu after-dinner musical sessions or recitals was a regular feature of the course. It was reported that a great 'spirit of camaraderie' pervaded the course – its informality and variety of activities encouraging a real friendliness and zest amongst its members to enjoy it to the full. Its atmosphere was claimed to be as invigorating as sea air.[17] Celebrating its tenth anniversary in 1932 it was grandly claimed in *The Teachers World* that it '*...has become in a single decade, an annual institution which is known to educationist in all parts of the world.*'[18]

ORGANISATION, LOCATION AND FUNDING

All three of these vacation courses followed a similar format in terms of overall concept. They were held for a fortnight during the summer holidays at the end of July and beginning of August; they were residential and took the participating teachers out of their home and school context; and they included a formal lecture/education programme as well as social and recreational opportunities. One was located in a provincial Diocesan Women's Teacher Training College in the Midlands, another in an all-male Oxford College and another in various grand hotels right in the heart of London. Regardless of this shared format, location and venue alone marked each of these vacation courses as distinctive and would have created a very different experience for participants. In addition, course ownership, as well as arrangements for funding, selection of participants and organisation was also quite different, The Derby Summer School was endorsed by the Board of Education and subject to HMI inspection, but was part of the Training College's business plan and was marketed to teachers and local authorities as an important source of annual income for the College. The Welsh Courses were entirely organised and funded by the Welsh Department of Education, and were conceived of as high end, elite provision for relatively small groups of teachers. The CLVC was not approved by the Board of Education and was a private enterprise – competing with other providers, such as Derby Diocesan Training College.

For teachers attending the Derby Summer School, a strict timetable for residents was posted, which prescribed a fairly regimented daily routine, starting with Chapel first thing in the morning and last thing in the evening, set times for morning lectures, morning classes, afternoon classes and meals. It was an institutional regime resonant with any Training College regime of its time, including a 'lights out' policy at 11.00 sharp as well as other clearly stipulated 'rules' about noise, smoking and use of facilities that would have been very familiar to the teachers who would once have been College students. It was a serious working two weeks with teachers expected to participate fully and attend all sessions. Certificates were issued to those teachers who attended classes regularly – for at least twenty-one hours per week, which suggests that there was very careful monitoring of attendance and participation. These certificates were potentially valuable to teachers seeking promotion and it was recorded in an HMI inspection of the Derby programme in 1923 that some LEAs required evidence of attendance at vacation courses from candidates seeking promotion to headships.[19]

As a Board of Education approved and partially subsidised course, the Derby Summer School relied largely on local authorities to pay for their teachers to attend, and in some cases on individual teachers themselves. Each year the Derby Summer School produced a comprehensive course brochure which was distributed to local authorities and teachers were required to apply and to complete a detailed application form. The financial health of the Summer School was not straightforward and experienced numerous difficulties during the 1920s and 1930s, in spite of its status as a popular and successful course.[20] In 1922, the principal of Derby Training College and the man behind the foundation of the Summer School, Canon A. Bater, wrote to the Board of Education to complain about a fall in the number of applicants seeking to attend the Summer School that year, something which he stated might be due to an increase in the number of vacation courses being organised nationally and to a trend for LEAs to reduce the amount of grant offered to teachers seeking to attend such courses, in response to a 'cry for economy'.[21] The reductions in spending by LEAs during this year would have been in response to the drive for national economy which had resulted in the appointment of the Geddes Committee on National Expenditure in 1921, which had recommended that stringent cuts in public spending be made in 1922 and 1923. Concern over the drop in numbers applying for the course, and therefore in the income which the course would generate, led Bater to ask that the Board of Education intervene to subsidise the Summer School as he had engaged the staff for it based on the previous year's figures and was concerned that the fall in applications would result in a 'deplorable' adverse balance.[22] The Board of Education however, also under considerable financial pressure at this time, were reluctant to offer any further financial support to the Derby Summer School beyond the ten shillings per student per week which were already paid to the School[23] Whilst there was some suggestion that the way in which the course was organised was perhaps not optimal – with mention made of '*a large and somewhat expensive staff*' – within the Board of Education there was also some suggestion that the problems at Derby were not unusual and that in the future, '*we shall have to face the possibility of the Voluntary Training Colleges giving up any responsibility for Refresher Courses*'.[24] The Derby course remained solvent but there is evidence of on-going financial difficulties and negotiations with the Board over additional subsidy throughout the 1930s.[25]

The Welsh courses at Oxford were specifically developed by the Welsh Department to support and underpin some of its wider educational and political policy around Welsh identity and language. The idea for the 'Rural Lore as an Aid to Education' course had first been put forward by Sir Alfred T. Davies, permanent secretary to the Welsh Department from 1907–1925, in 1921. He asked the College to provide board and lodging for 40 teachers and course staff (in the end 36 teachers attended), as well as allowing the use of a common room and at least three lecture theatres, and access to libraries.[26] Teachers selected for the course paid a ten shillings per day fee to the College themselves but were then eligible for a maintenance grant of £1 per week and a third class return rail fare to and from Oxford, provided that they attended the course for its specified hours.[27] This was a tightly controlled, highly selective course which was generously funded, monitored and evaluated by HMI.

Though for the first three years the Welsh Language, Literature and History course was held in Welsh Universities, it then moved in 1925 to Jesus College, Oxford.[28] The particular role of Jesus College in these in-service courses for Welsh teachers is significant as the College had long-lasting ties to Welsh education as well as to the study of Welsh literature and culture.[29] The College would therefore have seemed a natural home for the courses which the Welsh Department was organising for Welsh teachers, and would have been a prestigious place for those teachers to visit. There were also strong personal connections between the course organisers and staff and the college – as noted above, Sir Alfred T Davies' son, Mervyn, was employed on the 1922 course and was a student at Jesus College at the time, and a list of course staff includes a handwritten note that one of them, an Inspector named R.E. Hughes, was '*an old Jesus man.*'[30] Though there was little or no involvement of College staff on the courses – they were organised and run by the staff of the Welsh Department and HMI – the College does seem to have had a good working relationship with the Department when making arrangements to hold the courses, and on one occasion delayed accepting another booking which would have clashed with the Rural Lore course, stating that '*we, of course, would prefer to have the Welsh Schoolmasters.*'[31] On another occasion, the College Bursar referred to the running of the courses as seeming to be '*a very successful arrangement*'.[32] The Bursar's favourable attitude to the courses may have due to more than just the prospect of filling the college rooms during the summer, as after the first course held there in 1922, Alfred T Davies had written that the teachers who had attended were '*so impressed by the advantages which Oxford offers to young Welshmen, that I believe they mean, individually, to do what lies in their power to direct to the College the steps of many a young Welshman who may come under their influence.*'[33]

HMI played a critical role in selecting teachers for these Welsh courses. In 1923, 36 attendees were chosen by the Board solely on the personal recommendation of local HM Inspectors.[34] Inspectors were required to ensure that the teachers whom they wished to recommend for the course were willing to attend it and that their local authority would be willing to release them on full pay for the duration of the course, as that way the time spent on the course would be eligible to be counted towards salary increments and for pension purposes.[35] In seeking to have teachers released from their duties for the course, Inspectors were encouraged to impress upon local authorities the '*very substantial advantage*' that their county would see from one of their teachers attending the course.[36] Inspectors were asked to consider, when recommending teachers, whether they had already shown an interest in the Rural Lore Scheme or were likely '*under the stimulus of such a course, to become capable and keen in applying it in future*'.[37] Arrangements for the Welsh Literature and History course in 1925 were a little different as HMI were instructed to bring the course to the attention of suitable candidates for the course but in this instance teachers were to apply for a place on it themselves, directly to the Board of Education, rather than having to be specifically recommended for it by an Inspector.[38] It was desirable for this course that the teachers attending it should speak Welsh as the lectures were to be given in that language.[39]

The exact rationale for and origins of the CLVC are somewhat hazy, but some insights can be gleaned from Robert Evans' own personal tribute to Lord Burnham, President and long-term supporter of the course from its beginnings in 1922 until his death in 1933. Evans wrote, '*I remember the occasion some twelve or so years ago when I first spoke to Lord Burnham about the status of the teaching profession, the absence of public recognition, the fact that the State did not really know its teachers, and that there was nothing to bring the teaching profession into touch with our great national institutions and with the leading people responsible for the government of the country.*'[40] Unlike the Derby Summer School and the Welsh courses which were held in more confined institutional college institutional environments, albeit of different character, the CLVC convened around Holborn, using lecture rooms in the Royal College of Surgeons, College of Preceptors, Kingsway Hall and the Connaught Rooms with participants residing in the Imperial Hotel. Participants were self-selecting – and paid for the course themselves. The inaugural 1922 course brochure advertised an all-inclusive cost of sixteen guineas per person, which could be paid in three instalments.[41] At that time, the average salary for an elementary teacher was around £300 per annum – so expenditure on the CLVC would have represented a significant outlay.

The Board of Education was always suspicious of the commercial nature of the CLVC. In July 1922 Frank Roscoe wrote to the President of the Board of Education, H. A. L. Fisher inviting him to attend and present an after-luncheon talk to teachers. His invitation was declined, though in the following year Fisher was to become the new Principal of the course and thereafter fully supported and championed its cause.[42] Relationships between the Board of Education and the course remained difficult – even though Board officials both attended and gave speeches in subsequent years. In an official memorandum on the course written in 1928 it was suggested that, *'There is no doubt that it is a "good show" and has real educational merit, but we have always felt a little difficult about it.'*[43] The independence of the course from the Board of Education is significant and was commented upon favourably by observers. *'...the enhanced value of a course which was inspired from within, which was unhampered by official direction, and was free from the taint of "charitable grants-in-aid". We, who are tied and bound by the chains of an official outlook or by the leading strings of the Board of Education, confidently expect this Course to show the value of independence and the "self-help" method.'*[44] Being outside of the control of the Board of Education, the course became a significant public platform for debate on educational policy.[45] In contrast with the Derby and Welsh courses, the CLVC had more of a liberal 'holiday' feel and though there was a programme of lectures and classes, participants were free to choose which sessions they wished to attend and also to select which aspects of the social, cultural and recreational programme they wished to join.

COURSE CONTENT

In examining the educational content of these three vacation courses, it is possible to see greater similarities between the Derby Summer School and the CLVC as the Welsh courses were so highly specialised. However, common to all three courses was a commitment to bringing the teachers in touch with up-to-date and modern educational methods, new educational ideas and, above all, a strong practical focus which would enable them to take back their new knowledge, understanding and skills to their classrooms and to their colleagues.

The Welsh courses were both highly specialised and drew upon leading experts on Welsh language, history, culture and education. The course on 'Rural Lore as an Aid to Education' was led by Dr William Williams, HMI, aided by other inspectors and by Mr. Mervyn Davies of Jesus College, who was Sir Alfred Davies' son and a student at the time.[46] Mornings were given over to either lectures or 'study circles' in groups of ten or twelve teachers with a tutor, whilst afternoons were given over to visits to museums or other places of interest before the teachers returned to further lectures or study circle work after tea.[47] Alongside Dr Williams and the core course staff, there were lectures from several guest speakers on a variety of subjects, following on from an inaugural lecture from Sir Alfred Davies himself which addressed the aim and purpose of the 'Rural Lore Scheme'. Much of the lecture programme was delivered by Welsh HMI, such as Hugh Davies whose particular expertise was 'Welsh Furniture', F.O. Mann who gave a lecture on 'History and Oral Literature from Local Sources' and G.K. Sutherland who gave a lecture on 'Plant Surveys and Mapping in Connection with Botanical Studies'.[48] However, there were also talks from a variety of other speakers including university lecturers discussing phonetics and the Welsh Language, and the use of parish records as a source material.[49] Furthermore, the teachers were to hear lectures from Dr Mortimer Wheeler, who was then working at the National Museum of Wales and who would go on to become one of Britain's pre-eminent archaeologists, as well as from the Chief Inspector of Ancient Monuments for Great Britain, C.R. Peers.[50] The programme of lectures from 1927 also contains a similar mix of speakers and topics, with lectures covering 'Permanent Values in Education', 'Education and the Spirit of the Age', 'Folklore', 'Place Names', 'Welsh Folk Songs', as well as 'School Journeys' and a talk on 'The language we speak and the grammar we teach.'[51] Although the course's title suggests quite a narrow focus, the programme of speakers makes clear that in fact it included reference to a number of subject areas – such as Language, History, Geography, Botany, Craft – and was therefore rich and wide-ranging, addressing subject content as well as teaching methods. It was intended that the teachers who followed the course would practise the scheme in their own schools and that they would also *recommend it to others and make themselves sources of information about it.* [52]

In 1923, the 'Welsh Literature and History' summer course focussed on 'Welsh Literature and thought in the eighteenth and nineteenth centuries in relation to the social life of the period.'[53] It was aimed to promote better teaching of Welsh and to improve the methods used in its study so as to enable the language to take its place in schools as 'an instrument of culture'.[54] This course in particular therefore formed part of a drive to increase and improve the use of Welsh in schools in Wales, especially at secondary level, which saw a Departmental Committee established at the Board of Education in 1925 to enquire into this matter, amidst considerable debate about the question of encouraging bilingualism or introducing compulsory Welsh-teaching.[55] In 1924 its focus was confined to the eighteenth century only, which was reported by the Board to have *'resulted in an improvement both in the treatment of the subject and in the appreciation of the lectures by the students'*.[56] The course covered topics including economic, social, political, and religious aspects of Welsh life and history alongside literary study, and the teachers were also given advice about school text books available in Welsh and were provided with a selection of reference books to use on the course by the National Library of Wales.[57] Teachers selected for and attending both of these Welsh courses were exposed to a rich curriculum and were expected to be ambassadors for its possible implementation and influence back in schools.

Both Derby and the CLVC had a much more broad-based educational programme aimed to attract and interest a more diverse and differently experienced group of teachers. They both offered a daily programme of general education lectures delivered by external speakers, in addition to specialist classes. Claiming to be varied, differentiated by stage and curriculum subject and, perhaps most importantly, supported by leading educationists and 'expert teachers, with an unrivalled knowledge of classroom needs'[58] who were 'far removed from "mere theorists" as well could be,'[59] the CLVC lecture programme claimed to be designed to be both inspiring and practical. The general course consisted of keynote lectures by leading educationists, designed to present each subject in its larger setting and to demonstrate how traditional school subjects could be approached in novel ways by teachers. It also looked at wider subjects in relation to education such as Philosophy, Law, the British Commonwealth, Science and Literature. The lecture courses covered most of the subjects of the school curriculum such as English, Arithmetic, History, English Literature, Geography and Handwork, and were organised according to a strictly prescribed and organised timetable, to allow members to move between sessions, according to their own individual needs. The ethos of the lecture programme was one which sought to promote and develop new educational principles and methods and to discuss up-to-date ideas about teaching. It was hoped that the course would give teachers the satisfaction of a, '*thorough 'overhauling of their pedagogic ideas and teaching methods.'*[60]

> Amidst much that is flattering and pleasing it must not be forgotten that day by day the members of the Course, under the direction of their famous Principal, Mr Fisher, are pursuing in the lecture-rooms the main purpose of their visit to London. They are refreshing their knowledge of teaching methods, renewing that professional skill which requires stimulating after long and perhaps monotonous usage. They are, in short, utilising a holiday to gain a fresh grasp of all that teaching comprises; to view its difficulties and opportunities afresh, and to gain new energy for the years ahead.[61]

At Derby the pool of external speakers was more modest that the CLVC and included a range of topics such 'Music in the School', 'Voice Production and Song-Singing', 'Education and Reality', and 'Technique and Inspiration in Teaching'.[62] The themes of these lectures, as their titles suggest, were often broad, and focused on the wider nature, theory, and practice of education as well as sometimes on specific subjects.

Running alongside the general lecture programme, The CLVC timetable was broken down into separate classes for four groups: senior teachers; junior teachers' infants' teachers' and foreign students. Classes ran each morning apart from Sundays, from 9.00 am to 12.45 pm, typically with three one hour sessions and short breaks in between. Each day classes comprised formal academic and theoretical input on key subjects as well as a focus on 'Methods'. Lectures were combined with demonstrations, workshops and practical classes. By the early 1930s, the overall pedagogy changed to included formal 'Class Discussions' at the end of each morning's input. Although the sessions were differentiated there was plenty of opportunity for teachers to mix together – so that barriers between senior, junior and infant teachers could be broken down in shared discussions about general educational and pedagogical principles. There was a strong sense that the lecture courses were not designed to be formal – rather to help teachers with their practice and to engage them in the discussion and exchange of ideas. For example, a report on the 1926 course claimed that: 'The lectures, whose practical achievements in the classroom fill the teachers with professional pride, give expert guidance based upon actual classroom practice. Their lectures are intimately friendly. Discussion, inquiry, help with personal difficulties, all point away from formality to pleasant and sincere helpfulness. From each lecture there is immediate practical benefit to be gained, and more, and enthusiasm which fires the teacher with new energy and confidence.'[63]

The Derby programme, whilst not dissimilar to that offered by the CLVC had more of a Creative Arts and Handwork bias with an emphasis on subjects such as Art, Music and Dance, Basket-Weaving, Needlecraft, Woodwork and Pottery. In 1925, the Summer School featured a course for kindergarten and junior school teachers. This course was a broad-ranging one, led by two lecturers from Southlands Training College, which covered several different subjects of relevance to teachers of children aged from 3–11 years, including Nature Study, Story Telling, Needlework and Toy-making, as well as showing teachers how to make apparatus suitable for use when teaching Reading, Arithmetic, English, History, Geography and Scripture.[64] As with most of the courses at Derby, there was a mix of lectures and practical work, for which teachers were expected to supply their own materials, as indicated in the prospectus:

> Teachers who intend to take this course should bring some or all of the following apparatus: Paint box, scissors, penknife, drawing paper, brown paper, coloured paper, wall paper, gummed paper, tracing paper, Indian ink, Higgins' vegetable glue, counters, cardboard, small cardboard boxes, match boxes, match sticks, cotton reels, wooden skewers, corks, pins, scraps, children's pictures, advertisements, sale catalogues...

This extensive list of supplies clearly indicates that teachers would have engaged in making a variety of apparatus whilst being introduced to ideas which they could later make practical use of once back in their classrooms. Teachers were asked to bring examples of children's work with them for discussion in the sessions. Whilst most of the courses at the Summer School were based in the College rooms, some gave teachers the opportunity to undertake excursions, such as the Geography course which was offered in most years and a course on the organisation of school trips which was offered in 1925 and 1927.[65] Excursions included trips to various locations in the Derbyshire Peak District, such as Dovedale, Wirksworth, Cromford and Matlock. Teachers looking to apply to a Geography course advertised in the 1929 prospectus were warned that they would need to be able to undertake long walks and told that they 'should be prepared to incur a moderate expenditure with regard to bus fares, maps, etc.'[66]

During this particular period or educational history in Britain, experiments with individual work, project work and the Dalton Plan as well as a focus on creative work in arts, crafts and the performing arts were 'cutting-edge' and this was reflected in both the CLVC and Derby courses. By the early 1930s, the CLVC was offering senior teachers special sessions on how to work with 'backward children'. For junior teachers the focus was on individual work, projects, Handwork and Drawing and for infant teachers the emphasis was on the '3 R's', Handwork, Music, Language-training and Story-telling. Practical classes in Drawing, Woodwork and Metalwork, Book-craft and Weaving, as well as demonstrations and performances of percussion band work, speech training, and Dancing, were also organised. The course tried to adapt and respond to wider changes in the system. It showcased the potential of new technologies in radio broadcasting and film as well as new teaching apparatus, such as the episcope. In 1928 the programme was specially modified to provide help to teachers who had to carry out in their schools the new junior re-organisation plans which were then being implemented across the country.[67] By the early 1930s demonstrations from the BBC were an integral part of the main programme. Provision for the special need of the rural school was also made. Displays of latest text books and up-to-date apparatus were routinely arranged as part of the course. The cohort of overseas members was specially catered for with classes in the 'Speaking of English', 'Speech Practice', 'English Literature' and 'English Schools.' The Derby Summer School also hosted an exhibition of books, diagrams and material, arranged by the Central Educational Company, Derby and the Dryad Handicrafts Company, Leicester. It also showcased a progressive approach to music teaching - 'Musical Appreciation and Rhythmic Work (or the De Rusette Method)', led by Louie de Rusette of the Rachel McMillan Training Centre, aimed at teachers of children aged 4–7 years.[68] De Rusette advocated the view that Music teaching in schools should focus on allowing children to express themselves through rhythm, rather than on imitation, and that it should concentrate on fostering children's own creativity and imagination.[69] This theoretical outlook is reflected in the course she led at Derby, as each morning began with a demonstration class to a group of children, which was followed by practical training '*so that all attending the course may themselves fully enter into Miss de Rusette's musical method of child development*', and on different days the training focused on, for instance, rhythmic movement, band training, or rhythmic expression. Teachers attending the course were asked to wear loose clothes or short skirts so as to be able to move around freely, as well as shoes without heels, and were also asked to bring some materials, such as scissors, paints and cardboard, if they wished to make materials. As well as the De Rusette method, teachers attending the Derby Summer School in 1925 had the option to follow a course on Dalcroze Eurythmics, another method of Music education which had been developed in the early twentieth century.

Though staffing of the Welsh courses was primarily HMI, as outlined above, core staffing for both the CLVC and Derby courses was bought in either from teacher training colleges, demonstration schools or from schools engaged with cutting-edge curriculum or pedagogy.

For the CLVC there was a loyal core of main lecturers who appeared each year and who were central to the course. These included, for example, Mrs J. Murray MacBain who ran the 'Course for Teachers of Little Children' and who also acted as resident 'hostess' responsible for introducing new members of the course who had travelled alone and needed to make friends. She published fifteen educational textbooks for teachers on poetry, nursery rhymes and Music, including the use of the gramophone for children with Evans Brothers between 1923–1965. In 1922 she was described as a headmistress of a large school in London who had experimented with new teaching methods and was subsequently asked by the *'highest authorities for her help in the training of teachers.'* Other regulars some of whom were also authors of educational text books, included: Mr Robert Finch; Mr Frank Jones; Miss Rosa Bassett; Mr George Green; Miss Punnett; Miss Mabel Campbell; Miss Margaret McCrea; Miss Salt; and Miss Hancock.[70] Rosa Bassett was the Headmistress of Streatham County Secondary School for Girls in 1922 and had written about the introduction of Dalton Plan assignments in her school – she was considered a pioneer of this method.[71] Frank Jones and E. Hasluck were both teachers and lecturers. Jessie Mackinder was headmistress of a college demonstration school in London and a special feature of her lectures was their practical aspect – '...*at each lecture there will be exhibited the latest and best apparatus suitable for the carrying out of the principles so ably enumerated by the lecturer.'* Mabel Bisson was an expert in Froebel teaching and a Lecturer on Handwork at Southlands Training College as well as an Inspector for Schools in Croydon. Miss Salt was also a Lecturer at Graystoke Training College. With considerable practical experience, an important feature of their work was made very clear – they were all *'expert teachers, with an unrivalled knowledge of classroom needs.'*[72] The Derby Summer School had a similar staffing profile, though on a smaller-scale and with different individuals. In addition to a number of 'home' Derby Training College lectures, such as Miss Carpenter, Handwork Lecturer and Miss W. Alexander, Art Lecturer, there were staff from London schools, such as Miss Roe, Headmistress of Burghley London County Council (LCC) School and Miss Kipps, Headmistress of the LCC West Hill Demonstration School for Whitelands Training College and other training college staff, such as Miss Marjorie Davies, Music Lecturer at the Rachel Macmillan Nursery Training College and author of 'Music Making' published by the London University Press.[73]

SOCIAL AND CULTURAL OPPORTUNITIES

If the educational programme of the vacation course model formed its backbone and provided its main purpose, then the opportunities afforded to teachers to share their professional and personal experiences, to socialise, network and enjoy some 'holiday' recreational time together formed its soul. Though there is limited detailed evidence of this aspect of the Welsh and Derby courses, with much more available for the CLVC, the social and cultural dimension of a residential programme and its contribution to the formation of a strong group identity amongst the teachers involved is an important part of the vacation course model of professional development.

What is known of the Welsh and Derby courses suggests quite a low key, 'home-grown' social programme. The Welsh teachers were ensconced in the arguably lofty and privileged world of an Oxford college with an emphasis on intellectual after-dinner debate and intimate group discussions. Afternoons at Oxford were spent visiting local museums, libraries and enjoying the Oxford experience. Welsh teachers were also encouraged to meet up with other groups of teachers, also in Oxford for similar purposes but on different courses. The value of networking was recognised by HMI initiating the Welsh programme, which was deliberately held in the same week as other courses for English teachers held at Balliol College as it was hoped that there would be some opportunity for the two groups of teachers to mix.[74] Prospectuses for the Derby Summer School indicated time allocated for social activities, though the organisation of social events was largely be left to the teachers themselves. Applicants for the programme were asked to indicate if they were instrumentalists, suggesting that some kind of musical ensemble might have been arranged. Tennis courts were made available to participants who were also strongly encouraged to organise themselves into groups for walks or even drives in the nearby countryside.

The CLVC was much more organised and the social and cultural side of its programme was an integral part of the overall experience. Following the hard work of the morning lecture sessions, afternoons were given over to organised visits and tours. Each year visits to famous London landmarks and other places of educational interest were arranged including the British Museum, Windsor Castle, Eton College, Houses of Parliament, Hampton Court, Westminster Abbey, St. Paul's, the Port of London, Greenwich Observatory, Kew Gardens, London Zoo and the National Gallery. These visits were specially designed and often provided tailored talks or introductions. If, for example, the trip was to the Houses of Parliament, then members were promised to be shown around under the personal guidance of serving Members of Parliament. If the trip was to the Tower of London, then it was the Yeomen of the Guard who would guide the group. A special opening of the Tower Bridge was arranged for the visit of the CLVC in 1922. Trips to Oxford for tea parties at New College, hosted by its Warden and also Principal of the Course, H.A.L Fisher, and to an annual garden party at Cliveden, hosted by Lady Astor, were memorable highlights.[75] In 1925 Lord and Lady Eustace Percy (President of the Board of Education 1924–29) hosted a garden party at Sutton Place near Guildford for 300 CLVC members.[76] Annual receptions were held for the CLVC by the Worshipful Livery Companies in the Halls of the Ancient Guilds of London. In 1925 an evening soiree was hosted by Gordon Selfridge at his famous Oxford Street store and the '... guests were delighted at the generous scale on which this soiree was arranged. The floral and other decorations were most beautifully done, musical entertainment was provided by a distinguished band of artistes, and supper was served in the sumptuous Oak Hall and other salons.[77]

The after-luncheon speech programme was a distinctive part of the course and it was in this forum that members had the opportunity '...*to meet some of the great personalities in Letters, Art, Science and Politics.'* The idea was that members '...*will be able to hear addresses by some of the outstanding figures in Britain to-day – men and women who are making history, and whose work and ideals are moulding and shaping the world of tomorrow.'*[78] The after-luncheon speakers can be categorised into three groups: politicians and ministers; educationists; and literary, artistic or other 'celebrities' of the time, including members of the aristocracy. Perhaps the major highlight, in terms of public patronage for the CLVC, was the attendance of the Prince of Wales at its inaugural Guildhall Reception in 1926.[79] Also, the Prime Minister, Stanley Baldwin, was all set to address the CLVC in 1925 but at the last minute was called away, so his speech to the teachers was read instead by the Duchess of Atholl.[80] That royalty could identify itself with the course was seen as a great honour and also a real vote of confidence for the social status of that '...*once much despised profession*'.

> It is indeed a remarkable change in the history of the relations between the teacher and the general public that so brilliant an assemblage of notable men and women should have gathered to pay tribute to the rank and file of the profession on an occasion – a holiday refresher course – that but a few years go would not have received a line of notice in the Press. It sets an example which will undoubtedly have its reactions in bringing the teacher's work, aims and ideals more fully to the notice of the public, which has been too apt to associate the profession with salary squabble and pension grievances.[81]

Politicians, including Ministers for Education, were regular speakers and there was representation from across the political spectrum including, for example, Lord Irwin, Sir Charles Trevelyan (both serving Presidents of the Board of Education at the times of their visits), Harold MacMillan, Clement Atlee, Leader of the Labour Party in 1935, Ellen Wilkinson, Margaret Bondfield, Mr Herbert Morrison, Minister for Transport in 1931, Lord Hailsham the Lord Chancellor of England and, in 1929, Sir Oswald Moseley. In 1935 the former Prime Minster, himself a former school teacher, Ramsay MacDonald spoke at the Guildhall ceremony and was reported to have said that '...*behind the teacher he saw the high purpose of the teacher's quest.'*[82] Leading educationists in addition to the course organisers included Sir Henry Hadow, Vice-Chancellor of Sheffield University and Chairman of the Hadow Report, Cyril Burt, P. B Ballard, the Headmaster of Rugby, the Vice Provost of Eton College, Professor Fred Clarke, Professor Campagnac, Dr F. J. Schonell and Professor John Adams. In 1936 Maria Montessori who was meant to be a star attraction eventually managed to get to London and give her '*eagerly awaited lecture*', after she had been held up in Barcelona, caught up in the cross-fire of the Spanish Civil War.[83] Other more artistic and adventurous speakers included writers such as Hilaire Belloc, J.B. Priestley, G. K Chesterton, Storm Jameson and L.A.G. Strong, the famous aviator Tommy Rose, the explorer Captain Kingdom Wood, the pianist Harriet Cohen, the actress

Edith Evans, the Everest expeditionist the Marquis of Clydesdale MP and the famous American blind educationist Helen Keller and her teacher Miss Macy. The informality of these speeches and visits was stressed. In a report, supposedly written by a course member in 1927, there was an interesting description of how regardless of their importance or status, the speakers mingled with the teachers – it was not a 'them and us' situation – more of an occasion of mutual respect. '*They get up with cigar or cigarette alight and chat to us rather than address us.*'[84]

If the trips, excursions and celebrity speeches were not stimulus enough, then members could always engage in a less formal programme of events. These usually took place in the lounge of the Imperial Hotel for an hour every day after dinner and included private dramatic performances, dance demonstrations, recitals, concerts, whist drives, bridge parties and dances. A special musical feature of the course was the annual formation of a Vacation Course Choir under the direction of two of the lecturers, Robert White and Mrs MacBain. This choir would give a performance at the end of the course. As with the Derby Summer School, CLVC members were encouraged to bring music and instruments. Reduced cost theatre tickets were available to course members and a list of popular entertainments in London was posted up for guidance.

The vacation course model, with its intensive two week residential approach brought together groups of teachers who had the opportunity to join together in a shared sense of professional identity and educational endeavour. Social interaction and communal living was encouraged and teachers would have had the opportunity to discuss and share ideas about their work. It can only be assumed that friendships and relationships were struck up on these vacation courses and that the members went on to form informal networks, possibly reuniting at subsequent courses. A description of the 1923 CLVC evokes the shared sense of professional identity and camaraderie fostered. '*...As the great company broke up, and the members dispersed to their hotels, it was obvious that one of the great objects of the course had been achieved. The members had already begun to know one another, the spirit of good fellowship was patent everywhere, and that atmosphere, in which the happy interchange of ideas can most readily be made, already pervaded the course.*'[85]

THE VACATION COURSE AND TEACHER PROFESSIONALISM

Key features of the vacation course as a model of teacher professional development have been examined across three different cases and, though they shared common features, it has been suggested that each case was quite distinctive in its focus, scope, intentions and ambition. The CLVC was arguably superior in terms of the richness of experience on offer – from the London location, accommodation in hotels, extensive social and cultural programme and also because of the high calibre and prestige of visiting speakers and lecturers. The Derby Summer School appeared more modest yet continued to attract similar numbers of teachers each summer as the CLVC. Though it was marketed nationally and drew teachers from across Britain, most of its cohort appeared to derive from nearby Derbyshire, Nottinghamshire and Leicestershire, suggesting that it was more of a 'local' example.[86] Its strong emphasis on Handwork subjects, particularly during the 1930s, differentiated it somewhat from its more glamorous metropolitan counterpart. The Welsh courses offered something quite specialised in a particular academic environment for a small group of selected teachers. The Oxford surroundings were regarded as the 'main factor' in making the courses '...*quite outstanding as compared with previous courses in the same subject which have been held elsewhere.*[87]

Underpinning all three cases was an ethos founded on a belief that teachers needed to be removed from their quotidian experiences and exposed to new ideas and practices in order to re-invigorate them and their teaching. Derby Summer School prospectuses for the late 1930s emphasized the need for teachers to stave off boredom or apathy towards their work by renewing their interest in it. The Summer School was presented as having the power to re-invigorate teachers by providing '... an opportunity for beginning new interests and for recovering interest in work that has become tedious.'[88] The CLVC was explicitly billed as a '...*great 'adventure', designed to lift the elementary teacher out of their normal existence, with ...new scenes, new manners, new customs, a sense of being in a bigger world, and, of a freedom from the narrow routine and limited social opportunities'.*[89] The Welsh courses deliberately took their teachers out of Wales and put them into an Oxford college to expose them to the possibilities of a different world.

Both explicitly through their educational programmes and implicitly in their conception and ethos these vacation courses, different though they were, all subscribed to a very particular model of the idea of teacher professionalism. This was made particularly explicit in the case of the CLVC but was very much implied in the Derby and Welsh examples. This model of teacher professionalism was committed to teachers having their practical teaching skills and knowledge extended and honed, for the benefit of their pupils – but was also concerned with personal development and growth. This idea of teacher professionalism was very much embodied in the 1925 Departmental Committee Report, discussed in Chapter Two, which suggested that in-service training should seek to meet two main functions: first, to refresh subject knowledge and learn new developments, and to improve teaching techniques and introduce new methods; and secondly, to have a generally positive effect 'upon the teacher's mind and outlook'.[90] The vacation course model certainly seemed to fit this bill.

Though contested, salaries, pensions and conditions of service for teachers were significantly improved during this period, providing scope for teachers to engage in their own wider professional development and education. In his speech at the inaugural dinner of the CLVC in 1926, Lord Burnham captured some of this change and was reported to say that '...*the teacher has shown, since the Fisher Act has begun to change his working conditions, and since the national scales have bettered his material prospects, that he knows how to use his improved position wisely and well. He is using his leisure for the better furnishing of his mind, as the large attendance at the CLVC each year shows, in order that he may be a more effective member of what Mr Fisher has called "one of the great liberal callings of the country".*[91] There was no place in this new order of teachers' work for old stereotypes of the 'narrow' elementary teacher – the technical pedagogue keeping at bay hoards of unruly Board School children, but there were fears that popular perceptions lagged behind changes in the profession. A report on the 1925 CLVC argued that it was up to the teachers themselves to apply themselves '*...determinedly to the task of lifting their profession out of the shameful morass of shabby-gentility and sweated conditions in which they had been grovelling for a couple of generations.*'[92] In 1933, educational commentator Horace Shipp reporting on the course suggested that, '*There is a tendency sometimes for teachers to accept the old-fashioned poor opinion of their profession. Remembering some specimen of the early strident-voiced keepers of order in disgracefully over-crowded classrooms, they will disguise and all but deny their calling, having as an ideal that they should not be recognised as teachers. Whereupon the world goes on judging teachers by the avowed specimens complete with the strident voices.*'[93] Shipp went on to describe the teaching profession as a noble calling but warned that it would only become as valued as other professions, such as law and medicine when it learned to value itself. First teachers had to recognise value and believe themselves and then the public could be better educated.

Existing historical work on wider aspects of teacher professionalism, notably by Cunningham and Gardner and Ozga and Lawn, has raised important questions about how the new teacher professionalism of the 1920s and 1930s could be interpreted as a State-imposed ideological model which sat uncomfortably alongside the working-class, craft and union roots of elementary teachers.[94] Both Simon and Lawn have drawn attention to the potential social danger of teachers, who with their working-class roots, extended education and position of authority in communities where, for the first time, the political franchise had been extended, were seen as the touchstone of public attitudes.[95] This new professionalism, according to some interpretations, represented a 'selling-out' on the part of elementary teachers, as they 'bought-in' to dominant establishment discourses of the teacher as a cultured, responsible public servant, with a civic and patriotic responsibility to the future of Britain. These discourses represented a major shift away from, what Cunningham and Gardner refer to as, '*...the continuing official suspicion of and dislike for, the traditional classroom teacher understood as a characteristically narrow, uncultured and uninspiring figure.*'[96]

Where then does the vacation course model of teacher professional development fit into these existing interpretations of inter-war teacher professionalism? The CLVC and the Welsh Oxford courses in particular might well be interpreted as a patronising attempt on the part of both the educational and the political establishment to improve teachers who, because of their relatively humble origins and limited education and training, were somehow found wanting. The glittering social and cultural programme of the CLVC and the privileged Oxford world of the Welsh courses might convincingly have transported teachers into a more bourgeois, high culture world than that to which they were accustomed. It could be argued that they neatly exemplified a highly visible vehicle for the inculcation of an externally engineered ideal of teacher professionalism, as well as a very public platform for its exposition. On the other hand, the Derby Summer School, with its more institutionalised 'training college' ethos, could be viewed as least likely to lift teachers towards higher cultural and social aspirations, bringing them back to the very modest type of establishment in which they would have completed their initial training. However, its educational pedigree was robust and there was a clear objective to refresh and invigorate the potentially stale teacher and renew their professional enthusiasm. The relationship between teachers, the vacation courses available to them and the new teacher professionalism of the 1920s and 1930s is difficult to unpick. This is because so much of the historical record overlooks the lived experience of the teachers themselves and, most importantly, tends not follow up on the impact of these vacation courses on teachers' professional work and personal lives, other than through rather anodyne and formulaic HMI reports. Though the vacation course model engaged teachers in social and cultural activity as part of the overall experience, not least because it was meant to be a working holiday, there was also a very powerful commitment to providing new professional learning for teachers which would be of direct practical relevance to their classroom practice. A deficit model of externally imposed and engineered teacher professionalism offers an overly simplistic interpretation of a highly complex phenomenon, and takes away any agency from the teachers themselves – those teachers who actively chose to engage with these vacation courses in their own time and sometimes a their own expense. The vacation course model offered teachers an opportunity to meet together, to share professional experience and to share professional learning and potentially to form a strong sense of professional identity. It also raised aspirations and expectations that teachers could refresh both their professional and personal knowledge and keep abreast of new ideas, new methods and new skills. Though modest in scope, for its time it went some way towards shaping the idea of the learning profession.

NOTES

[1] See for example Gosden, P. (1972). *The evolution of a profession.* Oxford: Basil Blackwell; and Dent, H. (1977). *The training of teachers in England and Wales 1800–1975.* London: Hodder & Stoughton.

[2] See Tropp, A. (1957). *The school teachers.* London, UK: William Heinemann Ltd. Simon, B. (1974). *The politics of educational reform 1920–1940.* London, UK: Lawrence & Wishart.

[3] Simon, *The politics of educational reform 1920–1940*, p. 198.

[4] Tropp, *The school teachers.*

[5] Dobson, M. (1951). *1851–1951: The first hundred years of the Diocesan Training College Derby.* West Bromwich: Kenrick & Jefferson, p. 36.

[6] Dobson, *1851–1951: The first hundred years of the Diocesan Training College Derby*, p. 36; Derbyshire Record Office (hereafter DER RO), D6845/Box 34/5: Derby Training College vacation course prospectus 1934, p.1.

[7] The UK National Archives (hereafter TNA), ED 82/126, letter from Bater, dated 26/6/1922; DER RO, D6845/Box 34/5: Derby Training College vacation course prospectus 1927.

[8] DER RO, D6845/Box 34/5: Derby Training College vacation course prospectus 1925.

[9] Ibid.

[10] DER RO, D6845/ Box 34/5: Derby Training College vacation course prospectuses 1925 and 1927.

[11] TNA, Ed 82/126, Derby Summer Vacation Courses, 1935 Brochure, p. 1.

[12] Board of Education, *Report of the board of education for the year 1934*, pp. 153–4. (hereafter cited as BoE, Annual Report with date); BoE, Annual Report, 1934, p. 88; BoE, Annual Report, 1935, p. 92.

[13] BoE, Annual Report, 1921–22, p. 67.

[14] BoE, Annual Report, 1923, p. 140.

[15] BoE, Annual Report, 1925, p. 156.

[16] BoE, Annual Report, 1930, p. 83; BoE, Annual Report, 1936, p. 61; on shift to elementary teachers due to Departmental Committee report, see University of Oxford, Jesus College Archives (hereafter Jesus), BU.COR.3, letter from Watkins (Welsh Department) to Hazel, dated 20/12/1927; and see BoE, Annual Report, 1934, p.88. Watkins' letter suggests the change to elementary teachers occurred in 1928 but it is first mentioned in the annual reports in 1934.

[17] *The Teachers' World* (hereafter TTW), August 10 1932, p. 682.

[18] *TTW*, July 27 1932, p. 642.

[19] TNA, ED 82/126, HMI report on Derby Summer School dated 8/10/1923.

[20] TNA, ED 82/126, internal Board of Education note, dated 24/07/1922.

[21] TNA, ED 82/126, letter from Bater, dated 26/6/1922.

[22] Ibid.

[23] TNA, ED 82/126, internal Board of Education note, dated 24/07/1922.

[24] Ibid.

[25] TNA, ED 82/126, letter from Helen Hawkins, dated 13/12/1932 and replies.

[26] Jesus, BU.COR.2 CN, letter from Davies to Hazel, dated 26/04/1922.

[27] Jesus, BU.COR.2 CN, course programme 1922.

[28] BoE, Annual Report, 1925, p.156.

[29] http://www.jesus.ox.ac.uk/about/the-welsh-college [retrieved 25/09/2011].

[30] Jesus, BU.COR.2 CN, undated staff list, probably from 1922.

[31] Jesus, BU.COR.2 CN, letter to AT Davies from Jesus Bursar, Dr Hazel, dated 18/02/1924.

[32] Jesus, BU.COR.2 CN, letter to AT Davies from Hazel, dated 29/02/1924.

[33] Jesus, BU.COR.2 CN, letter from AT Davies to Hazel, dated 19/07/1922.

[34] TNA, ED 22/173, Memo to inspectors (Wales) no.309, dated 1/05/1923.

[35] Ibid.

[36] Ibid.

[37] Ibid.

[38] TNA, ED 22/175, Memo to inspectors (Wales) no.342, dated April 1925; Jesus, BU.COR.2 CN, form 105U, 1925.

[39] TNA, ED 22/175, Memo to inspectors (Wales) no.342, dated April 1925.

[40] *TTW*, July 26 1933, p. 612.

[41] TNA, Ed 24/1810, City of London Vacation Courses in Education for teachers: papers, 1922–1935.

[42] *The Times*, March 5 1923, p. 9, reporting that the Advisory Council of the CLVC had secured H. A. L. Fisher as its Principal and that 600 teachers were expected at the forthcoming 1923 meeting.

[43] TNA, Ed 24/1810, City of London Vacation Courses in Education for teachers: papers, 1922–1935.

[44] *TTW*, August 9 1922, p. 902.

[45] *The Times*, July 28 1928, p. 8.

[46] Jesus, BU.COR.2 CN, course programme 1922.

[47] Ibid.

[48] Ibid.

[49] Ibid.

[50] Ibid.

[51] Jesus, BU.COR.3 CN, lecture programme 1927.

[52] TNA, ED 22/173, Memo to inspectors (Wales) no.309, dated 1/05/1923.

[53] BoE, Annual Report, 1923, p.140.

[54] Ibid., pp. 140–141.

[55] See Jones, G. (1982). *Controls and conflicts in Welsh secondary education, 1889–1944*. Cardiff: University of Wales Press, pp. 123–130. This Departmental Committee produced a report in 1927 entitled '*Welsh in Education and Life*'.

[56] BoE, Annual Report, 1924, p. 126.

[57] Ibid.

[58] *TTW*, May 15 1929, p. 369.

[59] *TTW*, May 24 1922, p. 381.

[60] *TTW*, July 30 1924, p. 877.

[61] *TTW,* July 29 1925, p. 886.

[62] DER RO, D6845/Box 34/5: Derby Training College vacation course prospectus 1925 and 1929.

[63] *TTW*, February 17 1926, p. 1009.

[64] DER RO, D6845/Box 34/5: Derby Training College vacation course prospectus 1925, pp.11–12.

[65] DER RO, D6845/Box 34/5: Derby Training College vacation course prospectuses (various). Course on school trips may have run in other years but series of prospectuses in Derbyshire Record Office is incomplete.

[66] DER RO, D6845/Box 34/5: Derby Training College vacation course prospectus 1929, pp.10–11.

[67] *TTW,* July 25 1928, p. 883.

[68] DER RO, D6845/Box 34/5: Derby Training College vacation course prospectus 1925, pp.7–8.

[69] Cox, G. (2001). 'Teaching music in schools: some historical reflections', in C. Philpott and C. Plummeridge (Eds), *Issues in Music Teaching*. London, UK: RoutledgeFalmer, pp. 9–20.

[70] See for example, Finch, R. (1923). *A. & C. Black's world-wide geography pictures*. London, UK: A. & C. Black.

[71] Bassett, R. (1922). *Streatham County Secondary School for Girls Dalton Plan Assignments Compiled by the staff of Streatham County Secondary School for Girls*. London: G. Bell and Sons.

[72] *TTW,* May 15 1929, p. 369.

[73] TNA, ED 82/126, Derby Summer Vacation Courses, 1935 Brochure, p. 1.

[74] Jesus, BU.COR.2 CN, letter from Hazel to Davies, dated 5/11/1921, and letters from Davies to Hazel, dated 26/04/1922 and 04/05/1922.

[75] *The Times*, July 31 1924, p. 15.

[76] *The Times*, August 3 1925, p. 5.

[77] *TTW*, July 29 1925, p. 88.

[78] TNA, ED 24/1810, 1922 Course Brochure, p. 4.

[79] *The Times*, July 31 1926, p. 14.

[80] *The Times*, July 28 1925, p. 11.

[81] *TTW*, August 4 1926, p. 842.

[82] *TTW*, July 31 1935, p. 652.

[83] *Teachers world and schoolmistress*, July 29 1936, p. 831.

[84] *TTW*, August 10 1927, p. 990.

[85] *TTW*, August 1 1923, p. 843.

[86] TNA, ED 82/126, report by D.I. Mr C J Phillips, dated unclear but annotations refer to correspondence from 1932, so likely to date from around then; TNA, ED 82/126, an Interview Memorandum of interview with Miss Hawkins, 3/01/1934.

[87] Jesus, BU.COR.2 CN, letter to Hazel, dated 08/03/1926.

[88] DER RO, D6845/Box 34/5: Derby Training College vacation course prospectus 1939.

[89] *TTW*, April 6 1927, p. 37.

[90] BoE, Annual Report, 1924–25, p. 119.

[91] *TTW*, August 4 1926, p. 842.

[92] *TTW*, August 5 1925, p. 916.

[93] *TTW*, August 2 1933, p. 643.

[94] See Ozga, J. & Lawn, M. (1981). *Teachers professionalism and class*. London, UK: The Falmer Press; Lawn, M. (1987). *Servants of the state: The contested control of teaching 1900–1930*. London, UK: The Falmer Press; Cunningham, P., & Gardner, P. (2004). *Becoming teachers: Texts and testimonies 1907–1950*. London, UK: Woburn Press.

[95] Simon, *The politics of educational reform 1920–1940*, p. 71; Lawn, *Servants of the state: The contested control of teaching 1900–1930*, p. 59.

[96] Cunningham, P., & Gardner, P. (2004). *Becoming teachers: Texts and testimonies 1907–1950*, p. 229.

SPECIAL ADVANCED COURSES FOR TEACHERS
1945–1960

INTRODUCTION

Following the Second World War, programmes of in-service training for teaching became increasingly well-established. From 1948 the Ministry of Education began to fund 'special advanced courses for experienced serving teachers' which were aimed at a small, elite group of teachers whose potential as school leaders, teacher trainers or educational administrators was recognised as worthy of investment. These advanced courses required experienced teachers to be seconded for one year from the regular classroom and to study a full-time course at university, leading to an award-bearing Diploma in such subjects as child psychology, child development, nursery and infant education, special needs education and various special subjects. Developed at a time when the recommendations of the 1944 McNair Report were being implemented, with regional ATOs being established in partnership with selected universities[1], the special advanced courses for serving teachers arguably represented the pinnacle of in-service provision at that time, in terms of aspiration, process, duration, accreditation, subject focus and possible impact on career development. This model of in-service training, whose basic concept involved the serving teacher being removed from their immediate day-to-day classroom life into a university environment to engage in high level educational study for a sustained period of time, usually one year, leading to a higher qualification, continued to have currency in the landscape of teacher professional development throughout the twentieth century, albeit in various forms. It is also a model which embodies a number of perennial issues which have characterised the history of teacher professional development – namely the role and function of the universities; debates over the appropriate balance of academic theory and professional practice in teacher education and the relationship between the status of the teaching profession, the academic study of education and accredited higher qualifications for teachers.

This chapter will examine the development of special advanced courses for serving teachers by the Ministry of Education in the period 1945–70 with a focus on two case studies of provision. The chapter is in three main parts. First, the origins and development of the model by the Ministry of Education will be outlined, with a consideration of general policy, funding, selection and recruitment of teachers. Secondly, a discussion of the development of special advanced courses in two institutions, the University of London, Institute of Education (LIoE) and the Bristol

Institute of Education will be presented. Finally, the implications of this model of provision will be evaluated in relation to wider issues in the teaching profession and teacher professional development. Though mentioned briefly in standard histories of teaching, very little historical analysis of the special advanced course for serving teachers exists, with the general consensus being that universities did not really get involved in the creation of accredited programmes for serving teachers until the late 1960s and 70s onwards.[2] Archive data for this chapter is drawn from central government papers at the National Archives, as well as institutional archives for the LIoE and the University of Bristol.

THE DEVELOPMENT OF 'SPECIAL ADVANCED COURSES FOR SERVING TEACHERS' BY THE MINISTRY OF EDUCATION

Origins

During the 1920s and 1930s the Board of Education had developed a very modest scheme of studentships for serving teachers which laid the foundations for the idea of the special advanced course, subsequently taken up by the Ministry of Education in 1947. This earlier scheme contained similar core elements to its successor: it was aimed at the experienced teacher; it involved subsidised one year secondments for research or study at a UK or overseas university; and it represented highly elite provision for very small numbers of participants.[3] Though it fell into abeyance during the Second World War, discussions about whether to revive or replace it began in 1947. Initially, there was some suggestion that two distinct models might be funded by the Ministry: one would be a revival or reworking of the old studentship system, to be called 'educational fellowships'; the second would enable up to 100 teachers to undertake specially organised year-long courses at universities.'[4] Opinion eventually turned against the fellowships proposal.[5] Indeed, in reference to recipients of those earlier awards having been able to choose their own courses of study and to the relatively small number of such awards made each year, one civil servant described the studentships scheme as having been 'a frill', suggesting that in retrospect the scheme was viewed as having been inconsequential and costly, with limited return for the investment.[6]

By late 1947 the Ministry of Education had identified a more clearly defined aim for the higher level of in-service training that it wished to fund for serving teachers. Anxiety at the shortage of training college lecturers in the face of planned expansion in recruitment to the teaching profession generated an approach which aimed to channel experienced serving teachers on to courses of study which would equip them for training college vacancies, as well as other positions as head teachers of schools or LEA supervisors.[7] The focus of this level of provision therefore shifted away from individual teachers' personal interests as had been the case with the earlier studentship scheme, towards a much more centrally controlled programme of courses run by universities in line with government priorities. In the 1947–48 academic year, two 'proto-type' courses were being piloted: one at the LIoE, aimed at nursery and infant teachers; the other, at the University of Birmingham, focused on Child Psychology for teachers.[8]

Funding

In order to roll out this new scheme, the thorny question of funding had to be addressed. This issue was contested, as there was considerable resistance within the Ministry to any suggestion that LEAs might continue to pay salaries – or a part of them – to their seconded teachers in exchange for commitment from the teachers to return to the employment of that particular authority. Rather, it was the Ministry's intention that '...*the teacher going off to other service should indeed very often be the result of them.*'[9] A Ministry funded grant seemed the sensible option. Following protracted discussion and negotiation with the Treasury, it was eventually agreed that this grant should offer up to £300 per teacher for 1948–49, the first academic year of the programme, and a calculation was put forward which set an amount of £16,000 to be made available for this purpose (based on £200 for each of 80 teachers) to cover expenditure required for the two terms which would fall within the 1948–1949 financial year.[10] Additionally, teachers on the programme were eligible for annual pensionable increments on the Burnham scale.[11] The agreed grant of £300 was intended to satisfy the needs of teachers who had already been working for several years and who would have become accustomed to a certain level of income, though right from the outset there were concerns that it might be difficult to attract more experienced teachers to the scheme as they would be accustomed to a certain level of income and would also be more likely to have other financial commitments, particularly to family, to fulfil whilst on sabbatical.

With this funding mechanism in place, the Ministry of Education set out to organise a programme of 'special course for experienced serving teachers' for the academic year 1948–1949. By the beginning of 1948, alongside the courses at London and Birmingham Universities, it was known that Darlington Training College was to run a course, and Manchester and Bristol Universities were also considering doing so.[12] However, even as the Ministry was seeking to get the programme up and running for the following academic year, teachers and LEAs were already expressing their concerns about the funding situation. In March 1948, Mr Longland, the County Education Officer for Dorset, wrote to the Ministry's Teachers Branch to request advice on whether or not the LEA could provide a further grant to a teacher considering taking one of the new courses in order to meet the shortfall between his salary of £468 and the Ministry grant of £300.[13] The Ministry was well aware that there would be a gap between the amount of grant it provided and the salary level to which experienced serving teachers had become accustomed, as this had formed part of the discussions when the level of grant was set. It had already been calculated that a four-year training graduate, with five years' teaching experience would be expected to be earning in the region of £420 for a man and £366 for a woman per annum.[14] The question of how to respond to the query from Dorset was discussed between Ministry officials, as it was considered that the response to this letter would act as a test-case in setting a precedent in dealing with the new courses.[15] The reply was eventually split into two elements, with the first being to note that a 'teacher's contribution' for course tuition fees would be calculated based upon his or her income during the year of the course, though, in practice, unless the teacher had significant income from other sources he would not be required to make a contribution as such.[16] The second part of the response focused on the thorny issue of the shortfall between the teacher's normal salary and the £300 grant, and on this issue it was clearly stated that '...*the Ministry intended that the teacher should make some financial sacrifice in order to take a course, particularly in view of the better prospects which satisfactory completion of it would give him.*'[17] On these grounds, the letter continued, whilst it was open to an LEA to make a grant for incidental expenses to a teacher if it so wished, to do so would be contrary to the Ministry's intentions.[18] Therefore, it is evident that at this stage in the scheme the Ministry viewed some element of financial sacrifice on behalf of the seconded teacher was necessary, perhaps seeing it as evidence of their commitment to their own personal or professional development. What was on offer was intended to be of mutual benefit – both to the Ministry and to the teacher, who in the long term should benefit from career enhancement and improved remuneration.

Recruitment and Selection of Teachers

In February 1948, details of the new courses were sent out to LEAs in 'Administrative Memorandum No.266'.[19] The courses were open to qualified teachers with not less than five years' experience, and the teachers were selected from amongst the applicants by the institutions hosting the courses in conjunction with the Ministry and with advice from HMI if necessary.[20] Documents from the early years of these courses show the complex process of negotiation between the Ministry and institutions selected to run one of these one-year courses, illustrating some of the challenges of organising the programme in a context where several parties were responsible for its development. For example, documents relating to the development of a 'special course for experienced serving teachers in Domestic Subjects', illustrate the involvement of multiple agencies. Letters from J.V. Stephenson at the Ministry of Education to W.O. Lester Smith, Chief Education Officer for Manchester, suggest that a course in Domestic Subjects at Manchester Domestic Science Training College should be organised for the academic year 1949–1950. Some of the letters mention that the recently formed ATO should be informed of the development of this course and involved in its operation, but there is no clear indication of what involvement this organisation came to have, if any.[21] There was also correspondence on this course between the Ministry and the Training College, and the Ministry and the University of Manchester.[22] Several points emerge from these letters – one is that funding for these courses was at this time being agreed between the Ministry and the Treasury on a year by year basis, so confirmation to the institution that the course would definitely be able to go ahead would not be forthcoming before early 1949.[23] This made forward planning difficult. A further point of interest is that by 1949, a change in the grant regulations meant that a teacher's contribution and grant level were assessed based upon their own and their spouse's salaries, if appropriate, subject to some deductions.[24] Finally, the Manchester course in Domestic Subjects illustrates the strong focus of these special courses on Educational Psychology, as even for a course whose title suggests a subject focus, the advertised programme actually reveals a three part structure, with part one focused entirely on theories of Educational Psychology, part two on the organisation of secondary education and only part three on 'The Educational Principles of Housecraft.'[25] At this time Educational Psychology was the dominant discipline within university education departments and had been since their development in the late 1890s. The complex history behind the influence of Psychology and the growth of university departments of education in the twentieth century has been well documented in the work of Adrian Wooldridge.[26] With its 'scientific' credentials, Educational Psychology as a discipline had gone some way in securing the legitimacy of Education as a subject worthy of adoption within the academy, and it is not surprising that the majority of the special advanced course endorsed by the Ministry of Education had a strong Psychology bias.

Letters relating to the operation of a course in Child Psychology at the LIoE reveal that financial sacrifice was not the only barrier that teachers faced if they wished to be considered for this programme. A discussion between Dorothy Gardner, the course leader and Stephenson at the Ministry about the exact wording of a question on the application form for this course suggest that teachers might have been selected according to a hidden set of criteria. Although one of the main rationales for the programme was to provide a route to career progression out of the classroom, how this was managed and made explicit was not so clear. Gardner, writing about a suggestion that the question *'Please state what special purpose you have in taking the course?'* should be altered, wrote that *'If they state promotion as a main purpose it immediately puts us on our guard and we are then careful not to accept people if we feel this really represents their point of view.'*[27] She went on to write that there were some who might be seeking promotion who were 'genuine educationists' but that there were also those who were merely 'promotion-hunters', and that it was difficult to discern which was which simply through their written answers, and she went so far as to describe some of the applicants as 'the dangerous people'. The idea that actively pursuing promotion was a negative trait was also held by Stephenson who wrote to Gardner about the need to 'sift' the applicants carefully in order to ensure that 'their aims are both honest and good.'[28] Reconciling personal ambition with a dedication to education for its own sake was clearly an issue here, with the traditional notion that teachers should have a 'higher purpose', calling or vocation, not to be sullied by an individual career ambition prevailing. Stephen Wiseman, a contemporary university academic working in the field of teacher education, wrote a short feature in a very early edition of the *British Journal of Educational Studies* in 1953 on 'higher degrees' in education, and was explicit in his belief that through the special advanced courses '*....the practising teacher may gain advancement within his profession for a more responsible post or to a headship; or he may enter educational administration, or become an inspector of schools. For many it leads to posts in teacher training colleges and university departments of education.*'[29] It is hard to imagine, given the evident financial sacrifices involved, that teachers embarking upon this programme would not have been motivated by the promise of career advancement

Between 1947 and 1951, the Ministry of Education, in collaboration with universities and LEAs, had established its special advanced courses programme. By 1951, eight courses for experienced teachers were being held in eight institutions for a total of 79 teachers.[30] Outside of the London course, numbers of teachers per course were modest, though courses would have been larger with private paying students from home and overseas. However, by 1951 there was concern that the programme was not performing as intended, due to inadequate funding arrangements. In reality, the programme was deterring candidates with 'domestic responsibilities' – often those very teachers with the experience and length of service that were '*... the kind of teachers we really want*'.[31] In the years 1948–51, a total of 225 teachers had been selected to take part in the special courses, and the issue was not that this number was too small but that the quality of recruits was not that which had been originally desired.[32] The courses were intended to attract the 'cream of the teaching profession' but were not doing so due to the financial sacrifice which the teachers had to make, and it was noted that as a result there was pressure to accept applications from teachers with less than five years' experience.[33] These difficulties led the Ministry, following consultation with the ATOs which were by then responsible for the general organisation of these courses, to approach the Treasury for approval to change the funding arrangements, by shifting to a system whereby the Ministry would pay tuition fees as well as a separate maintenance grant.[34] Appeals to the Treasury emphasised that there would be no attempt to increase the number of teachers being recruited to these courses, as the focus was on 'quality over quantity'.[35] The cost of the proposed new funding arrangement was estimated at £29,000 for the year 1951–1952, increasing to £40,000 by 1953–54.[36]

The Ministry's Annual Report for 1955 recorded that 82 teachers (19 men and 48 women) had attended twelve of these courses in 1954, but also stated that as many teachers again had been unable to take up their places due to their financial domestic responsibilities. Inappropriately matched funding was clearly a systemic problem. At the request of the National Advisory Council on the Training and Supply of Teachers (NACTST), LEAs and Institutes of Education were then asked to cater for the needs of these teachers through local short and part-time courses.[37] By 1960, the programme had been further developed and was roughly divided into four types of course: General Diplomas in Education (nine courses, 109 students); Educational and Social Psychology (six courses, 84 students); The Education of Handicapped Children (four courses, 65 students); and courses focused on particular subjects (six courses, 37 students).[38]

The Robbins Committee proposals for the expansion of higher education in 1963 recommended a much closer and more coherent administrative and academic collaboration between universities and training colleges and the introduction of an all-graduate teaching profession. The impetus of Robbins drove further expansion of university-based programmes of study for seconded teachers – not just for full-time courses, but also for more flexible, local, part-time opportunities. If the need to expand the pool of possible teacher trainers had spurred the early development of the special courses programme in the late 1940s, then the post-Robbins expansion signalled another wave of demand. Circular 7/64 emphasised their importance in the context of expansion of the school system and of colleges and called for an increase of around 50% in the number of students taking special advanced courses by the end of the 1960s.[39] In the same year the Department for Education and Science announced its intention to increase recruitment to the courses to 1000 teachers per year on a full-time basis by the end of the decade, with an additional increase in the number taking these courses on a part-time basis.[40] In 1964, there were 578 teachers taking government funded special courses, not including those attending courses for teachers of handicapped children.[41] Recruitment to these courses exceeded 1,000 teachers in 1967 and reached a peak of 1,840 in 1974[42]. By this time it was clear that the control exercised by the government in approving special advanced courses had weakened. Whilst some institutions had been actively encouraged to offer courses by the Ministry of Education in the early years, other programmes had begun because universities, seeing the potential financial gain and opportunity for capacity building within their education departments, had sought Ministry approval and funding. In practice, this meant that by the 1960s, there were numerous institutions offering approved courses, with LEAs topping up government grants to support their teachers in attending them. By the late 1960s and early 1970s, with wider in-service opportunities developing for teachers, not just in universities or by the LEAs but also in the new emerging teachers' centres, the special advanced course for experienced serving teachers, as it was originally conceived in the late 1940s and 1950s was very different. The introduction of a new four-year B.Ed. degree for intending teachers created different opportunities for university departments of education and colleges of education to develop new education programmes for undergraduates as well as targeting the large numbers of non-graduate experienced teachers who wanted to bring their own qualifications up to date, either of a part-time or seconded basis. With the emergence of an all-graduate profession, Diplomas gave way to the development of Masters and even Doctoral level degree programmes, which offered higher level academic qualifications for career-oriented professionals, though they had left an enduring legacy which continues to shape teacher professional development in universities to the present day.

CASE STUDIES: THE UNIVERSITY OF LONDON INSTITUTE OF EDUCATION
AND THE BRISTOL INSTITUTE OF EDUCATION

In collating archive material for this brief historical overview of the special advanced courses organised by the Ministry of Education there was more detailed data available for the London Institute of Education courses which was then followed up with further archival research in the London Institute of Education archives to develop a deeper case study. In addition, Bristol University archives were consulted to generate a second institutional case study, different from the London Institute example, but also representing a significant ATO at that time.

The University of London, Institute of Education

The Centre for Child Development at the LIoE was one of the first institutions to offer a special advanced course for experienced serving teachers. Its Director, Dorothy Gardner, was in close contact with the Ministry of Education about the issues surrounding recruitment to the Diploma in Child Development which she ran and which formed part of the Ministry's programme. Formed in the 1930s, under the leadership of Susan Isaacs, this specialist Centre had a history of delivering progressive, cutting-edge courses to teachers and training college lecturers in new methods and approaches to child study, and it is likely that its contribution to the special course programme was an extension of existing provision rather than an entirely new offering.[43]

Though Ministry of Education archive data at the National Archives first refers to a Diploma course in Child Psychology being run at the Institute in 1947–1948, the Institute's own records suggest that in fact the Ministry began to fund students to take the course in 1946–47, as the Centre for Child Development's Annual Report for that session states that 24 students had taken the course having been funded by grants from the Ministry.[44] In 1947–48, that number increased to 29 and was expected to rise again to 39 for the next session, although the report – written by Gardner – notes that the new grant system meant that existing training college lecturers were no longer eligible to take the course.[45] Though it is not expressly stated, it does seem likely that this was indeed the Ministry according 'special course' status to this course, though the discrepancy between the timelines given in the different sources of documentation is puzzling.[46] Although apparently unhappy that the restrictions which prevented training college lecturers from taking the course, which she wrote 'had excluded some particularly able candidates', Gardner did express satisfaction that the new grant system had enabled more students to take the course, and mentions especially that an increased grant – it was raised from £200 to £300 for the 1948–49 session - would enable more English men to take up places.[47] Of the five men accepted for grant in 1947–48, only one had been able to take up their place, with the others presumably having found the gap between their usual salary and the amount of grant too big a drop in household income to bear.[48] The reference to English men specifically reflects the fact that between ten and twenty 'private' students took the course each year, many of whom were foreign. It also highlights the fact that the majority of the English students accepted onto the course were women, as it was mainly aimed at nursery and infant teachers and the teaching profession at those levels was largely dominated by women at that time.[49] The gender divide was ongoing as in 1956–57, of a total of 62 students – both grant-aided and private – there were 15 men and 47 women.[50]

The number of grant-aided students taking the Diploma in Child Development varied considerably during the 1940s and 1950s. The number of grant-aided places available was set by the Ministry of Education, in consultation with the Institute, and seems to have been largely based upon budgetary concerns. After the steady increase in grant-aided places available during the 1940s, in the early 1950s a need for 'national economy' during the age of austerity caused the Ministry to reduce the number of places that it would fund.[51] As the Ministry only set the quota of grant-aided places for each session during the preceding session, there was not a great deal of time for Gardner and her staff to prepare for significant changes in the number of students. For example, in 1956–7, when the Ministry raised the number to 40 and was also open to admitting more, plans had to be made for Institute staff to be carefully shared across the courses then running to ensure 'adequate tutorial supervision'.[52] The retrospective departmental report on that session admitted that 'though the staff have been very much aware of the department being over-large for fully adequate supervision and the students have regretted not having more opportunities for discussion in smaller groups.'[53] Furthermore, a note included in the 1957–8 report, looking forward to the 1958–59 session, sees Gardner explaining that the Ministry had offered to fund 50 places on the course and that she had at first been inclined to refuse to admit such a high number, but that as '*it becomes increasingly difficult to discriminate between good applicants*', she had accepted the increased quota although with plans to compensate by reducing the number of foreign and privately funded students.[54] However, she says that the course would again be too large for its staff, and that the existing staff spent so much time with students that their other responsibilities, such as research, were suffering.[55] This clearly shows that a sudden significant increase in numbers had impacted upon the functioning of the course and upon the experience of those following it, as well as upon the functioning of the Department as a whole. However, in some years a reduction in numbers was due to a failure to attract enough applicants of the desired standard to fill the quota allowed by the Ministry, so the number accepted onto the course each year was not solely determined by the Ministry and was not set on exclusively financial criteria.[56]

As well as documenting the numbers attending the course and the relationship between the Department for Child Development and the Ministry of Education, the annual departmental reports written by Gardner also touch upon the experiences of those who followed the course, particularly with reference to the social life of the Department. For example, the report for 1951–52 notes that the students '*have been very united this year*', that there had been an '*absence of cliques*' and that locally-based students had '*entertained overseas students in their own homes on many occasions*'.[57] Gardner also reported that students had organised, at their own initiative, expeditions and social gatherings, and had undertaken fundraising activities for the Susan Isaacs Memorial Fund.[58] In other years though, particularly 1955–57, Gardner noted that the social life of the department had been much quieter and suggested that this might have been due to the fact that many students now came from the London area and were spending more time at their own homes.[59] However, in the 1957–58 report, Gardner retracted this idea as she reported that the social life in the Department had improved once again.[60] As well taking part in social activities together during their time on the course, an Old Students' Association was founded in 1948–49 to keep former students in touch with each other and with the Department, and by 1952 there was a London sub-group in operation.[61]

In terms of course structure and content, information is limited. A reference for a teacher who had taken the course, written by Gardner, describes how the course addressed '*the psychology of children, recent educational developments, the training of teachers, and the special needs of backward and difficult children*', through a programme of lectures and seminars, and also included visits to schools, child guidance clinics, and other social and educational institutions.[62] The teacher in question, Amelia Bullen, had also conducted research into the issue of children on waiting lists for places in nursery schools or classes, both in London and in her home town of Grimsby. This research had involved the compilation of 100 sample case histories, with the analysis of the reasons of mothers for wanting to place their children in nursery, as well as '*a careful study of the needs of children and young mothers in relation to their home life*' which Gardner stated was a valuable contribution to the wider study of the subject being undertaken by the department.[63]

Annual course reports provide further insights into some of the research projects which other students undertook, including individual and group projects, as well as ongoing projects, led by academic staff, which enabled different students to work on the same topics year after year, to build up a 'longitudinal study' and body of research. An example of such a project was mentioned in 1947–48 report, which described a study of the effect upon young children of longer hours in nursery, whilst the 1951–52 report refers to group projects, also continued from previous years, which saw two students studying 'spontaneous stories told by children living in institutions compared to those living in their own families' and four students investigating 'the therapeutic value of play in infant and junior schools.'[64] At least some of these projects were staff research projects on which the students assisted.[65] Individual research projects looked at topics including the teaching of handwork in training colleges, the relationships between training colleges and their practising schools, and a study of children with speech difficulties and their responses to playgroup.[66] The range of topics show that as well researching issues relating purely to 'child development', students on the course could also focus their research projects on matters relating to pedagogy, or on matters of policy or on how educational institutions operated, as in the case of those looking at the role of training colleges. Although it is not possible to determine from the annual reports which projects were undertaken by those students sponsored by funding from the Ministry of Education, it may be that some of these topics were chosen due to the student's interest in furthering their career by moving into training college work or school management. Related to this, it is worth noting that students also sometimes had the opportunity to lecture at training colleges and on courses for nursery nurses and matrons, as well as to parents' associations, which Gardner states was useful experience for those seeking to move into training college posts.[67]

Significantly, the annual reports do provide some information about the post-course destination of students. For example, in the report for 1949–50, details are given for 39 students (three more than the number of grant-aided students, so including some privately funded students) of whom one became a lecturer at Durham Institute of Education, nine became training college lecturers, one became a lecturer with the National Nursery Examinations Board, and one a tutor on training courses run by the National Under Fourteens Council.[68] In these cases, the students had clearly moved out of teaching and into other roles within the education system. Other students returned to teaching, either to new positions – three were appointed heads and five were appointed to assistantships – or to their old jobs, with four returning to headships and six returned to assistantships.[69] The special advanced course in Child Development was therefore, producing teachers able to take up school management roles but it was also recruiting at least some of its students from those already in such positions. In addition to those taking up new roles or returning to old ones, the report also noted that nine other students were still awaiting new appointments.[70] Dorothy Gardner, in her role as head of the department, provided references for students who had followed the course. Amelia Bullen, referred to above, and a teacher for whom Gardner provided references which survive in the archives, was appointed as the Superintendent of a Buckinghamshire Nursery School after having completed the course.[71]

As well as the special advanced course in Child Development, by the late 1950s, the LIoE also ran a special course for experienced serving teachers in 'Education of Children in Junior Schools' led by a Christian Schiller.[72] Information on this course can be gleaned from the papers of one teacher who attended it in 1958–59, Dietrich Hanff. Following an interview with Schiller, due to a high number of applicants to the courses, Hanff was offered a place on the course provided that he was seconded on full salary by his LEA, which was Bath.[73] Due to having been seconded on full pay, the grant which Hanff received from the Ministry was limited to eligibility for free tuition, which the course programme shows would otherwise have cost £62 10s, and he was told that he would have to meet any further expenses himself.[74] The course programme was to consist of a mix of lectures and seminars, which would address three main areas: 'a) A general survey of how children grow physically, mentally and emotionally before adolescence; b) The history and organisation of Primary education, and the place and function of the Junior school; c) The fields of learning which form the Junior school curriculum.'[75] Course programmes for the

Autumn term 1958, reproduced in Table 3. below, and the Spring term 1958, show that the structure of the course meant that students spent Mondays either in schools for observation visits, or at Goldsmiths College undertaking practical work in Arts and Crafts.[76] The remainder of the week was filled with the course lectures, from a range of lecturers including Dorothy Gardner, alongside seminars and tutorial discussion classes, but also featured movement classes on Wednesday mornings for which students were required to wear soft shoes.[77]

The Institute's archives contain a bound volume of Hanff's notes, taken during the lectures on this course, which shed further light on its range and content.[78] The handwritten notes are fragmented, featuring keywords jotted down as reminders, as well as recommendations for further reading alongside notable phrases and concepts. However, it is clear that the course was a very thorough and in-depth study, with lectures on Child Development beginning from birth focusing on how babies are affected by the cultural beliefs and attitudes of the adults around them. Hanff's notes show that theories of Psychology featured strongly on the course, with topics examined including gender identity and sibling rivalries. The course was also wide-ranging, with other lecturers addressing issues such as how to use play equipment to assess mental development and abilities by testing perception, memory and decision-making; considering how to teach topics of personality development to teachers during their initial training; or looking at language usage in primary school and how teachers might best communicate with children. There were also lectures on specific subjects taught in junior schools, such as Music, Poetry and Nature Study. Hanff's notes also record some discussions of teaching techniques and their pros and cons, such as whether to correct individual pupils' written work whilst circulating around the class or whether to correct common mistakes during a whole class session, as well as showing suggestions for books to use in school, such as books for 'backward readers'. The course, therefore, seems to have contained a mix of the theories of Psychology and pedagogy, alongside more pragmatic and prosaic information. The Institute did not award a Diploma for this course, unlike some other special advanced courses which did offer such rewards, but would provide students with a statement to confirm that they had followed the programme.[79] Overall the ethos and focus of the LIoE special advanced courses for serving teachers combined a mixture of theoretical and practical elements, with a strong professional focus for teachers, with a distinctive emphasis upon conducting empirical research in the field.

Bristol Institute of Education and Special Advanced Courses

As the programme of special advanced courses for experienced serving teachers was in its infancy in the late 1940s, with the courses operating at the LIoE, Birmingham University and Darlington Training College being the first confirmed for the 1948–9 session, other institutions began to develop courses to fit into the programme. Among those interested in developing a course was Professor Basil Fletcher, Director of the University of Bristol, Institute of Education.[80] Fletcher initially proposed a course on Educational Psychology for the session 1949–50 which would have been similar in content to those existing courses at the LIoE and also at Birmingham.[81] If successful, this proposed course would have formed part of the early activities of the Bristol Institute of Education, a body set up to lead the regional ATO following the recommendations of the McNair Report of 1944 '*to further training of teachers and youth leaders [...] in the counties of Gloucestershire, Somerset and Wiltshire, and the cities of Bath, Bristol and Gloucester.*'[82] Professor Fletcher was the first Director of this Institute, whose constituent institutions were Bristol University and nine teacher training colleges spread across Bristol, Bath, Cheltenham, Gloucester and Salisbury.[83] However, although the idea of introducing a special advanced course in Educational Psychology was discussed by the Board of the Bristol Institute of Education, and plans for it became far enough advanced for it to be included in the Bristol University Department of Education's prospectus for the 1949–50 academic year under the title of a 'Diploma in Child Study', in the end the course did not take place.[84] At first, it was pushed back to a proposed start in October 1950, but was then further postponed until 1952 due to a lack of accommodation.[85] However, it seems as though the plans then faltered further, due to 'little progress' having been made in 'national negotiations' about advanced courses, and that therefore the Bristol Institute of Education decided in 1952 to 'make a break' in their attempts to set up 'more substantial courses' of in-service training and to 'start afresh' in 1953–54.[86] Though the files held by Bristol University do not specify what these national negotiations were, papers in the National Archives from 1951 refer to discussions between the Ministry of Education, HMI, and the newly established ATOs about the funding arrangements for these courses and for teachers wishing to follow them, and suggest that the delay in resolving this issue was due to the need to consult the ATOs.[87] Following this delay, it seems that a special advanced course in Child Study was never established at Bristol, perhaps because courses of this nature were operating at several other centres.

Despite the failure to establish the course in Child Study, the programme of professional development training offered to serving teachers by the Bristol Institute of Education did develop to include advanced courses, notably a Diploma in Education and an Advanced Certificate. The programme of courses which was offered by the Bristol Institute of Education in the 1950s and 1960s offer a good illustration of the evolution of the advanced course model after its initial introduction in the late 1940s.

Originally, in the 1930s and early 1940s, Bristol University Department of Education offered a one-year 'Diploma in Education' course as a fourth year of study which enabled students who had graduated to gain a teaching qualification immediately after the completion of their degrees.[88] However, in 1947–48 the University renamed this course as a 'Certificate in Education' and offered a new Diploma in Education course which was to be open to those already in possession of a Certificate in Education or equivalent initial teaching qualification and would be awarded to those who had pursued '*a period of supervised study or research in some specialized field* of education so that their total professional training amounted to not less than five years.[89] The Diploma in Education course came to consist of at least one year's full time study, or two years' part-time, after which the teachers were required to complete a thesis or 'special study' on an area of education in which they had a particular interest.

Although these terms of admission read slightly differently to those set out by the Ministry of Education for the selection of teachers for special advanced courses, the Bristol Diploma in Education did fit into this category with regards to funding. A document from 1963 shows that, by that time, full-time Bristol Diploma students were seconded on full pay by their LEAs for one year and then presumably completed their dissertation work in their own time during the period following this, and also had their tuition fees paid.[90] This document also notes that this funding was available to teachers with five or more years' teaching experience, in line with the standard terms for special advanced courses although the course was open to those with only three years' experience. It was also possible for teachers to follow the Diploma course on a part-time basis, and although the part-time course had accepted a new intake only every other year initially, from the 1963–64 session it was anticipated that this would change to allow an annual intake because the course was increasingly popular as an entry qualification for teacher seeking to undertake MA courses.[91] Part-time students were offered grant-aid by their LEAs, the extent of which varied between authorities but *'normally at least half of the tuition and travelling expenses'* were paid.[92]

Lists of students on the Diploma course in 1962–63, show that the course attracted a mix of headteachers, assistant teachers, training college lecturers and teachers' centre wardens.[93] These lists also show that Bristol University also accepted a significant cohort of foreign students each year onto special Diploma courses for overseas teachers. A list of thesis subjects from 1956 illustrates that the Diploma in Education was broad-ranging and allowed those taking it to focus on their own particular subjects or on an element of educational theory or history. Examples included: 'An enquiry into the attitudes of boys towards authority in a Secondary School'; 'William Barnes (1800–1886): his theories and practice of education'; 'A survey of the development of infant schools in Bristol during the nineteenth century'; and 'The influence of home background on the teaching of religious instruction.'[94]

Between 1953 and 1962, 77 full-time and 72 part-time students had completed Part I of the Diploma (the taught element) and 56 had completed Part II (the thesis).[95] Evidently, there was a significant proportion of those enrolling in the course who either did not complete Part II or who took several years to produce their thesis. Perhaps this was the reason behind the decision that from 1960 onwards those who had completed Part I of the Diploma course would be awarded an 'Advanced Certificate in Education.'[96] This Advanced Certificate was first proposed in 1957 and was intended to sit somewhere between an initial Certificate in Education and the Diploma, with teachers admitted to it required to have three years' teaching experience but not the five years' professional study which was required for the

Diploma.[97] In fact, the Advanced Certificate came to be synonymous with the first year (i.e. the taught element) of the Diploma course. Teachers admitted to study for the Advanced Certificate were expected to study on a part-time basis for between two to four years, whilst continuing to work in schools.

Further documents reveal that, although in the late 1940s and 1950s, the Diploma had evidently accepted graduate teachers – their undergraduate years were counted towards the five years' prerequisite professional study no matter what their subject had been – by the early 1960s, the award was aimed at those who had entered the profession as non-graduates originally. By this time, graduate teachers were channelled towards the M.Ed. programme after having completed the Advanced Certificate in Education. This relationship between the Advanced Certificate, the Diploma and the M.Ed. programmes remained in place throughout the 1960s. However, discussions about the range of advanced courses offered to serving teachers continued throughout the decade, often with reference to the national picture. In 1968, plans emerged for a restructuring of Bristol's advanced course programme with effect from 1969.[98] These plans took into account the general expansion of the advanced course programme across the country, as well as the development of the relatively new M.Ed. programme, which Bristol offered from 1965.[99] The main aim of this restructuring was to achieve a *'unified and expanded programme of studies'* and cited a *'growing national concern over the lack of coherence in educational studies'* as having been taken into account during the formulation of the new structure.[100] The scheme described was to cover the period 1969–71 and would be subject to ongoing reassessment with further recommendations to be formulated for the period after 1971, which highlights the fact that this was a time of considerable change in this sphere. The principles underlying the new structure were that admission onto advanced courses should be increased and that the relationships between the various post-initial qualifications available to teachers should be clarified. The proposals for advanced courses stated that the separate Advanced Certificate and Diploma qualifications would be abolished and replaced with a single new Diploma course which would run alongside the M.Ed. programme. Students on both the Diploma and the M.Ed. would be required to undertake a course of general studies in education, a special subject, and to produce a minor dissertation or portfolio of work, although the exact content of what they studied would depend upon their interests and previous experience in the profession. General studies would account for 50% of their final assessment and their special subject, including their dissertation, would also account for 50%. The distinction between full time and part-time courses was to be abolished but there would still be full-time and part-time students, who would attend classes at a frequency which suited them. Teaching would take between 3.30pm and 8pm in order to accommodate working students.

This restructuring of advanced courses offered at Bristol was part of a wider process of national debates and developments which surrounded advanced courses during the 1960s. From the files in the archives of Bristol University, it is also possible to trace the reactions of the institution and the wider institute to national policy initiatives, such as the landmark Circular 7/64. It is clear from these documents, which originate both from the University itself and from the Department of Education and Science, as well the Conference of Institute Directors and UCET that the advanced course programme had developed due to local, institutional initiatives – with different universities and training colleges developing course programmes according to their particular specialisms.[101] The Bristol archives contain a document responding to this by a group of tutors on advanced courses, following a meeting held by them in London in February 1965.[102] This response welcomed the government's favourable attitude towards advanced courses but called for further standardization so that a Diploma from one institution might be accepted at other institutions as an entry qualification for courses of further study, such as the M.Ed. The tutors suggested that the situation as it stood meant that teachers might, taking advantage of their one-year secondment, take their Diploma course at a distant university but might later find that this caused problems for them if they then sought admission to their local university to undertake further part-time study as the new institution might not recognise their Diploma.

Evidently, the restructuring of Bristol's advanced courses during the 1960s and the ongoing process of their development, was a part of this bigger national picture. Few documents are available in the Bristol archives from post-1970, but the few that are show that this development was an ongoing process, with disagreement over the place of the Advanced Certificate as a qualification following its abolishment in 1969, and a sense that the James Report and the development of the in-service B.Ed. degree, were seen as signalling a shift away from Diploma courses towards the B.Ed.[103]

CHAPTER SUMMARY

Key features of the special advanced courses for serving teachers discussed in this chapter were that they: were government controlled, validated and funded, albeit in collaboration with higher education institutions; were elite and high-end in terms of resource and numbers; targeted an extremely small number of participants from the wider teaching population; focussed on full-time year-long secondments from the classroom for the study of education at a high level; were intended to provide a route out of the classroom into positions of greater responsibility for teachers; and carried some personal cost, particularly in their earliest form, to the teachers involved. As with all the other models of teacher professional development discussed in this book, lack of adequate funding was a constant source of tension for all those involved, at the level of the government, LEA, university and the individual teacher. There was never quite enough resource available to facilitate the desired expansion and this meant that the programme could only ever reach and benefit a chosen few. Those teachers that did become involved would experience an opportunity not just for their professional development and career progression but also for personal development with the expansion of their general education and the award of formal university accreditation on successful completion of their year of study. The two institutional case studies developed here to flesh out some of the detail from the history constructed from government sources, would suggest that the special advanced courses were academically rigorous, theoretical and research-oriented in their approach. At the same time, in the case of the London Institute courses, as well as the Bristol Institute programme to a lesser degree, there also appeared to be a strong practical and professional focus. Though limited, data does indicate that the special advanced courses did act as springboards for teachers to move into training college lectureships, headships or local authority positions. With their extended knowledge and understanding of education, they would then be well placed to influence and enrich other trainee or even experienced teachers in their care. The special advanced courses programme, whatever its limitations, was designed to build capacity within the education system as a whole – though the extent to which it really effected this is impossible to ascertain.

As I have discussed elsewhere, educational reorganization after 1944 marked the abolition of an uncertificated route into the teaching profession, the ultimate vision being for an all-graduate profession. At the same time the post-war period witnessed the expansion of education as a field of study both within the universities and training colleges to embrace broader philosophical, historical, sociological and comparative approaches.[104] This period in the history of the teaching profession marked an increasing valuing of the universities as the custodians of high quality teacher education, whether directly through their own training programmes or indirectly in the accreditation of training college courses, which in itself was intricately bound up with ambitions for raising the status and all-round education of the teaching profession.[105] However, at the same time, the relationship between the university and 'education' both as an academic discipline and as a vocation, with practical training needs, was an uneasy one – and this has also been discussed elsewhere by historians, both in the UK, and in the US.[106] Writing in the 1980s, Helen Patrick, for example, argued that in the UK '...*despite the introduction of higher degrees in education, the move towards concentration of postgraduate secondary training and the work of a number of distinguished educationists, departments of education were not held in high regard.*'[107] At the same time, there were long-held concerns about the appropriate balance between academic or theoretical aspects of teacher education and those more practical and professional dimensions. Though Phil Gardner has pointed out that the 'practice versus theory' debate is an old chestnut - a century old debate which remains unresolved to this day[108], this contradictory and potentially volatile world into which the special courses for experienced serving teachers were born raises some interesting issues about the particular model of teacher professional development they embodied and, indeed, the legacy they have left behind for future generations of teachers. These concern: the premium placed on university accredited programmes of higher study in the specialised field of education; the vexed relationship between the study of education as an academic discipline within a university environment, the health and livelihood of university departments of education and teacher professional learning; the high financial and time cost involved; the removal of the serving teacher from the regular classroom for extended periods of time into a higher education institution; and the greater likelihood that successful completion of this type of programme would lead to promotion. Part of a wider capacity and status enhancing agenda for teachers, the special advanced course programme in the period 1945–1970 raised the stakes for government, universities and the wider teaching profession and framed a new conception of professional learning.

NOTES

[1] For further detailed discussion of the McNair report and the development of Area Training Organisations, see Crook, D. (1995). 'Universities, teacher training, and the legacy of McNair, 1944–94', *History of Education*, 24(3), 231–245.

[2] See for example, Gosden, P. (1972). *The evolution of a profession*. Oxford: Blackwell, p. 269; Dent, H. (1977). *The training of teachers in England and Wales 1800–1975*. London: Hodder and Stoughton, 119–20; Crook, D. 'In-service education and professional development for teachers in England: historical perspectives from the late twentieth century', 4–12.

[3] Board of Education, Annual Report (hereafter BoE, Annual Report) for 1919–1920, p.80; BoE, Annual Report, 1920–1921, p. 58. See also The UK National Archives (hereafter TNA), ED/22/129, Memo to Inspectors TC, No. 65, dated 23/7/1923.

[4] TNA, ED/86/222, letter from Posener at Ministry of Education to Mrs Rossiter at the Treasury, dated 16/06/1947; also other documents within ED/86/222.

[5] TNA, ED/86/222, note dated 11/10/1947.

[6] Ibid.

[7] Ibid; TNA, ED/86/222, letter from Pearson at Ministry of Education to Mr Hale at Treasury, dated 14/10/1947.

[8] TNA, ED/86/222, note dated 11/10/1947.

[9] Ibid.

[10] Ibid; TNA, ED/86/222, letter from Pearson at Ministry of Education to Mr Hale at Treasury, dated 14/10/1947; reply from Hale, dated 3/11/1947.

[11] TNA, ED/86/222, note dated 11/10/1947.

[12] TNA, ED/86/222, note dated 1/1/1948.

[13] TNA, ED/86/222, letter from Mr Longland, dated 11/03/1948.

[14] TNA, ED/86/222, note dated 9/10/1947.

[15] TNA, ED/86/222, handwritten note (undated, attached to Dorset letter and response).

[16] TNA, ED/86/222, reply to Dorset letter from JV Stephenson, dated 5/04/1948.

[17] Ibid.

[18] Ibid.

[19] TNA, ED/86/222, Administrative Memorandum No.266, dated 26/02/1948.

[20] Ibid.

[21] TNA, ED/86/222, letters from Stephenson to Smith dated 21/10/1948 and from Smith to Stephenson dated 29/10/1948.

[22] TNA, ED/86/222, letters from Stephenson to Miss Weddell, TC Principal, dated 17/02/1949, and from Stephenson to Professor RAC Oliver, University of Manchester, dated 8/12/1948.

[23] TNA, ED/86/222.

[24] TNA, ED/86/222, letter from Stephenson to Weddell.

[25] TNA/ED/86/222, note from Lester Smith detailing course content and prerequisites.

[26] Wooldridge, A. (1994). *Measuring the mind: Education and psychology in England 1860–1990*. Cambridge: Cambridge University Press.

[27] TNA, ED/86/222, Gardner to Stephenson, dated 15/11/1949.

[28] TNA, ED/86/222, Stephenson to Gardner, dated 19/09/1949.

[29] Wiseman, S. (1953). 'Higher degrees in education in British Universities', *British Journal of Educational Studies, 2*, 54–66.

[30] TNA, ED/86/222, series of internal notes beginning 21/07/1951.

[31] Ibid.

[32] Ibid.

[33] Ibid.

[34] Ibid.

[35] Ibid.

[36] Ibid.

[37] Ministry of Education (hereafter MoE), Annual Report, 1955, p. 64.

[38] MoE, Annual Report, 1960, p. 85.

[39] MoE, Annual Report, 1964, p.70. and Circular7/64.

[40] MoE, Annual Report, 1964, p.70.

[41] Ibid.

[42] Figures drawn from annual volumes of Statistics of Education.

[43] University of London, Institute of Education Archives (Hereafter IOE), DC/DG/A/1 – contains annual reports on the Centre's activities from 1930s through to the 1960s and these do not detail any reworking or restructuring of the course offered in order for it to achieve Special Course status. See also: Thompson, F. (Ed.) (1990). *The University of London and the World of Learning 1836–1936*. London: The Hambledon Press; Aldrich, R. (2002). *The institute of education 1902–2002: A centenary history*. London, UK: Institute of Education.

[44] IoE/DC/DG/A/1 – annual report 1946–47.

[45] IoE/DC/DG/A/1 – annual report 1947–48.

[46] Ibid.

[47] Ibid.

[48] Ibid.

[49] See for example: Partington, G. (1976). *Women teachers in the twentieth century*. Windsor: National Foundation for Educational Research; Robinson, W. (2003). 'Frocks, frills, femininity and representation of the woman teacher in *The Woman Teacher's World*: reconstructing the early twentieth century English 'schoolmarm', *Journal of Educational Administration and History, 74*(2), 87–99; Widdowson, F. & de Lyon, H. (1989). *Women teachers: Issues and experiences*. Milton Keynes: Open University Press.

[50] IoE/DC/DG/A/1 – Annual report of the Institute of Education pamphlet, 1956–57.

[51] IoE/DC/DG/A/1 – annual report 1951–52.

[52] IoE/DC/DG/A/1 – annual report 1955–56.

[53] IoE/DC/DG/A/1 – annual report 1956–57.

[54] IoE/DC/DG/A/1 – annual report 1957–58.

[55] Ibid.

[56] IoE/DC/DG/A/1 – annual reports 1953–54 and 1954–55.

[57] IoE/DC/DG/A/1 – annual report 1951–52.

[58] Ibid.

[59] IoE/DC/DG/A/1 – annual reports 1955–56 and 1956–57.

[60] IoE/DC/DG/A/1 – annual reports 1957–58.

[61] IoE/DC/DG/A/1 – annual report 1951–1952.

[62] IoE/DC/AF/2/3 – Amelia Fysh papers: reference dated 30/06/1955.

[63] Ibid.

[64] IoE/DC/DG/A/1 – annual reports 1947–48 and 1951–52.

[65] IoE/DC/DG/A/1 – annual report 1950–51.

[66] IoE/DC/DG/A/1 – annual report 1951–52.

[67] IoE/DC/DG/A/1 – annual report 1950–51.

[68] IoE/DC/DG/A/1 – annual report 1949–50.

[69] Ibid.

[70] Ibid. Note that the 1951–52 report also gives information about the destinations of English students on the course, and shows a similar mix.

[71] IoE/AF/2/3 – Amelia Fysh papers: references dated 30/06/1955 and 6/10/1955.

[72] IoE/DC/CS/M/2: London Institute of Education Course, 1958.

[73] IoE/DC/CS/M/2: see letters to Hanff from Schiller, dated 19/02/1958, and from EH Warmington, Acting Director of the London Institute, dated 28/05/1958.

[74] IoE/DC/CS/M/2: see note from Ministry, dated 2/06/1958, and course pamphlet which gives tuition fees.

[75] IoE/DC/CS/M/2: course pamphlet 1958–59.

[76] IoE/DC/CS/M/2: course programmes autumn term 1958 and spring term 1959.

[77] IoE/DC/CS/M/2: course programme spring term 1959.

[78] IoE: CS/M/1: Institute of Education course (Schiller, London, 1958–1959).

[79] IoE/DC/CS/M/2: course pamphlet 1958–59.

[80] TNA, ED 86/222, Ministry note, dated 1/1/1948, and letter from Ministry to Fletcher, dated 3/11/1948. See also Humphreys, D. (1976). *The University of Bristol and the education and training of teachers.* Bristol: University of Bristol School of Education.

[81] TNA, ED 86/222: letter from Ministry to Fletcher, dated 3/11/1948.

[82] Bristol University Special Collection (hereafter BUSC) DM2076/Box 4/File 1 – Board of the Institute of Education, Minutes: minutes 28/05 1947.

[83] Ibid.

[84] BUSC, DM2076/Box 4/File 1: minutes 7/06/1948, minutes 22/11/1948, and minutes 28/02/1949; BUSC/DM2076/Box 74 – Prospectuses 1925–1969: Prospectus 1949–50.

[85] BUSC, DM2076/Box 4/File 1: minutes 21/11/1949 and minutes 13/03/1950.

[86] BUSC, DM2076/Box 4/File 1: minutes 9/06/1952.

[87] TNA, ED 86/222: Internal note/discussion paper dated 21/07/1951 and others following.

[88] BUSC, DM2076/Box 74/Prospectuses 1925–1969.

[89] BUSC, DM2076/Box 74/ Prospectus 1947–48.

[90] BUSC, DM2076/Box 4/File 2: Annual Report on Advanced Courses 1962–1963.

[91] Ibid.

[92] Ibid.

[93] Ibid.

[94] BUSC, DM2076/Box 4/File 1: annexe to minutes 17/06/1957.

[95] BUSC, DM2076/Box 4/File 2: Annual Report on Advanced Courses 1962–1963.

[96] BUSC, DM2076/Box 4/File 1: annexe to minutes 17/06/1957.

[97] BUSC, DM2076/Box 4/File 1: minutes 17/06/1957.

[98] BUSC, DM2076/Box 8/File 2: 'A Revised Structure for Advanced Courses', October 1968, BAS/68/16; 'Structure for Advanced Courses' BAS/68/20

[99] BUSC, DM2076/Box 8/file 1: 'Relationship between Advanced Certificate, Diploma in Education and M.Ed', dated 11/11/1963.

[100] BUSC, DM2076/Box 8/File 2: 'Structure for Advanced Courses' BAS/68/20.

[101] BUSC, DM2076/Box 8/File 1: 'Conference of Institute Directors: Review of Special Advanced Courses Programme – Note by the Ministry of Education', October 1963.

[102] BUSC, DM2076/Box 8/file 1: Memorandum following Meeting of Tutors of Full-time Advanced Courses held at London University Institute of Education on February 19th 1965.

[103] BUSC, DM/2076/Box 8: File 5.

[104] Robinson, W. (2008). 'Teacher education in England', in T. O'Donoghue & C. Whitehead, C. (Eds.), *Teacher education in the English-speaking world: Past, present and future.* Charlotte, NC: Information Age Publishing.

[105] See Dent, *The training of teachers in England and Wales 1800–1975*, pp. 119–20; and Gosden, P. (1976). *Education in the second world war: A study of policy and administration.* London, UK: Methuen, 291–2.

[106] See Labaree, D. (2004). *The trouble with Ed Schools* (New Haven: Yale University Press; Craft, M. (1971). 'Social process, social change and English teacher education', *International Review of Education, 17*(4), 425–441; Crook, 'Universities, teacher training, and the legacy of McNair, 1944–94'.

[107] Patrick, H. (1986). 'From Cross to CATE: the universities and teacher education over the past century', *Oxford Review of Education, 12*(3), 243–261. See also H. Knox, (1951). 'The study of Education in British universities', *The Universities Review, 24*(1), 34–40 for a more contemporary analysis of the historical period under consideration.

[108] Gardner, P. (2007). 'The "Life-long Draught": From learning to teaching and back', *History of Education, 36*(4), 465–482.

THE TEACHERS' CENTRE 1960–1990

From the late 1960s to the late 1980s teachers' centres emerged in England and Wales as a popular focus for teacher professional development, bringing groups of teachers together from across a local area and offering a central forum and physical space in which teachers could access resources, meet together and engage in various professional courses. Energised by new directions in curriculum development, particularly through the work of the Schools Council, and responsive to ambitions of the 1972 James Report, the teachers' centre model appeared to offer a promising new conceptualisation of grassroots professional learning. It promoted a distinctive philosophy with a rhetoric of democratized teacher professional learning which valued organic, teacher-led transformation; was responsive to local demand and expertise, and was committed to teacher autonomy. Regarded by some educationists as a distinctive 'movement' for democratic, practical and genuinely teacher-led professional development, but by others as incoherent, divisive and highly differentiated in terms of quality of provision, the teachers' centre phenomenon divided professional opinion. A real challenge with evaluating the contribution of the teachers' centres is that this was not a homogenous national model with clearly shared practices, resources and leadership. Centres varied enormously across England and Wales in terms of vision, purpose, role and function, physical space, resourcing, staffing, governance and management. For this reason, this chapter seeks to provide an illustrative snapshot of the teachers' centre phenomenon, drawing upon existing secondary source material as well as new archive data and oral history testimony to raise important questions about their place in the history of teacher professional development and learning and their promise as a model which might still have currency in the contemporary educational context.

The chapter is in four parts. First, the emergence of the teachers' centres will be located in the wider social, political and educational context, which both fostered their growth in the 1960s and 1970s and which ultimately led to their demise by the late 1980s. Secondly, a broad overview of the work of the centres will be developed. Thirdly, the leadership of the teachers' centres and the work of the National Conference of Teachers' Centre Leaders (NCTSL) will be examined. This offers a useful lens through which to probe the distinctive democratic educational vision and ethos for the teachers' centres espoused by some of their most enthusiastic advocates. Finally, the international appeal of the British teachers' centre model will be explored. Research for this chapter drew upon a number of contemporary studies, unpublished theses, books and papers on the teachers' centres[1], including a report commissioned by the Schools Council in the late 1970s[2] and a survey on teachers' centre staff and resources published by the National Union of Teachers in 1972[3]; an extensive range of archive material on the teachers' centres, both from the National Archives and the London Institute of Education Archives; and oral history testimony from 31 interviews, of which seven were with former teachers' centre leaders and staff who had actively been involved in the work of the teachers' centres in their professional careers, across a total of 13 different centres across the country.

TEACHERS' CENTRES IN CONTEXT

Teachers' centres evolved during the 1960s and early 1970s, during a period of relatively expansive, liberal and progressive thinking in the field of education. Chapter Two has already described the 1960s as a time of rapid educational change, with a range of initiatives all demanding responsiveness from the teaching force and highlighting more than ever before the need for sustained and systemic in-service training and development.[4] A focus on curriculum reform led by the Nuffield Foundation and the Schools Council, comprehensive school reorganisation with significant revisions to GCE and CSE examinations, and planning for the raising of the school leaving age to sixteen years all helped to shape a climate which demanded the modernisation of teacher professional development. There was also greater experimentation with curriculum, methods and pedagogy. More widely, this period also witnessed unprecedented social and technological change and economic prosperity which had a profound effect on the nature of schooling and the business of teaching.[5] During the 1960s, government spending on education more than tripled and was twice the amount spent on defence. Changing youth culture and more permissive social attitudes and values began to challenge some of the traditional hierarchies and practices in the school context. In a speech delivered to the National Conference for Teachers' Centres Wardens at Exeter in April 1974, Harry Ree argued that teachers' centres were filling a necessary and previously unmet need for teachers. He described the broad social and educational changes of the 1960s and argued that these had left a large number of teachers in a state of malaise - utterly bewildered and unprepared for the new world of education in which they found themselves.[6] He also suggested that the blurring of social class distinctions and a more assertive youth meant that young teachers were very different and had higher expectations than their older counterparts. For Ree, teachers' centres offered a social and recreational space for teachers and also provided the mechanism for change, with the wardens of the teachers' centres taking a pivotal role in managing the rapidly changing educational landscape and supporting the teachers in adapting to such change as well as equipping them with new skills, knowledge and understanding.

It was into this climate of change in the 1960s and 1970s that the teachers' centres emerged and flourished - a time often described in the oral history testimony as a 'golden-age' in English education, where teachers had more freedom, autonomy and opportunity than ever before and ever since. It is not within the scope of this particular chapter to unpick this notion of the professional golden age which will be examined more fully in Part Three of the book – though M. Plaskow's defence of the 'rose-tinted view' does capture some of the spirit of the age in which the teachers' centres thrived. Plaskow wrote,

> It is fashionable to deride the 1960s as culturally aberrant and wildly idealist. Healthy idealism may be preferable to entrenched ideology parading as pragmatism, which has been the chief characteristic of subsequent decades. Many of us who were active in education in the 1960s look back on a time of optimism, a spirit of shared concerns, and the beginnings of an articulation (in every sense) of an education system which would offer the greatest possible opportunities to everyone as an entitlement, not a privilege.[7]

In seeking a balanced evaluation of the teachers' centres, it is difficult to escape from some of the unashamed bias and enthusiasm for their work and contribution to be found in much of the written literature – often produced by pioneer teachers' centre leaders. A good example of this can be found in Robert Thornbury's 1973 book *Teachers Centres*.[8] Thornbury was the warden of Sherbrooke Teachers' Centre, London and a great advocate of the teachers' centre movement. He regarded teachers' centres as fundamental to educational reform in the late 1960s and suggested that they represented a 'silent educational revolution'. Some contemporary critics were more guarded. In a scathing review of Thornbury's book, Harry Ree argued that Thornbury was overly preoccupied with ideas that local authorities and the Schools Council were conspiring to undermine the organic, democratic development of teachers' centres and that his perspective was far too London-centric.

> Teachers' Centres have grown like beans on wet blotting paper, but they have developed unevenly, and haven't always justified the delight and optimism felt by their planters in the early days.[9]

The teachers' centres were very much of their time. Their demise in the late 1980s and early 1990s corresponded with a critical juncture in the recent history of Western education when political, social and economic changes began to inform neo-liberal reforms, dominated by a discourse of public accountability, performance management, regulation and central control. This education reform movement mandated radical structural changes to teachers' professional engagement and practice, in which the organic, local, teacher-led and democratised forms of professional learning reflected in the ideal of the teachers' centre model no longer had a place. As a consequence, their particular contribution and influence have either been overlooked in current debate or have been relegated to the untested educational folk myth of a past golden age. A central position of this chapter is that, in their relatively brief historical moment, teachers' centres held out a promise radically to shape and influence the teaching profession and educational reform, but that this moment was overtaken by a different set of political and educational priorities.

TEACHERS' CENTRES: AN OVERVIEW

Teachers' centres emerged in England and Wales in the early 1960s, initially as a means to disseminate to teachers the materials generated through curriculum development projects. The first centres were Mathematics subject centres, such as the specialist Wythenshawe Mathematics Centre in Manchester, which provided courses for teachers on Nuffield curriculum schemes.[10] These were soon followed by centres on a variety of other models. There were subject specific centres, for example a Language Education Centre in Leeds and an Art Centre in Lewes, Sussex, established in 1965.[11] There were also phase-specific centres, catering either for primary or secondary teachers, resource-only centres and general centres. The majority of centres were general centres funded by LEAs with one established per town, city or LEA district. Teachers' centres were run by individuals known as wardens or leaders, who, although employed by LEAs often enjoyed a high degree of autonomy in their work. By the late 1970s it was estimated that there were over 700 teachers' centres across England and Wales.[12]

There was a great variety of teachers' centres across the country, with differences in the physical space, size and location of the centres, and clear rural/urban disparities. Initially, many were housed in former school buildings though some were also in Nissan huts, disused fire stations and ambulance stations, or shared buildings with other local authority services. Rarely were purpose-built centres established. Data from the Schools Council commissioned survey of teachers' centres in the late 1970s highlighted some of this variety. For example, in commenting about physical space, one centre warden suggested that, 'The centre itself is a pleasant Victorian house and the LEA allowances, although modest, have enabled it to be improved in furniture, decoration and equipment over the past few years.'[13] In contrast, another centre warden wrote, 'My centre occupies old buildings of uncertain future. Sad state of internal decoration deters custom.'[14]

The location of a centre and its easy accessibility for teachers at the end of the school day was crucial to its use and popularity – and this was a particular problem for dispersed rural areas. A number of oral history participants who had worked in rural areas recalled that without cars it was difficult for them to get to the centre so they only went if there was a special in-service course. Some centres were well equipped with a number of rooms for seminars, meetings or workshops, a library and resources facility and social space, including bars, refreshment areas and snooker tables. City based centres – such as in London or Coventry appeared to be better equipped and very popular as a social base for younger teachers. One oral history participant, Bill Parkinson, recalled having used the Coventry teachers' centre as a second home in his early days of teaching in the late 1960s. Living in fairly primitive bedsit accommodation he would even go to the centre for a bath!ived[15] Another suggested that '...there were good social centres that teachers would have for their wedding receptions.'[16] A teacher working in Hackney, London in the early 1970s recalled the popularity of the Hackney Centre with teachers who would routinely go after school three or four days a week. She was a member of the social committee and used the centre for recreational as well as professional activity.[17] Some centres specialised in providing teaching materials and resources for teachers, as well as reprographic and photocopying equipment so that teachers could make their own resources and share them with others. For example, from 1967, the Bradford Teachers' Centre invested in audio visual and duplicating resources which were made available to teachers, with a small charge made for materials. The centre experimented with a loan scheme for teachers, but found that the damage rate on audio-visual equipment too high to sustain. In addition, a 'reasonably comprehensive teachers' reference library and a text book collection' was available for teachers and periodically kept up to date.[18] Kate Moorse, warden of a subject centre in Hackney in the 1970s and 1980s, recalled that teachers,

> …could go through the centre for learning resources. They would come and they'd look for the sources that they might use, copy them, put them into resource packs…[19]

In a paper presented at the annual DES/NATHFE Conference at Bristol Polytechnic in September 1978, Vin Davis, warden of the Kendal Teachers' Centre, described the holistic function that teachers' centres could provide for local teachers, with in-service education being one part of a much bigger service. He wrote.

> It is the success of the whole Teachers' Centre which nourishes the contributory parts, especially INSET provision. A successful combination of uncomplicated and useful services is seen as an essential base from which to build and support Teachers' Centre-based INSET activities. Workshop facilities, a library of teaching aids and resources, audio-visual equipment, reprographic facilities and mobile support for sparsely populated areas, are the wherewithal which allows a Teachers' Centre to readily respond to the immediate and varied needs of teachers. The creditability of the Teachers Centre depends on the availability of human and material resources, the knowledge and experience to utilise these resources, the accurate identification of teachers' needs and wants, and above all – good will.[20]

The funding, management, staffing and governance of the centres varied. The NUT survey of teachers' centres in 1972 found that, though LEAs were totally responsible for allocating grants to the centres, resourcing varied between authorities. 'By means of weighted average, to the nearest ten units, urban centres receive the most generous allowances: urban £3,660 per annum, rural £630 per annum; specialist £930 per annum.'[21] Data from the Schools Council Survey highlighted a specific tension inherent in the teachers' centre model – the nature of the relationship between the centre staff and the LEA, with considerable confusion over who had the ultimate power and authority. One warden wrote,

It has never been made absolutely clear whether a centre and its staff are operating (a) on behalf of the LEA – as an instrument of dissemination on communication of the policies and views which are formulated by senior colleagues in the administrative hierarchy or (b) on behalf of the teachers – gauging their wishes and needs, identifying their problems, supporting them in the classroom, and defending their interests.[22]

There was a sense that teachers' centres were very much subject to the whims of local authorities – with some regarding centres as useful institutions worth investing in, whilst others treating them grudgingly in terms of resource allocation. Whilst enthusiasts for the teachers' centres were keen to point out their teacher-centred, democratic and organic management and organisation – with centres being run for the teachers and by the teachers, management structures and responsibilities also varied. Keith Martin suggested that in his time as warden of the Purbeck Teachers' Centre there was a strong commitment to teacher-led centre activity. He said,

At the centre, they had a representative from all schools. They didn't all go but there was the chance for every school to have a representative and yes, and that, that more or less ran the place. They were supposed to just run the Teachers Centre so it was teacher led.[23]

Similarly, Alec Fellows in discussing the management of his centre in Nuneaton remembered that the management committee was heavily represented by teacher union officials and he emphasised that teachers' centres were quite literally *teachers centres*.

There was a managing body and quite hefty union representation on that managing body although it was funded by the local authority it was, it was largely governed by the teachers themselves.[24]

Many centres had a teachers' management committee comprising elected teacher representatives from local schools who would work with designated centre leaders/ wardens to design programmes of activity, make decisions about resources and funding and take responsibility for the centre building and social programme. These management committees would also have co-opted LEA representatives and sometimes representation from teachers' professional organisations or unions. Sub-committees focussing on specific aspects of the centre, such as library facilities, resources, specific curriculum areas, catering and social programmes were often established.[25] Joslyn Owen, Deputy Chief Education Officer for Devon, wrote a paper in 1968 which probed the extent to which teachers really engaged in the organisation and management of the teachers' centres. His experience was that teachers' centres appeared to thrive on a fine balance between teacher and local authority control. He argued that,

The management of centres has some effects on teacher participation: much again, seems to depend on how far the local education authority is involved and on how far the teacher members of the management committees are chosen on the basis of their proportionally representing teacher associations. Teachers are said to participate less suspiciously in centres where the management committee is one in which the local education authority voice is not dominant and where the representation of teachers is based not simply on association membership but also on the individual's contribution to the curriculum.[26]

Whilst acknowledging the ambition for teachers' centres to respond to local need, he queried the extent to which local teachers were either able or willing to take ownership of their professional development through the work of the centres and suggested that,

> Apart from areas which are taking part in the trial stages of national projects, there is as yet comparatively little planned local experiment: the emphasis seems almost entirely to be on open discussion and exchange of views rather than on the devising of specific contributions to teaching within particular subject areas. The dangers are obvious: as long as the lecture/seminar/discussion group method of traditional in-service training are regarded as the principal methods appropriate to curriculum development, teachers seem unlikely to provide, and to work within, their own framework of activity.[27]

In a survey of the activity of Bradford Teachers' Centre in 1968, it was reported that considerable thought had gone into ensuring effective communication between local teachers, teachers' centre advisers and the local authority in relation to centre activities and the generation of teacher-led centre activity, through meetings, face-to-face meetings in schools and in regular newsletters and was considered that the centre had been fairly successful in involving a large number of teachers in planning and organisation. However, the Chief Education Officer in Bradford at that time was not convinced that teachers were as active in the centres as they could be. He suggested that,

> The teacher representatives tended to be nominees of the teachers' associations, did not involve themselves in curriculum development work and rather wanted to stress the 'social' nature of the centre.[28]

With such a variety in practice between centres, for geographical, professional, administrative and financial reasons, understanding what they actually did in terms of in-service provision, providing support for teachers, creating opportunities for teacher discussion and sharing of resources is also difficult to define, as there were numerous permutations of activity. By way of illustration, three examples have been drawn from the archive material consulted for this chapter. By their very nature, these examples cannot be viewed as representative – but they do capture something of nature of teachers' centre work. The first is taken from a copy of a detailed newsletter from Kendal Teachers' Centre in September 1978.[29] Newsletters such as this one were a common feature of teachers' centre life and were used to communicate with the local teaching population and to disseminate information about forthcoming events and activities. This newsletter offers an interesting insight into the local organisation, activities and community of this centre, set in a rural context.

The overall tone of the newsletter, written by its warden, Vin Davis, is very informal and inviting with a strong encouragement for teachers to feedback their views and ideas. New teachers were '...most welcome to call into the Centre anytime and have a chat with the staff and a look around the building'. The newsletter referred to the activities of the Teachers' Centre Management Committee and various teacher representative meetings in the creation of the forthcoming programme which was designed in response to suggestions from teachers. This included practical sessions on primary school Maths, a practical guide to using AV equipment, cooking in the classroom, infant screening techniques and 'get out and about in Kendal' social evenings, back by popular demand having run previously and attracted over 250 local teachers and their friends and families. Termly themes around which practical workshops, seminars and discussions were planned were adopted. The programme consisted of a combination of after-school twilight sessions, as well as more formal 'courses' held during the day and a daily plan of forthcoming events, with timings was published. The centre building was also used by other community groups, including the local Scout group, WEA meetings and a local choir. The impression of the centre from the tone and content of the newsletter is one in which there was a strong sense of a local teacher community, with the centre fulfilling an in-service, educational, cultural as well as social and recreational function.

A second example is taken from an HMI report of in-service courses for teachers in East Sussex in 1968–9, where there were three teachers' centres across the county. The report stated that the centre premises had been made attractive and it was hoped that in time they would become places where teachers would wish to meet socially. Their primary function was to provide space for lectures, for discussion and for the practice of classroom skills in well-equipped workrooms. In East Sussex the teachers' centres were originally established to meet immediate curriculum needs in modern Mathematics and Science, Art and Craft, and trends in new methods. With East Sussex schools taking part in trials of the Nuffield Secondary Science Project at that time the Lewes Teachers' Centre was a focus for special meetings for teachers involved in the new programme. These informal meetings were for teachers to share their experiences, with a focus on 'O' level Science Courses and the particular needs of the raised school leaving age. Primary school teachers were invited to primary Science focussed evenings at the centres, which comprised of lecture demonstrations followed by discussion. In addition, longer curriculum courses led by local head teachers, college of education lecturers and HMI were organised in the teachers' centres.

A specialist County Art Centre was regarded as popular with teachers and the diary of events contained 28 meetings of various kinds concerned with Art and Craft in schools. One particular practical course, 'The Will to Form', which comprised five consecutive Tuesday evening meetings covering a variety of techniques and media, was oversubscribed. HMI reported that the course,

…was notable for the thoroughness of the preparation, the provision of a rich variety of well-chosen visual stimuli, and the enthusiasm and liveliness engendered by the personality of the adviser. The County Art Centre itself provides small but attractive and stimulating accommodation for courses, meetings and exhibitions. The series of exhibitions held there is of high quality and is very well presented, providing an unusual opportunity for teachers, students and pupils to study original works or art at first hand. The standard of the activities seen was high and deserving of every support for future development.[30]

At the time of writing this report, East Sussex teachers' centres were still fairly new, but HMI reported that the teacher advisers who had been given responsibility for running the centres had high hopes for their potential development. They wished to develop the centres as educational workshops for experimental groups, for the making of apparatus and for learning how to use teaching equipment, and as centres for the display of books, equipment and teaching aids. They are also anxious that the teachers themselves should take a more active part in the running of the centres and in planning programmes. To this end committees were being established which included a proportion of both primary and secondary teachers.

A third example can be found in an LEA report on the City of Bradford Teachers' Centre for 1969/70. This centre was the focal point for in-service training in Bradford and was funded by the LEA from 1964 in a vacated boys' grammar school building. In April 1967 a Curriculum Development Officer was appointed by the LEA with sole responsibility for the day to day running of the centre. In September 1970, with plans for its expansion, the centre relocated to Rosemount, Clifton Villas, a large Victorian residence with two pre-fabricated blocks in the grounds, which was shared with a local Technical College. The report considered the numerous ways in which particular courses in the centre were generated, with the LEA advisory staff playing a prominent role in response to seeing a need in the schools or in a particular subject or phase. Need arising from Schools Council projects in humanities, primary French and middle school reorganisation were also influential in the shaping of the centre's activity. Teachers were also identified as possible stakeholders who could make practical demands for particular courses, such as Creative Music in primary school, making musical instruments and guitar playing. Local phase-specific initiatives also created demand for courses at the teachers' centres. At primary level this included an induction and refresher course for nursery staff, a course on Reading Readiness for nursery/infant school teachers, Maths for teachers of young children, animal welfare in schools and integrated studies. For middle years, courses on Modern Mathematics, French, Sex Education and Home Economics were developed. At secondary level, courses on Home Economics, Counselling, Science, Art, and Kodaly Methods of Music Teaching, Computer Education, School Sailing, Physical Education and Careers Advice were developed. More general courses included School Management, Theatrical Productions in Schools, School Safety, and AV Support. In addition to a specific programme of courses for teachers, the centre also hosted meetings for the local Guild of Teachers of Backward Children (*sic*), Teachers' Associations as well as regular displays of school furniture, Physical Education equipment, books, scientific, handicraft materials and educational exhibitions.

Overall, oral-history participants interviewed for this project reported quite mixed views about the centres. For some they were a fundamental part of their professional development and growth and were highly significant, whilst for others they were less important. This was very much contingent on the leadership, location and ethos of the teachers' centres in a particular area. Contemporary critics of the centres, including Dick Weindling, who was commissioned by the government-funded School's Council to review their effectiveness in the late 1970s, identified key strengths as well as weaknesses.[31] Strengths included the supportive environment fostered in the centres, their innovative approaches to in-service education and their relative neutrality, which gave teachers a professional space outside of their immediate school contexts. Weaknesses included their ad-hoc development nationally, with gaps in provision, particularly for rural teachers, as well as very different types of centres emerging. He also observed a tendency for teachers' centres to attract disproportionately more teachers from the primary sector and questioned their appeal to secondary school teachers. Weindling noted that the ambition of the centres was to enable teachers to take control of their own professional development and practice, but he was concerned that for some centres this claim was being overstated. Above all, teachers liked the idea of the centres – though the extent to which they benefited from and engaged with the centres is less clear and varied enormously from region to region and teacher to teacher. Another contemporary commentator, Bob Gough attributed to the centres certain 'unique qualities' including their local nature, the freedom they provided from the normal hierarchies of school or local authority systems and the 'tendency they have to involve the teachers themselves in the decision making, the design and the implementation of their in-service programmes'.[32]

TEACHERS' CENTRE LEADERS

Knamiller's study of teachers' centres in the 1990s argued that all of the contemporary survey and reviews of teachers' centres were keen to emphasise the importance of the role of the teachers' centre leader, with centres often being judged as only as good as the wardens that ran them.[33] Thornbury referred to centre leaders as 'dogs bodies with many talents'[34], and Weindling found that centres relied heavily on the key role of the leader. Research for this book has also found that with such a diversity of teachers' centres, a crucial key variable was the teachers' centre leader. Qualified and experienced teachers with enthusiasm for in-service education and an ability to work well with a range of education professionals both in the schools and in the Local Authorities characterised teachers' centre leaders. The exact terminology of the formal title of a teachers' centre leader was different from LEA to LEA – with some designated as 'leaders', many as 'wardens' and a few given the title of 'in-service adviser'. These professional titles were telling in themselves and reveal something of the uncertainties around their status within the professional hierarchy. For Keith Martin, who worked in three different teachers' centres across three different Local Authorities during his career, his title changed. '*I was a leader to begin with. Then when I moved to Somerset I became a warden for a year and then I became a director*'. Alec Fellows, who worked in Rugby and Nuneaton Teachers' Centres in the West Midlands recalled, '*my official designation I think was warden but I just changed it to head.*'[35] Arguably, the distinctive personality, vision, values and professional ambition of a particular teachers' centre leader had a significant impact on the work, reach, impact and ethos of the individual centres. The Schools Council evaluation of teachers' centres was clear in its findings that, '*A factor which facilitates is the personality, drive and initiative of the warden.*'[36] Occupying a new and rather anomalous position within the normal school or LEA appointments hierarchy, centre leaders broadly enjoyed comparable status with senior school staff school in terms of their remuneration and conditions of service, though not always necessarily at the level of headship, and with subject specific advisers or assistant inspectors in an LEA context. Operating as they did outside of the schools and outside of the confines of County Hall, within their own newly designated professional space – the teachers' centre - centre leaders were between and betwixt two different but, nevertheless, connected, professional worlds. This created both tensions and opportunities for their role. Joy Williams who was appointed as 'organiser' of the Winchester Teachers' Centre in the late 1960s described the potential conflict of identity inherent in her own role.

> because we were neither fish, fresh foul nor good red herring. And head teachers thought we were just lackeys, arranging things. We got very little respect from headteachers. Some we did but then they were probably the ones who realised what we were actually doing but, and of course several of them thought that we were failed class teachers which of course is the way that people think, used to think, but they always liked coming to the Teachers' Centres.[37]

Kate Moorse, warden of a large, generously funded subject centre in London which focussed on History and Social Sciences and which, she claimed, catered for 150 secondary schools and 1000 primary schools, recalls a different status for the centre wardens, but did identify with the notion of status anxiety. As a newly appointed warden in the late 1970s she was keen to maintain a teaching presence in a school one afternoon a week, to ensure that she had credibility with teachers and was still embedded in the school culture. She suggested,

> Now I'm out, when I left and when I've met up with people subsequently, I think the status was probably better than I was aware of at the time, in that sense. I think it was a tricky one. In a way the Head Teachers didn't particularly know much about the subject centres, because they didn't have a direct connection with them. They related to the ...you know, multipurpose. So, I think

in retrospect, I think there was quite a lot of respect towards you as being the repository of subject knowledge. But, I don't think...they wouldn't necessarily think of you as a Head Teacher, you weren't presented as a Head Teacher or anything like that. But I think they thought that we were sort of treated as a Head Teacher of a largish primary school, that's how you were thought of...[38]

Previous professional experience, the circumstances surrounding their selection and appointment to teachers' centre leadership, their working relationship with serving headteachers and LEA Inspectors and whether they saw themselves as leading-edge teacher educators or simply managers of centres who could broker various opportunities for local teachers or even as custodians of the physical centre building all helped shape the centres under their leadership. However, as one oral history participant, formerly the warden of Plymouth Teachers' Centre said, '*I found how diverse the profession was, the conditions that people were working under, so very diverse.*' For some there were clear job descriptions and for others there was a real sense that they were 'learning on the job'.[39] Harry Ree suggested that in the early days there was a lack of clear direction with '*hundreds of centre wardens, lifted from their classrooms and a little uncertain of what they should be doing...*'[40] Evidence from the oral history testimony with former teachers' centre leaders suggests that for some, becoming a centre leader was a happy accident – being in the right place at the right time when an opening came up. During the 1960s, with school reorganisation and school closures, appointing a redundant headteacher to a centre position so that he could see out his days until retirement was not unknown.[41] For others, involvement with the centres, particularly in their early days, created a clear career path and an opportunity to work with teachers to bring about change.

Centre leaders appeared to enjoy relatively high degrees of autonomy and a flexible approach in their role, possibly because their positions were so new and they were in unchartered territory. Alan Forster, for example, interviewed for the study, described how he became a 'curriculum development leader' in Oxfordshire in 1967 and how this led him to take up a post in Devon in 1972 where there was '*...nothing, a bare room with paper peeling off the walls and a small budget to set up a teachers centre.*' He described the early days of his role and how, '*...it just suited me to be working on my own initiative, getting to know the teachers the schools for which I, wouldn't say was responsible for, but which were in my area and setting up projects.*'[42] For Keith Martin, in his first post as warden of Purbeck Teachers' Centre in Dorset, the local authority provided very little guidance on how he should run the centre and he found that networking with wardens from the other three centres in Dorset to be the best strategy to build his practice.[43] Alec Fellows, on his appointment as warden of Nuneaton Teachers' Centre at the age of 29 years, made the move because he was ambitious and he took an Open University course in his own time to build his own personal expertise and capacity. He recalled that, '*...I was, well thrown in at the deep end. But first of all management was one of the things that I wanted - a role and management was one of the things that didn't seem to have* *been covered by the inspectorate so I took an Open University course in Educational Management and did what, grabbed whatever knowledge I could and that became useful in lots of ways, it meant that I could then regurgitate what I'd learnt.*[44]

Vin Davis, a keen advocate of the centres argued that as centre leaders were the only full-time permanent professionals associated with the centres they were synonymous with all of its functions and activities. He suggested that, *'The function of the Warden appears to be controlled by three main factors: the teachers' needs; the LEA's expectations and the Warden's aspirations and capabilities. Only when all are congruent will the Teachers' Centre have a chance to begin to achieve success.'*[45] Still, data from the Schools Council evaluation suggested that *'...the amount of autonomy which a warden may have is very largely dependent on who holds the purse-strings – and how tightly they are held. Even in instances where a warden has established a democratic system of management and control for his centre, the overriding constraint of the method of funding still applies.'*[46] There were concerns that systemic under-resourcing was directly linked to the low status of the centre leader and their lack of influence and authority in relation to direct resources. This might go some way to explain the real variety of experience of teachers' centres nationally – with some enjoying relatively generous funding and resources and others struggling. If a warden had a good working relationship with the Local Inspector of senior adviser responsible for resourcing the centre, then matters could be easily resolved. Joy Williams, in her oral history testimony suggested that in her experience at Winchester,

> I always managed to get what I wanted actually, to be honest. There was a lovely man who was in charge of the money for the Teachers' Centres in the main, in the County Education office and I was introduced to him by my predecessor and he always said to me…"look if there's anything you want come and ask and I'll tell you whether we can have it or not". So it was like that. And if he could fix it and he thought it was the right thing to do he gave me the money or had it funded.[47]

Joy Kell, as professional development coordinator in Cornwall in the 1980s talked about a struggle to get centres properly funded and recalled teachers' centres in Cornwall as being pretty basic, with only one being reasonably well supported as a resources centre for teachers because of the tenacity of a *'...a very far-seeing county inspector and she'd set up a resources centre which was very forward-looking and she begged, borrowed and stole the money for it and so we had our Teachers' Centre but any others were located, based in schools.'*[48]

How centre leaders developed programmes of activity and worked with schools and local teachers seemed to be very contingent on a relationship of trust between the centre leaders and the schools and an ability to be responsive to local need. There was also an important relationship to be brokered with the local authority advisers and inspectors. An article in *Insight* the journal of the National Conference of Teachers Centre Leaders (NCTCL) in 1981 provides an interesting example of how a teachers' centre leader developed some work with a school, based on the delivery of a new initiative in pupil profiling and in response to specific demand from a school. Geoff Hall, warden of the Knowsley Teachers' Centre described how he had worked on an innovative project to use pupil profiles as part of ongoing student assessment and reporting pupil progress with a local secondary school. The centre worked with the school to develop focussed in-service training for teachers on the use of pupil profiles and this then became an important tool for the school's evaluation strategy. For Geoff this was a very good example of a '*...a situation where a school requested support and advice and a Teachers' Centre was able to supply it.*' The trusted relationship between centre and school was crucial and Geoff wrote,

> It is worthwhile considering the role of the centre leader in this project – centre leader has relevant professional experiences – knowledge and experience of the curriculum process. But of most importance is – the crucial nature of trust between the centre leader and the school leaders and teacher. '...no matter how well qualified a centre leader might be in academic terms, he will be of little use to that school unless a trusted relationship is developed.[49]

Being responsive to teacher demand was something that Alec Fellows was keen to promote for his centre in Nuneaton. He relied heavily on the teacher committee to recommend activities and described the centre as '*...a bit of a booking agency*', following up teachers' requests to bring in certain advisers or speakers.[50] Kate Moorse had a similar experience and described meeting regularly with her team and the committee to identify appropriate activities and support and also close working between local authority advisers and local headteachers to identify specific needs, with '*...people ringing up and saying, I've got a real issue with X or Y...and then if you, you know, we'd meet quite regularly as a team...well we'd meet every week as a team. It was an intelligence gathering place, really, so we would think a bit about what we could do...*'[51] She described the particular working culture of her centre as one which really fostered educational discussion and debate. Recalling a period in the 1980s when National Curriculum debates were highly contested, Kate described how the centre became a meeting place where advisory teachers would come for hours at the end of the day and '*...people would stay there until eight at night, talking education.*'[52]

Given their relative newness on the educational scene and the fact that they occupied a middle ground between schools and local authorities, teachers' centre leaders found support and encouragement from networking with each other. Keith Martin suggested that many centre wardens felt isolated - '*I think some teacher centre leaders had a very hard time and you know were very cut off in that respect.*'[53] Initially, informal local or regional networks sprang up. Joy Williams recalled the Hampshire Teachers' Centre group, which met termly to discuss progress and share ideas. Alec Fellows was a member of the West Midlands Teachers' Centre group and Keith Martin and Alan Forster, members of a Somerset and Devon group which continues to meet today as a social group for retired teachers' centre leaders. Kate

Moorse described the scene in London as comprising a number of different warden's groups, depending on their particular focus and role. She recalled, '*I think maybe we had a rota, and so one month we'd meet as wardens and another month we'd meet as specialist wardens, and another month we'd meet as multipurpose, you know, we had our interest group meetings.*' Kate found these groups to be '*...quite blokey... which is one of the reasons why the women wardens group set themselves up, to offset the blokeyness of it.*' Interestingly two of the other female centre wardens interviewed referred to their more domestic approach to running the centre – with a special focus on ensuring that tea, cakes and refreshments were in plentiful supply – something that they did not think that their male counterparts would have been so concerned with.

In 1973 these regional groups came together to form a national association which was first known as the National Conference of Teachers Centre Leaders, which published a journal *Insight* to promote networking between teachers' centres nationally and internationally as well as the sharing of ideas, practice and meetings and an annual national conference. NCTCL changed name several times, becoming the National Council of Teachers in Professional Development, then the National Association of Professional Development, and then the Association of Professional Development in Education. Regional branches retained their own distinctive identity and it is clear that some regional groups were more engaged with the organisation and activism of the national group than others, with the South-East grouping perhaps being more 'political' in its engagement with the Schools Council and the teacher unions than other regional groups, possibly reflecting the strength of London-based centre leaders at the time. As the only professional organisation catering solely for teachers' centre leaders, one of the objectives of the group was to look at the varied employment conditions and salaries of centre leaders in an attempt to create some kind of equity. Vin Davis, a founder member and South West regional representative recognised the challenges facing the NCTCL when he wrote;

> There still remains a mass of basic problems to be solved before Teachers' Centres and the NCTCL may feel satisfied with their national role, influence and usefulness. The absence of a definition of what makes a Teachers' Centre something other than a centre for teachers, still remains.[54]

The NCTCL came into direct conflict with the Schools Council when its evaluation of teachers' centres was set up in the late 1970s, suggesting that there was a power struggle between the teachers' centre leaders, with their own particular vision for the centres and that of the Schools Council and possibly local authorities. This power struggle appeared to involve NCTCL members believing that the Schools Council did not recognise the significance of individual teachers' centre leaders as part of a wider conspiracy to reduce the autonomy of teachers' centres and their teacher-led mission. Schools Council papers document an irate exchange of correspondence between leading members of the NCTCL and the Schools Council over the lack of consultation over their evaluation of centres, the nature and appropriateness of their survey instruments and the extent to which the evaluation would really get to the heart of ongoing tensions around the status of the teachers' centres and their leaders and their relationship with local authority in-service provision and teacher development programmes, as well as the core philosophy underlining the work of the centres.[55] More research is needed on the NCTCL, as oral history testimony for this study has generated very contradictory evidence as to its role and impact, with some participants suggesting that it was a highly politicised organisation which lobbied government, local authorities and the Schools Council and others suggesting that it was nothing more than a rather parochial support group for isolated centre teachers. Data to illuminate the NCTSL is fragmented and there is no single archive of its activity, which makes a thorough historical analysis a challenge. However, it was clearly a body which sought to bring together a very diverse group of centre leaders, each with very different experiences of their centres in their local contexts. Even to find an agreed shared definition of what a teachers' centre was for and how its leaders should be formally designated was difficult for this group. It wanted to find coherence and to identify a shared experience and, in doing so, highlighted the very essence of the teachers' centre phenomenon which was both its strength and its weakness – its diversity. In the opening to Harry Khan's handbook *Teachers' Resource Centres*, written in 1984, Kathleen Devaney, an experienced American teacher educator who had observed the development of teachers' centres in England and promoted their development in the US noted:

> The basics of a teachers' centre are its personality, leadership, followership, grassroots, idiosyncracies. Try to segment someone else's experience, you will lose their essence – and not find your own.[56]

TEACHERS' CENTRES AND INTERNATIONAL DEVELOPMENTS

In the opening to his 1973 book *Teachers' Centres* Robert Thornbury painted an evocative picture:

> A New Zealand Teachers' Union Official, a New York elementary school principal, a sari'd administrator from Delhi, 20 Brazilian class teachers, a West German director of education, a lecturer planning the raising of the Hong Kong school-leaving age, a teaching sister from Connemara, and the education minister for a Middle East oil sheikdom – this mixed group of educationalists – visiting London in summer 1972 all made the same request. They all asked to see a teachers' centre. In fact, they all visited Sherbrooke Teachers' Centre, three converted classrooms in a Hammersmith primary school. Other teachers' centres all over the country were at the same time welcoming a similar flow of visitors.[57]

He went on to describe a proliferation of international interest in teachers' centres – because they were what he regarded as a 'British First'[58] so fundamental to educational reform in the late 1960s and early 1970s that they represented a 'silent educational revolution'. According to Thornbury, so successful were the early teachers' centres that he argued that they had become one of the country's major invisible exports both to the developed and developing world.[59] Having presented a snapshot of the teachers' centres as they developed in England and Wales, it is also instructive to consider the way in which this model of teacher development influenced and was adopted in a number of other countries, including the Netherlands, Spain, Japan, South Africa, the United States, Australia and New Zealand. The NCTCL supported a series of study visits and exchanges with sister institutions in the US, South Africa and Europe. In addition, the British Council was also influential in funding networking conferences which brought together teacher educators committed to the particular teacher-centred model of professional development that was embodied in the teachers' centre model.

The idea that the teachers' centre was an exportable commodity was recognised very early on by Thornbury and other early pioneers of the movement. Given that my study, as well as other earlier reviews of teachers' centres has suggested that there was no such thing as a homogenous 'model' for the teachers' centre, its popularity overseas as a peculiarly 'British' model seems somewhat ironic. Indeed, some contemporary observers noted that '...The British teachers' centre concept would seem to have caused more interest, excitement and sponsorship in countries copying the British prototype, than in the country of origin.'[60] The mechanisms by which the idea of the teachers' centre were taken up in different international contexts included frequent visits and delegations from other countries to the British centres, dissemination of materials and literature about the centres in international contexts, structured international exchanges between British teacher centre leaders and host countries and shared conferences, seminars and networks. Teachers' Centres flourished in a number of other countries, including the United States, Australia and New Zealand, and across Europe.[61] There is now, therefore, as then, clear scope for more systematic research into the internationalisation of the teachers' centre model, and the place of English centres in this development.

Thornbury's 1973 book on the centres, the first book of its type, was a powerful catalyst in itself. For example, a brief article in an Australian journal *The Age* in 1974 suggested that teachers' centres were springing up all over Australia and that Thornbury's book was specifically being used to guide their development.[62] Indeed, 300 copies of this book were pre-ordered by Australian teachers prior to publication. Thornbury himself was invited to undertake a study visit of Australia and New Zealand, December to March 1975 and acted as a consultant for new centres. Later on Vin Davis, warden of the Kendal Teachers' Centre, was seconded to Australia in the late 1970s to become Director of the Freemantle Teachers' Centres. A similar story can be found for the US, with Thornbury's book being chosen as 'book of the month' for an American educational book club.[63] Elizabeth Adams' 1975 book on teachers' centres reported a discussion about the international phenomenon of teachers' centres at a conference at Syracuse University in 1972, which discussed whether a British model of Teachers Centre should be introduced in the United States.[64] In the US a network of funded teachers' centres based on the English model was seen as the way forward. Writing in *Insight* in November 1978, Jack Burd, Director of Education Programmes in Missouri, lamented how far behind the British the Americans were in relation to in-service education, which was piecemeal and offered limited opportunities for agency on the part of teachers. He suggested that part of the Jimmy Carter presidential election campaign included a pledge for funding of teachers' centres along British lines.[65] A structured programme of teacher centre leader exchanges between the US and UK was critical for the expansion and growth of the American system, as was reported by Roy Edelfelt and Merrita Hruska in their article on 'British-American Exchange on Teachers' Centres' published in the *British Journal of In-Service Education* in 1982.[66]

Oral history data from my study suggested the value of exchange programmes between the England and the US. For example, as late as 1988, Keith Martin, warden of the Somerset Teachers' Centre, received funding from the British Council to go to America to visit teachers centres in the Chicago area. He also attended a conference for US TC leaders held in New Orleans. He was away for three months on this trip and recalled:

> Well it was good, it was great I went round all the centres seeing what they were doing and seeing how they compared with ours and what we were doing and... so I went to this place south of, near Chicago and they wrote up my visit and they called me Doc Martin.[67]

Keith had a copy of this 'write-up' in an American newsletter in an article entitled 'British Educators Feel the Weight of 'New Initiatives' Overload' which quoted Keith describing his own Centre in Somerset as a place '...*firmly committed to the principles of teachers' involvement in their own in-service training... and it provides a place where they can use the services, find resources, join a workshop or "just have a chat and a cup of coffee." Or tea, perhaps?*'[68]

Keith went on to write up a report for the trip for the British Council. He was particularly impressed that the American centres '.....*really believed in applauding success and making sure that the teachers were really up there and they had teacher of the year and things like this...*',[69] and thought more could be done in Britain to celebrate achievement. There is evidence to suggest that this 'exchange' was a two-way learning process and not all one-way.

In the following year Keith was involved in running an international seminar for the British Council on 'Teachers' Centres: Purposes, Principles and Practice' held at the Norwich Teachers' Centre, May 7–19 1989. When interviewed he still had a copy of the programme to hand which outlines the lectures and workshops, all focussed on sharing the model, purpose and concept of the teachers' centres ideal, with a range of speakers from across the UK, including Centre wardens. The list of invited participants included 16 participants from Austria, Belgium, Brazil, Canada, Denmark, Greece, Israel, Spain, Sri Lanka, UK and Pakistan. Later on Keith was involved in another international conference organised by the ADPE (formerly the NCTCL) in Dublin in 1992. Delegates involved in teachers' centre work came from the UK, Palestine, Israel and all over Europe. This conference represented the culmination of Keith's career and soon after it he took early retirement at a time when centres were being closed and funding for in-service work devolved directly to schools. For Keith, the networking with other teacher educators outside of his home context was really important.[70]

Alan Forster, former warden of a centre in Devon, also described the importance of exchange programmes, specifically with teachers' centres in New England, New Hampshire and Vermont in the early 1980s. He recalled the novelty of the centres in America at that time but had warm memories of the benefits of mutual exchange between teachers.

> I'd set up a link with a university in America and I would take teachers across to, just for a short time and then American teachers would come back. They'd live in each other's houses…. did share a lot of things.[71]

At his interview Alan produced a brief written report from one of his exchange teachers, describing her experience. She wrote '…*This exchange programme is I hope just the tip of the iceberg, we have so much to share and what better way to do it than living and working alongside one another even for a brief period of time.*'[72]

Another oral history participant from the project, Gill Brown, a head teacher from Rotherham, also recalled a teacher visit to South African schools and teachers' centres, funded by the British Council in the late 1990s. Her role was to try to advise organisers on how to improve the system – but recalled that the teachers' centres were always empty as they were difficult for teachers to access because of distance. She said:

> …we were ambassadors and all that kind of thing and we visited teacher centres out there which were always empty, and we tried to explain to them why they were empty, and the reason why they're empty is because the teachers hadn't got the funds to travel right across the city to a teachers centre. So they had all these lovely facilities…They were pretty well resourced, some of them, yes and they were an opportunity to meet and discuss things but nobody put any transport in and most of the teachers didn't have cars and they had long days, started at eight and finished at two. We started at eight and finished at two and then we went off to various places, and then we had to do something else as well, really long days and the teachers had had enough by two, they wanted to go home, sort their shopping out, do their lives so we said, they said no the teachers don't come here and we said "you need to get a bus and go out to the schools and you need to be…" it's hard to say this isn't it but you need to take your bus at the end of school for an hour and talk to the teachers there. They had brand new books and all sorts of stuff. Hopefully they've sorted that out now.[73]

The British Council was instrumental in the dissemination of the British teachers' centre model overseas – particularly to commonwealth countries. It certainly funded some of the early teacher exchanges described above. In the early 1980s it commissioned a group of experts to produce a 'handbook' which could be '*applicable to those setting up or developing teachers' centres in widely differing social, economic and educational conditions'*. Harry Kahn, Warden of the Enfield Teachers' Centre and also actively involved in producing this handbook reported on the preliminary discussions about this book at a conference held in Auckland, New Zealand, in May 1982.[74] The book, *Teachers' Resource Centres,* was first published in 1984 and revised in 1991, after reportedly being in 'constant demand', according to the Director of the Education programme for the Secretariat.[75] Kahn argued that the British teachers' centres had exercised a unique influence on the in-service education and status of teachers *'beyond the confines of the British Isles'*. He also suggested that:

> ...it is pleasing to note that the warning of all centre leaders in England, when receiving visiting educationalists from different parts of the word, to ADAPT and not to ADOPT the British pattern to their own circumstances has been heeded. Thus while today there is an underlying philosophy and a broad spectrum of common aims and objectives to Centres in different regions of the world, the actual patterns of interpretation on the ground are as widely different in other countries as they are in the UK, as between different areas and different Centres.[76]

Early pioneers, actively engaged in running new centres, like Vin Davis, Robert Thornbury, Harry Kahn and Bob Gough as well as other founding members of the NCTSL, were unashamed enthusiasts for their contribution to teacher professionalism, autonomy and learning. However difficult to define, given their *ad hoc* development in so many different forms, it could be suggested that there was something inherent in the philosophical ideal of the teachers' centres. Harry Kahn, with his unswerving enthusiasm for the work of the centres advised that a handbook he authored for international audiences should be read as a guide and not as a 'description of Utopia' – and that some adjustments would have to be made to local systems, resources and contexts.[77] Gough neatly summarised the nub of the philosophy of the centres as one in which '*... teachers' centres are teacher centred and should be quickly responsive to teachers' needs and wants'*,[78] whilst Kahn felt that the 'main plank' in the philosophy of teachers' centres was that they should offer support to 'the teacher as a professional'.[79] Various typologies of the 'ideal centre' emerged with practical suggestions for their day-to-day running. Kahn in particular used a very teacher-centred democratic language to describe centres as neutral, relevant, flexible, led by teachers, concerned with education (as opposed to mechanistic training), professional, realistic and above all focussed on immediate local need. Governance should be non-hierarchical and respectful of relationships between teachers, staff and visitors.[80] Khan concluded that:

> The Teachers' Resource Centre will weave the various educational agencies and the almost untapped expertise of the teaching force into its own democratic patterns through its committees, its co-operative style of work, and its empathy with its clients so that its work will win the confidence of the administration and the trust of the teachers and community. In this way the Centre will establish for itself an influential place in the evolution of educational advance.[81]

If the rhetoric of the teachers' centre was its democracy and its commitment to grass-roots professional development led by and directed by teachers themselves – then new historical data for this study suggests a much more mixed picture of teacher engagement.

CHAPTER SUMMARY

Undoubtedly, the histories of the British teachers' centres are multiple, varied and complex and more detailed research is needed to build a more coherent picture of their contribution to teacher professional development and teacher professionalism in their time. Much of the literature on the teachers' centres produced in the 1970s was promotional and verging on the evangelical, though in places doubts and questions did emerge. Weindling, for example, worried that the early literature on teachers' centres overstated the extent to which teachers could control and indeed wished to control their own in-service training. Jenny Williams, a New Zealand teacher educator who spent time studying teachers' centres in Britain in the late 1970s before returning to work with teachers in Wellington, New Zealand, wrote a fairly critical paper in the *British Journal of In-service Education* in 1981 describing the centres from her perspective as an 'Antipodean'. She recognised a gulf between the rhetoric about British teachers' centres and the reality on the ground. She wrote of the influence of the British centre in countries like the United States, Australia, Canada, Scandinavia and New Zealand where, '...*to many outside observers, the British Teachers' Centres appear neutral, supportive and readily transportable.*'[82] However, she went on to suggest that the centres were not always neutral, were unduly dependent on the quality and vision of the warden, were often underfunded, not necessarily democratic and subject to conflicting aims and directions:

> The British Teachers' Centre is reasonably cheap, efficient and apparently needed. Overseas interest and imitation show it to be a concept of considerable appeal to teachers. However, if Teachers' Centres are to avoid the danger of becoming a museum of pedagogical ideas, they have to continue to demonstrate their ability to respond quickly and change in new situations. Now the excitement of the cottage industry days are going the Teachers' Centres will perhaps have to operate as less of a 'pony express' and more of a service station on a high-speed motorway.[83]

From Williams' standpoint in the early 1980s she wanted the exported model to New Zealand to live up to the rhetoric – to be even more like the 'model' than the reality she had observed in Britain – so that New Zealand centres would be truly '*for the teacher, of the teacher, by the teachers*'.[84]

Though teachers' centres, as they were originally conceived, have now largely disappeared from the UK teacher professional development landscape, they appear to continue to thrive in a wider international arena, particularly in the US, parts of Europe, and in the developing world. A large study commissioned by the

British Department for International Development in the late 1990s with a team of researchers from the University of Leeds, led by Gary Knamiller, surveyed the legacy of the teachers' centres in the form of teachers' resource centres in developing educational systems in Andrha Pradesh, India, Kenya, Nepal and Zambia. This study identified strengths and weaknesses in the models – but also questioned the extent to which teachers were enabled to take ownership of activities within the centres and around their own professional development.[85]

By way of conclusion, it could perhaps be argued that the 'British 'export' of teachers' centres represented a classic case of 'smoke and mirrors', though this phenomenon does deserve some further questioning and research. This was a highly westernised model which flourished in England and Wales when, for a brief window of time at least, the economy and social milieu of the 1960s and early 1970s supported the ideal of teacher-led 'democratised' forms of professional learning – the 'golden age', as described above. How receptive to or indeed able to engage were other countries, particularly non-Western countries or more authoritarian countries, with core ideals of teacher autonomy and teacher-led learning? A key question relates to those factors which contributed to their demise in England and Wales and what factors currently contribute to their 'success', albeit modified 'success', in other international contexts. There is clearly scope for these questions to be addressed in the context of further systematic comparative in-depth studies of teachers' centres in Europe, the English-speaking world and in developing countries.

NOTES

[1] See for example: Townsend, H. (1968). *'The in-service training of teachers in the city of Wakefield'*, unpublished M.Ed. Thesis, University of Manchester; Ravenhall, R. (1971). *'Teachers' centres and their role in the pattern of in-service education for teachers.'* unpublished Dip. Ed. Thesis, University of Exeter; Richards, C. (1972). 'Teachers' Centres - A primary school view', *Trends in Education, 25*, 31–33; Brand, J. (1972). *'The in-service education role of teachers' centres'*, unpublished Dip. Ed. Thesis, University of Nottingham; Thornbury, R. (1973). *Teachers' centres*. London, UK: Darton, Longman & Todd; Midwinter, E. (1974). 'Teachers' centres: The facilitators', *British Journal of In-Service Education, 1*(1), 10–14; Adam. E. (Ed.) (1975). *In-service education and teachers' centres*. Oxford: Pergamon Press; Selby, D. (1976). *'The concept and growth of the teachers' centre movement, with special reference to the Lancashire area'*, unpublished M.Ed. Thesis, University of Manchester; C. Redknap, *Focus on teachers' centres*. (Windsor: NFER Publishing Company, 1977); Davis, R. (1979). *'A study of the Kendal Teachers' Centre in Kendal with special reference to the views of users'*, unpublished MSc. Thesis, University of Lancaster; Morant, R. (1978). 'Re-appraising the role of teachers' centres', *British Journal of In-Service Education, 4*(3), 198–205; Eggleston, J. (1979). 'Teacher's centres: a British development in further professional training', *European Journal of Education, 14*(3), 51–357; Martin, P. (1981). 'The role of teachers' centres', *Insight, 4*(2), 22–28; Newman, C., Shostack, R., & Sollars, R. (1981). 'Teachers centres: some emergent characteristics', *Professional Development in Education 8*(1), 45–50; Rutherford, T. (1981). 'The teachers' centre leaders: A partner in education', *Insight, 4*(3), 8–12; Weindling, D., Reid, M., & Davis, P. (1983). *Teachers' centres: A focus for in-service education*. London, UK: Methuen Educational; Gough, B. (1989). '20 years or so of teachers' centres: what have we learned? what can we share?', *British Journal of In-Service Education, 15*(1), 51–54; Gough, B. (1997). 'Teacher's centres as seen through the pages of the *British Journal of In-Service Education*', *British Journal of In-Service Education, 23*(1), 23–29.

[2]   University of London, Institute of Education Archives (Hereafter IOE), SCC /17175/385/01, Teachers' Centres, role and functioning, 1978–79.

[3]   IoE, SCC/385/416/01, A Survey of Centre Resources and Conditions of Service of Leaders, March 1972, published by the National Union of Teachers.

[4]   For a fuller discussion of educational change in the 1960s, see Lowe, R., (1997). *Schooling and social change 1964–1990.* London, UK: Routledge; and Jones, K. (2003). *Education in Britain: 1944 to the present.* Cambridge: Polity Press.

[5]   See Sandbrook, D. (2006). *White heat: A history of Britain in the Swinging Sixties.* London, UK: Little, Brown.

[6]   IoE, HR/6/32, Typed manuscript with handwritten notes/annotations of a speech delivered to the National Conference for Teachers' Centre Wardens, Exeter, 2 April 1974 entitled, 'Where is change?'.

[7]   Plaskow, M., 'It was the best of times', *Education*, 3 August 1990, p. 90 quoted in C. Chitty & J. Dunford, (Eds.), (1999). *State schools: New labour and the conservative legacy.* London, UK: Woburn Press, p. 22.

[8]   Thornbury, *Teachers' centres.*

[9]   IoE, HR/10/18, Manuscript for book review of Robert Thornbury's 1973 book on the teachers' centre, sent to the *Teacher's World* 13 July 1973 by Harry Ree.

[10] The National Archives, Kew, England (hereafter TNA), ED 272/3/1, Some aspects of in-service training for teachers of mathematics in the North West Division, 1968–9.

[11] TNA, Ed 235/7, In-service courses for teachers in East Sussex 1968–1969, Report by HMI on a survey on in-service courses.

[12] Thornbury, R. (1974). 'Teachers' centres', *New Society,* 28, p. 761.

[13] IoE, SCC/175/385/01, A Survey of Centre Resources and Conditions of Service of Leaders, March 1972, published by the National Union of Teachers.

[14] Ibid.

[15] BARDA Project 53026, oral history interview with Bill Parkinson, May 2011.

[16] BARDA Project 53026, oral history interview with Derek Cloke, May 2011.

[17] BARDA Project 53026, oral history interview with Diana Lucas, May 2011.

[18] TNA, ED 272/33, In-service training of teachers, 1970–1971, Survey on cpd for teachers in Bradford in 1969–70.

[19] BARDA Project 53026, oral history interview with Kate Moorse, February 2011.

[20] IoE, SCC/175/385/01, Teachers' centres, role and functioning, 1976–1982.

[21] IoE, SCC/385/416/01, 'A Survey of Centre Resources and Conditions of Service of Leaders, March 1972', published by the National Union of Teachers.

[22] IOE, SCC /17175/385/01, Teachers' Centres, role and functioning, 1978–79.

[23] BARDA Project 53026, oral history interview Keith Martin, May 2011.

[24] BARDA Project 53026, oral history interview with Alec Fellows, May 2011.

[25] TNA, ED 272/33, In-service training of teachers, 1970–1971, a survey of cpd for teachers in Bradford conducted in 1969–70

[26] IoE, SCC/175/385/01, Teachers' Centres, role and functioning, 1978–9, article on 'Curriculum and Teachers' from *Education* written by the Deputy Chief Education Officer of Devon, Joslyn Owen.

[27] Ibid.

[28] TNA, ED 272/33, In-Service training of teachers, 1970–1971, a survey of cpd for teachers in Bradford conducted in 1969–70.

[29] IoE, SCC/175/385/01, Teachers' Centres, role and functioning, 1978–9, copy of Kendal Teachers' Centre Newsletter, September 1978.

[30] TNA, ED 235/7, In-service courses for teachers in East Sussex 1968–1969, Report by HMI on a survey on in-service courses.

[31] Weindling et al, *Teachers' centres: A focus for in-service education.*

[32] Gough, 'Teachers' centres as providers of in-service education'.

[33] Knamiller, G. (Eds.). (1999). *The effectiveness of teacher resource centre strategy.* London, UK: Department for International Development.

[34] Thornbury, *Teachers Centres,* p. 28.

35 BARDA Project 53026, oral history interview with Alec Fellows.
36 IOE, SCC /17175/385/01, Teachers' Centres, role and functioning, 1978–79.
37 BARDA Project 53026, oral history interview with Joy Williams, September 2011.
38 BARDA Project 53026, oral history interview with Kate Moorse.
39 IoE, SCC/175/385/01, Teachers' Centres, role and functioning, 1978–9, copy of Kendal Teachers' Centre Newsletter, September 1978.
40 IoE, HR/10/18, Harry Ree Papers.
41 BARDA Project 53026, oral history interview with Derek Cloke, May 2011.
42 BARDA Project 53026, oral history interview with Alan Forster, August 2011.
43 BARDA Project 53026, oral history interview with Keith Martin.
44 BARDA Project 53026, oral history interview with Alec Fellows.
45 IOE, SCC /17175/385/01, Teachers' Centres, role and functioning, 1978–79. letter from RV Davis to the Schools Council Monitoring Committee on Teachers' Centres, dated 12 June 1979.
46 SCC /17175/385/01, Teachers' Centres, role and functioning, 1978–79.
47 BARDA Project 53026, oral history interview with Joy Williams.
48 BARDA Project 53026, oral history interview with Joy Kell, May 2011.
49 IoE, SCC/P/22, Manuscript dated December 1981 for an article to be published in *Insight*.
50 BARDA Project 53026, oral history interview with Alec Fellows.
51 BARDA Project 53026, oral history interview with Kate Moorse.
52 Ibid.
53 BARDA Project 53026, oral history interview with Keith Martin.
54 IoE, SCC/175/385/01, Teachers' Centres, role and functioning, 1978–79.
55 Ibid.
56 K. Devaney, quoted in Khan, H., (1991). *Teachers' resource centres,* Commonwealth Education Handbooks, London: Commonwealth Secretariat, p. 1.
57 Thornbury, *Teachers centres*, p. 1.
58 Note that contemporaries referred to the 'British' teachers' centres – though it would be more accurate to refer to them as 'English'.
59 Thornbury, R. (1974). 'Teachers' centres', *New Society 28,* 27th June, p. 761.
60 Williams, J. (1981). 'Teachers' centres in the United Kingdom: an Antipodean view, *British Journal of In-Service Education,* 7(2), p. 132.
61 Miles, M., 'The teacher centre: educational change through teacher development', in Adams, *In-service education and teachers' centres,* p. 163. See also IoE, SCC/175/385/01: Teachers' Centres, role and functioning, 1978–9 which refers to Vin Davies being seconded from Kendal Teachers' Centre to become Director of Teachers' Centres in Freemantle, Australia; Rust, V. (1973). 'Teachers' centres in England, *The Elementary School Journal,* 7(4), 182–192; Stabler, E. (1976). 'Teachers' centres: a comparative view, *Canadian Journal of Education,* 1(2), 37–50.
62 *The Age,* September 17 1974, p. 11.
63 Weindling et al, *Teachers' centres: A focus for in-service education,* p. 90.
64 Miles, M., 'Reflections and commentary on the Syracuse Conference on the Teacher Centre', in Adams, *In-Service Education and Teachers' Centres.*
65 Burd, J. (1978). 'INSET in the USA', *Insight,* 2(2), 19–22.
66 Edelfelth, R. & Hruska, M. (1982). 'British-American exchange on teachers' centres, *British Journal of In-Service Education,* 9(2), 80–87.
67 BARDA Project 53026, oral history interview with Keith Martin.
68 BARDA Project 53026, an extract from a report on Keith Martin's US visit 1988, personal papers given to the author,
69 BARDA Project 53026, oral history interview with Keith Martin.
70 BARDA Project 53026, copy of the conference programme, personal papers given to the author.
71 BARDA Project 53026, oral history interview with Alan Forster.
72 BARDA Project 53026, report on a US exchange from a teacher, personal papers given to the author by Alan Forster.
73 BARDA Project 53026, oral history interview with Gill Brown (p), July 2011.

74 Kahn, H. (1982) 'Teachers' centres their aims, objectives and philosophy: A Commonwealth perspective', *British Journal of In-Service Education*, 9(2), 75–80.

75 Kahn, *Teachers' Resource Centres*.

76 Khan, 'Teachers' centres their aims, objectives and philosophy: a Commonwealth perspective', p. 79.

77 Khan, *Teachers' Resource Centres*, p.1.

78 Gough, '20 years or so of teachers' centres: what have we learned? what can we share?', p. 51.

79 Khan, *Teachers' Resource Centres*, p. 8.

80 Ibid., p. 10.

81 Ibid., p. 113.

82 Williams, 'Teachers' centres in the United Kingdom: an Antipodean View', p. 133.

83 Ibid.

84 Ibid.

85 Knamiller et al, *The effectiveness of teacher resource centre strategy*.

TEACHERS' EXPERIENCES OF PROFESSIONAL DEVELOPMENT

Drawing exclusively on the oral history testimony generated for the research which underpins the book, this chapter considers how participants described their experiences of professional development at different times in their careers. For the most part, stories of professional development were very much associated with formal, structured opportunities broadly categorized as 'going on courses'. These 'courses' took many forms – and represented a wide range of different models of formal professional development provision. Key national initiatives as well as opportunities generated through the idea of teacher secondments were important drivers identified by the participants. In addition, there were some notable memories of informal professional development experiences generated organically amongst groups of teachers emerging from their accounts. The chapter presents the participants' testimony under five main themes: early career experiences; formal courses; the importance of teachers' secondment; the impact of national policy initiatives on professional development; and experiences of informal professional development.

EARLY CAREER EXPERIENCES: 'IN AT THE DEEP END'

When asked to consider any early career experiences of professional development in their first few years of teaching, a common theme which emerged from participants was a distinct lack of any formal professional development. Ann Dodd, who began her teaching career in 1968 in a primary school on the Braunston Estate in Leicester, then an educational priority area, recalled:

> ...you started your teaching, here you are a new teacher, there's no mentor in the school for you. I was befriended by one teacher and she was, she was more experienced than I, but basically you walk in your classroom, the door is shut and you just get on with it...[1]

Gill Brown, who began her career in 1976 teaching History and Religious Education (RE) in a challenging secondary school in the Moss Side region of Manchester, recalled a similar experience:

> The teacher next door had a strap. That was it. I was left to it - here's the classroom, here's the text books, this is vaguely what you're teaching, off you go.[2]

Bill Parkinson who began teaching in a Coventry primary school in 1969 recalled limited formal professional development on offer as a young teacher and very much felt as if he was '*thrown into the deep end*':

> I think when you're a new teacher you were just looked on as you didn't have that much to offer a school, I think there were some long established staff there who'd been there a long way and to an extent I always felt that they were looked after more than new teachers, if there was any training or any sort of in-service, the very little that there was in those days, it would go to experienced people because it was felt that if you've just come out of college you knew everything because you were just fresh out. I remember that being said to me, or, "you should be able to bring lots of things to school because you've just been to college". In reality it was quite the reverse.[3]

This 'deep-end' metaphor was used by a number of participants to describe their early career experience. David Howe recalled that as a newly qualified teacher in 1963, teaching English at a bilateral secondary school in Rugby, he never attended any courses and described in-school development as being confined to operational business-like staff meetings:

> I can't recall anything. I can't recall any concessions for teachers in a probationary year. I used to characterise it because I heard the phrase so often as the 'Deep End Theory', the way they learn is to push them in at the deep end and the argument you always got is, "that's what we had to do, that's what you'll have to do"…I just think the idea was, "well you've done your PGCE, the best way to learn now is do it, get on with it", and even department meetings, things like that were rare and if they were there, they were business like. They were about setting exam papers.[4]

Jim Christophers began his career as a Geography teacher in a Gloucestershire secondary school in 1972. Like David Howe and Bill Parkinson, he suggested that the attitude from more experienced staff and senior staff was that newly qualified teachers, straight out of college, were less in need of any further training because they were much more likely to be up-to-date than teachers who had been working for some time.

Though formal professional development might have been lacking, there did appear to be a range of informal support and encouragement from other teachers who would lend materials or books, support with classroom and behaviour management issues and generally provide some mentorship for the newly qualified teachers. Diana Lucas, who began teaching in 1972, working in an inner-London infants' school, recalled limited 'official' support for her as a new teacher but did stress the importance of informal support from other teachers in the school:

> There wasn't anything official I don't think, but the Head was supportive and the teacher in the next classroom, maybe she'd been asked to keep an eye on me. She'd been doing it for a year or so and she kept an eye on me. I remember

once taking a child and I can still remember his name, but he bit me in the neck and I lifted him gently, took him next door with tears in my eyes and she said, "come here...", you know....[5]

Hilary Cox, whose first teaching post was at a junior school in Southend-on Sea in the early 1960s, had no memory of anything being offered by way of courses or even what she referred to as proper 'in-house training'. However, she did remember that:

...the head and other members of staff were very supportive. The head particularly, he was very charismatic, you could go to him with any problem, but there was no particular training...[6]

For Peggy Jones, there was no formal professional development in her early career as a primary school teacher in Buckinghamshire in the late 1960s – '...*no you sort of went and did your teaching and then you just toddled off home.*'[7]

FORMAL PROFESSIONAL DEVELOPMENT: 'GOING ON COURSES'

Though participants did not often recall any specific support or training associated with their early career status – they did go on to describe a range of different formal professional development experiences that emerged as their careers progressed. These included engagement with what was happening in local teachers' centres, as described in Chapter Five, as well as a plethora of other experiences, including residential local authority or HMI/Department for Education courses, delivered at weekends and in school holidays, twilight sessions with advisers, curriculum association meetings and various teacher union activities. Participants commonly grouped under the umbrella phrase 'going on a course', their experiences of formal professional development which varied enormously in terms of quality, quantity, impact and memorability.

Memories of 'going on courses' resonate with some of the earlier chronological models described in the book – particularly the idea of a residential/vacation course. In spite of this variability, the 'residential' course, whether organised by HMI or by the local authority, or whether held over weekends or during holidays, appeared to stimulate participants' memories and stood out as something worth remembering. Joy Kell, as a primary school teacher in Devon in the late 1950s, was particularly impressed with a three-day residential Art course organised by HMI in the summer break, which was followed up later in the Autumn term to enable teachers to demonstrate new Art work they had completed with their pupils as a result of the course.

...it was in Exeter and it was three days and funnily the HMI was inspirational... And we went back into schools in the, it was in the summer holidays, we went back into school for the Autumn and then there was a follow-up near Christmas and we brought examples of what we had done with the children. Tie and dye was the third one. So that was the basis of the course. She talked about various types of art, she talked about fabric design, she talked about printing, wood block, that's potato printing for small children, and then we took samples back in the autumn near Christmas.[8]

Joy also attended evening classes in Exeter during the late 1950s on subjects such as Physical Education (PE), Music and Movement organised by the National Union of Teachers. Joy recalls the impact of wider trends and developments in education nationally – specifically the introduction of the Initial Teaching Alphabet and the Nuffield Council School Curriculum Projects – that provided stimulus for local authority short courses during the late 1960s. Later in her career as a primary head teacher in Cornwall and then as a professional development officer (PDO), Joy went on to develop strong views about the value of residential courses for teachers. She believed that teachers really benefited from working away from their immediate school and domestic environments, where there was more time and space, physically and emotionally, to concentrate on professional matters.

> You're out of it, you don't have to think, "what am I going to cook for dinner tonight?" Which I suspect many teachers are sitting thinking. You don't have to do that. You are divorced from your ordinary everyday mundane life which has terrific demands, and therefore you can concentrate and develop an awful lot in that week and I attended as a provider and as somebody learning from it because they were very, very valuable.[9]

Joy Williams who worked as a primary teacher in Oxfordshire and Hampshire from the early 1950s, and was appointed as 'organiser' of the Winchester Teachers' Centre in 1971, held similar views about the value of residential courses for teachers. Hampshire LEA ran a residential centre for teachers in the New Forest at Gurney Dixon, where courses were organised by advisers over weekends or holiday periods. Selection of teachers for these courses, which were regarded as a special treat, with good food, time for social interaction and a bar, appeared to focus on those teachers considered to be most in need of some new stimulation or ideas:

> Well we were all there for a specific purpose. We hadn't actually got to do the shopping on our way home and we hadn't done a day's teaching before we started. It was always seen as a bit of a sweetie. You know? To get on to a Gurney Dixon course.[10]

Jean Firth, working as an English teacher in Coventry secondary schools during the late 1960s and early 1970s, recalled how she had been most anxious to be accepted onto a Coventry LEA residential course held at Lincoln College, Oxford, over a series of long weekends during the spring term. For Jean, who applied twice to attend this course, paid for by Coventry and restricted to a small quota of teachers, this was one of the most worthwhile professional development experiences of her career. Jean regarded attendance at these courses a real privilege. Jean first attended an English subject course where teachers worked in discussion groups, attended workshops and lectures and later was accepted onto a course devoted to assessment and classroom management. She considered these residential courses to be most beneficial because they facilitated the exchange of ideas between education officers and teachers, but also enabled teachers from different schools to get to know each other, mix, share ideas and good practice:

> But you see it was an opportunity to meet people from other schools and the education officers who really joined in with great gusto. It was quite a social occasion as well, so the breaking down of some of those barriers and for them to find out what teachers on the ground floor were actually thinking... There were, yes, and we all ate together and, yes I remember them being very, very worthwhile.[11]

David Howe, after sixteen years teaching English and being a head of department in various secondary schools, became an English Inspector for Warwickshire Local Authority in 1979 and went on to become Chief Inspector. Whilst working for Warwickshire Local Authority, David was responsible for organising courses for teachers and he too favoured the weekend residential model, drawing in HMI and other advisers where possible. His courses were popular with teachers and generally oversubscribed. He described a typical weekend course:

> A typical one would be a Friday evening, welcome, hello, introductory remarks and then dinner and then a speaker. Often an HMI – we used HMI's a lot. The weekend would be an interspersal of further talks, you know, speakers coming in and groups with group work. On the whole we weren't doing much in the way of practical activities. Some were. We would sometimes have weekends which were wholly practical.[12]

David recalled that arrangements for these courses were pretty *ad hoc* with a lack of clarity over budgets and quota. Normally courses were limited to 40 teachers, but David was not averse to finding ways to bring more teachers in, even if it meant that they were put down as speakers and not participants. For him, the social interaction, being away from the immediate home and school context, made a big difference to teachers who were able to learn from each other in a more relaxed setting than their schools. He also valued the time available over a weekend, when much discussion, argument and debate took place between teachers. He considered this to be more meaningful for those teachers who attended than trying to cram in time for discussion at the end of a school day in a twilight staff meeting. According to David, teachers liked the residential nature of the courses, even though there was an option to be non-residential, given that the location was still relatively local.

> Well, you could be non-residential but most preferred to stay because why would you want at 9 o'clock on a Friday night, when you could have been drinking wine, to be driving twenty miles home to the kids screaming and phone messages and so on? I think they quite liked a weekend where everything was done for them as far as eating.[13]

David did suggest, however, that there was a core group of Warwickshire teachers who were 'regular professional course goers' – who were regulars both at the weekend residentials and other courses on offer at the local teachers' centre. He had concerns that the model was not particularly effective in reaching the majority of teachers in the area, and these issues of impact, evaluation and reach will be considered further in Chapter Seven.

In addition to a focus on residential courses, a number of participants who had been secondary teachers found their individual subject associations to be a useful source of professional development. Jean Firth was a member of the National Association of English Teachers, and attended local meetings at the Coventry Teachers' Centre when visiting speakers were brought in. Jean found this association to be useful to her in developing new ideas for her teaching. Jean, as an English teacher, found that there were so many changes to the teaching of English during her career that she was in a constant state of '...*relearning, retraining, relooking at the way you taught and what you taught*'. Support from her national association was valuable – in particular meeting other English teachers and sharing good practice:

> And it was just sharing ideas from other people as well. What you were doing in your school and, "what do you do in your English lessons?"[14]

At a more local level, David Howe was a founder member of the Hull Association for the Teaching of English in the late 1960s. Teachers involved with this group produced a magazine for local schools on new approaches to English teaching. Later in his career when working in Gloucestershire, David became involved with the Bristol Association for the Teaching of English, which ran lectures and discussion groups at various teachers' centres on regular evening and Saturday morning sessions.

Jim Christophers regarded his engagement with the national Geographical Association - attending conferences, keeping up-to-date with the journal and attending local meetings - as an important form of professional development, though he only considered this to be the case in hindsight, because he had always thought of it as a routine part of the job of being a Geography teacher. A number of other participants were members of the national Geographical Association. Sue Roberts who started teaching in 1971 in a girls' Catholic secondary school in Norwich and who went on to teach in various schools in Plymouth before becoming a deputy head teacher in the early 1990s, was a keen reader of the Geographical Association's circulars and materials for teachers but did not go to any meetings or national conferences. Derek Cloke, a Devon secondary school teacher, headteacher and subsequently warden of a Devon teachers' centre, regularly attended Saturday morning lectures organised by the Geographical Association in the early days of his teaching career in the 1950s. Keith Martin, though not actively involved in the Geographical Association, did recall an exhibition of the Geographical Association in which he showcased some of the teaching materials he had been developing as a Geography teacher in Bolton secondary schools in the early 1960s.

During her time as Humanities Adviser in Enfield during the late 1980s and early 1990s, Kate Moorse actively encouraged and funded local teachers to attend the Historical Association's annual conference in Leeds, which she regarded as very strong in terms of subject knowledge and innovative pedagogy for the teaching of history, with excellent practitioners.

Recollections of decisions as to who should go on courses, how these should be paid for, when and on whose recommendation varied between participants who were mostly pretty vague, unless they had been forced to fight particularly hard to get access. For Joy Willoughby, memories of having to select her preferred courses from a local authority booklet each year and then having to apply to attend were strong. She suggested that as time went on it became more difficult to go on courses and she thought this was bound up with reduced funding in the local authority. She believed that striking up a good working relationship with the local authority advisers was key to getting access to the courses she wanted to attend. Peggy Jones recalled having had little choice over which courses she went on – these decisions being made by the head teacher. However, after a ten year period in one school she moved to a different school where she experienced a very different approach. Here the head teacher would ask teachers which courses they wished to attend and then did her best to ensure that this was possible. Sue Roberts considered that access to courses was largely opportunistic and *ad hoc* – '...*of things coming along at the right time...*' - when she happened to notice a flyer in a staff room or read a course brochure and show an interest.[15] Sue never had to pay for any courses she attended and would have regarded any requirement for teachers to pay for anything themselves as a serious disincentive. For Gill Brown, however, she recalled having to really fight her corner if she wanted to go on a course. In her experience it was difficult to secure permission to attend any courses during the school day because there was a great reluctance to find supply cover:

> If you wanted to go on a course in this school you had to grovel and beg. It was just not done because you were out of the classroom and it involved spending money and so trying to get on a course whenever you chose to was really difficult. You had to go through your head of department, there would be formal structures of how you went on a course and yes, I think, they didn't like it.[16]

Andrea Finch recalled a generous allocation of time for courses, whether at twilight sessions in the teachers' centres or at weekends during her early career as a Modern Foreign Languages (MFL) teacher in Warwickshire secondary schools:

> I don't remember paying anything and I don't remember having to fight a corner to go, I just, it happened through the ether, as far as I was concerned.[17]

RESOURCED PROFESSIONAL DEVELOPMENT THROUGH TEACHER SECONDMENT

One clear way in which local education authorities actively resourced teacher professional development was through paid or partially paid secondments of teachers for sustained periods of time of up to a year. The most common form of secondment was for teachers to undertake accredited learning programmes, at degree or advanced diploma level, usually in universities or colleges of education, similar to the early model described in Chapter Four. Secondment also took the form of international exchange programmes, as well as specific short-term acting roles in positions of leadership in different schools or within the advisory service.

Paid secondment of teachers to undertake a sustained period of academic study training at a university, either to diploma or degree level, was viewed by a number of the participants as having marked a particular turning point in their professional careers. Being taken out of the immediate and often enclosed world of their school and supported to take a broader view of schooling and education was seen as liberating. Competitive and restricted though, there is a clear sense that opportunities for secondment were confined to those teachers who were regarded either as potential school leaders or as teacher educators. Joy Kell's secondment on full pay, still as a relatively young teacher in 1967–68, marked a significant stage in her professional and career development. Joy had become interested in child 'maladjustment' – children in her class who had behavioural and learning difficulties. Cornwall Local Education Authority seconded her to the London Institute of Education to undertake a year-long Diploma in Child Development. This was a nationally recognised and highly prized programme which was concerned with the whole child and was of interest to social workers, therapists and welfare professionals. Upon successful completion of this course Joy returned to a headship in Cornwall. She recalled:

> I was just about the youngest, in fact I was the youngest on the course. There were headteachers, deputy heads, social workers, I remember, and people from the medical profession. They must have been nurses or health visitors... but it did cover all child development, not just child learning in school.... it was broad based, fascinating, I loved it...[18]

For Joy, this one-year secondment reinforced her commitment to teaching, having worked with children in a more therapeutic, medical environment. This experience meant that she regarded herself as being '...*more tuned to actually changing children's lives and making a difference through teaching.*' Joy described the informal expectations placed on her by the local authority that she would return to Cornwall to become a head teacher and this was something she was happy to do:

> ...the only proviso from the authority was that, yes fine, you've got our full support and you're not hidebound by this, but we would like a sort of gentleman's agreement and when you have qualified we would be grateful if you would come back so Cornwall would benefit, but you're not held to it.[19]

Graham Jones had a one year secondment to study full-time at the University of Birmingham for a Masters in Education (MEd) degree programme in 1983, with a particular focus on Educational Management and Educational Psychology. Prior to his secondment, Graham had been involved in developing and rolling out an experimental vocational and careers learning programme across Warwickshire schools which had been relatively short-lived. Involvement with this programme had taken him out of his existing position as head of a languages department in a secondary school in Rugby and when a decision was taken not to continue with the programme, Graham was offered this secondment, which he believed was positioned both as compensation for the programme not continuing and as a bridging opportunity to enable him to move to a headship or an advisory position within the authority. Graham recalled how strange it was to become a full-time student after having worked in schools for over fifteen years:

> I mean it was really weird in that everybody went back to school in September and the university term didn't start until halfway through October, so I had the whole of September with nothing to do. I mean I'd got, I think, a reading list from the university but, in effect, I had a massive long holiday…But it was odd at first to have all that time to myself and then to go and be a full-time student with frankly just a few hours of contact time per week and acres of time to do all the reading, which I used. … And it was interesting stuff. There's no doubt, it was eye opening stuff at the sort of strategic level of it. None of it was about how you survived in a classroom on Friday afternoon and perhaps it shouldn't have been either. All of it was about the theory and practice of educational administration and the purposes of education.[20]

Though he was convinced that he did not need the academic content of the programme to improve his own teaching and wider management skills, he did find the time and space afforded by this secondment invaluable:

> No. I could have lived without it, but as a development thing, as an eye opener, certainly being able to stop, because it was, the career I'd had, had been quite hectic and very full and suddenly being able to stop and start thinking again about the purposes of the whole thing, why we were doing this, why were there schools even in the first place and what were the alternatives to schools and how should schools be run…[21]

As part of his degree, Graham wrote a dissertation on the new Technical and Vocational Education Initiative (TVEI), a scheme introduced by the conservative government to incentivise learning for work for pupils aged 14–19 years. This very much chimed with Graham's growing interest in careers education and when his secondment was finished, Graham became one of the first TVEI Coordinators in Warwickshire and an expert practitioner in the expansion of TVEI nationally.

Jack Scott began his teaching career in the late 1950s where he was involved in the new comprehensive system in Harlow before moving to work as a language teacher in a further education college in Suffolk. His subsequent career in education was stimulated by a year's paid secondment to study for an MSc in Educational Research Methods at the University of Bradford. Jack applied to the Suffolk LEA for this secondment and though at first the authority were reluctant to support him, because the MSc was very new, the programme tutor '...*wrote a sharpish letter saying the local authority were behind the times and didn't know the course had been recognised and so I got onto it...*'[22]

Jack regarded this secondment as, '...*probably the best thing, the best thing to happen because I was actually quite bored with teaching in the system.*' Jack went on to become an educational researcher and academic at a university education department. In his academic role, Jack himself developed courses for serving primary school teachers who were seconded by their local authority. Unlike his own secondment in the late 1960s, Jack's course, which was developed in conjunction with the local authority, was non-accredited. The model was that the local authority identified leading edge teachers who were known to be ambitious and seeking promotion to senior leadership positions in schools. Jack recalled:

> ...there wasn't any doubt about the nature of that programme. It was to get the best teachers and make them even better and prepare them for headship and if you were, as some of the teachers were, quite nicely cynical, this was basically a headteacher training course, preparation for headship. And they knew that and it meant that they were a pretty motivated lot, it was a pretty positive experience for them because nearly every course created a kind of social life for themselves and also they maintained a lot of their contacts afterwards, so it was interesting.[23]

For Valerie Jenkins, secondment in 1981 from her post as head of education at a girl's residential school (formerly an approved school) in Leeds ran by Barnardos, to become a full-time student at Newcastle University on a Diploma of Education course focussed on the specific teaching and learning needs of children in community homes and school, was as important for her own self-esteem as it was for her professional development. Barnardos funded Valerie who temporarily located to Newcastle and devoted herself to her year of study which she viewed as a proper sabbatical. At the end of this year she had the option of staying on and completing a degree. Valerie subsequently completed her BPhil in Education and went on to complete a Masters of Education degree in her own time, but still funded by Barnardos. Valerie had initially trained to teach in the late 1950s on a two-year certificate programme. She always felt that not having a degree meant that she was perceived by others a '...*second class citizen*'.[24] The valuing of accredited higher degree programmes as an important part of professional development, whether this was externally or self-funded was recurrent theme in participants stories – and is something which will be examined in greater detail as part of a wider discussion on professional identity in Chapter Eight.

Bill Parkinson enjoyed a different type of paid secondment in the late 1970s when Coventry LEA sent him to the National Agricultural College to further develop his Science curriculum resources. Bill was able to develop this opportunity in his own way and it did not lead to any formal accreditation. However, from a personal perspective he very much valued the opportunity to work in a different environment and believed that he went back to the classroom with fresh perspectives:

...it was the experience of working in an environment outside of education, because I'd been in school what for six, seven years by that point, possibly a bit longer...so it was really interesting for me personally working in an organisation like that and seeing the way that it's run in terms of a totally different to the way school is organised.[25]

In 1988, just as the new National Curriculum was being introduced, Joy Willoughby was invited to take a term's secondment from her position as a headteacher of a first school in Warwickshire to the local authority advisory service. She was given responsibility, along with six other colleagues, four of whom were also seconded from schools, to help develop and deliver a programme of training on the new National Curriculum for teachers in Warwickshire. For Joy, this was a challenging but rewarding brief as her main task was one of persuading teachers and headteachers who were anxious about such radical and fast-paced curriculum reforms. She was at the forefront of a group of teachers trying to make sense of the new curriculum and developing a '...*rolling programme of going around the county and introducing and making headteachers familiar with what the changes were going to mean*'.[26] She became involved in research on early years and National Curriculum attainment targets and also made instructional videos of teachers delivering the National Curriculum, to be used as training materials. This experience marked a turning point in Joy's own career as she then moved permanently into advisory work for a different local authority.

It was amazing for me. That's why I wanted then to become an advisor myself. Because I'd had that experience and really really enjoyed it. I really enjoyed working at my own level, away from children. It was about working with adults for a whole term.[27]

Alan Forster had a different type of secondment experience when he took part in a year-long teacher exchange programme in 1964 with an American school in Chicago. Alan started his teaching career in 1956 and worked as an English teacher in a North Oxfordshire boys' grammar school. After eight years of teaching in the same school, Alan was ready for a new challenge and applied to take part in an exchange organised by the British Council.

I had no choice about where I had to go. I was merely told and merely told whom my co-exchangee was. I met him very briefly and then landed in this large school...I mean, I went from teaching scholarship level in a small British grammar school to teaching the drop-outs, seventeen, eighteen year old drop-outs in Chicago. I was landed the worst classes, what we euphemistically called 'the basics' and the 'extra basics' and there I had to excite the kids, I had to get them on my side and that was absolutely fantastic in-service.[28]

Though Alan returned to his grammar school at the end of this year in America, the experience of the exchange and the opportunity it had generated for him to expand his professional experience as a teacher, prompted him to apply for a new post as a curriculum development officer in Oxfordshire working on preparing schools and teachers for the forthcoming raising of the school leaving age. Alan went on to become warden of a teachers' centre in Devon. Alan never forgot the value of his exchange experience and much later in his career, in 1988, set up a link with an American university in New England to facilitate teacher exchanges through a network of teachers' centres. Alan still retains personal copies of thank you letters from teachers who benefited from such teacher exchanges in the late 1980s. For him, the value was in the sharing of ideas and practice and in having a broadened professional experience.

NATIONAL INITIATIVES AND TEACHER PROFESSIONAL DEVELOPMENT

Whilst local authorities appeared dominant in the brokering and resourcing of professional development for teachers, participants also referred to a number of national-level initiatives which also stimulated different opportunities for professional development. These included various national meetings and discussions associated with examination boards; the introduction of the TVEI scheme in the early 1980s; and the large scale curriculum and assessment reforms of the late 1980s. These three key areas reflect the age profile and demographic of the participants, for whom the impact of new policies and practice associated with the education reform movement of the late 1980s marked a significant watershed in their professional careers, and possibly also in the strength of their memories about this period of education.

Involvement in examination boards was regarded by some participants as a very useful source of professional development, particularly around the strengthening of subject expertise and pedagogy. Jean Firth, a secondary English teacher in Coventry, was an assessor and marker for the West Midland Exam Board. In this capacity she enjoyed the opportunity to meet with teachers from different schools and to share ideas. When General Certificate of Secondary Education (GCSE) coursework was introduced, Jean was closely involved with detailed moderation meetings which would either take place in different schools in the region or in a teachers' centre. For Jean, this examination board work enabled her to keep up-to-date with all of the curriculum and subject changes and she definitely viewed it as a form of professional training:

> You just seemed to get used to one new thing, one new exam system and another new exam system would come in. So we've gone from CSEs (Certificate of Secondary Education) and GCEs (General Certificate of Education) completely separate teaching of that in schools, to combining the two exams for GCSES.... So there was training there, and meeting people from elsewhere and so on. So thinking back there was a lot of change and there were lots of new things to get used to and to put in place...[29]

Early in his career, Jim Christophers became involved in a local curriculum development project organised by Bristol University which was experimenting with new approaches to the examination of Geography, both at GCE and later at CSE level.

Working with colleagues on the project, Jim gained the support of the South West Examination Board and went on to work with it in the development of examination materials. Sue Roberts had fond memories of '*exciting times*' in Geography teaching, particularly when she attended regional and national coursework assessment meetings for GCSE Geography. For Gill Brown, CSE moderation was one of her most memorable and best experience of professional development. It not only got her out of the classroom, but enabled her to mix with a range of other teachers and to share and discuss ideas:

> So once a year usually in October, November everybody in the whole area would get together to standardise, because CSE was teacher moderated so that everybody who taught history would go to somebody's school and sit in the library usually and mark papers and come up with the standardised mark scheme for the work and you would meet other history teachers and that was the best, it wasn't meant to be formal training. You made contact, you met other people...It was the day you looked forward to in the year because you weren't teaching and you were off. It was hard work sitting marking twenty papers all together in a room and then justifying the marks and discussing them.[30]

The introduction of the TVEI programme, which was piloted in 1983, extended nationally in 1987 and continued in various formats until 1997, though primarily focussed on addressing a perceived lack of vocational input into the education of young people, had an indirect impact on the development of professional development opportunities for teachers because of the high levels of funding associated with the scheme.[31] Anecdotally, participants recalled how the introduction of TVEI brought with it a higher class of course experience in terms of the essential domestics, with the shabby rooms in teachers' centres or school staff rooms with tea and biscuits if you were lucky, discarded in favour of plush hotel venues and sit-down three-course meals. Graham Jones, a TVEI coordinator in Warwickshire recalled how the distribution of funding for TVEI was a matter of contention between local headteachers. Graham, however, eventually secured agreement to allocate some of the funding for the development of proper in-service training for any teachers associated with TVEI work. The focus of this training was on how to best engage children with their learning. For Graham, in spite of its political difficulties at local level and the way in which some teachers believed it to be elitist, TVEI did extend the reach of teacher professional development to a far larger group of teachers, which he thought had been previously far too dependent on the whim of advisors.

Cliff Harris, a local authority adviser at the time of the TVEI initiative, also recalls the generous funding associated with TVEI and the impact this had on teacher development. For him, TVEI was about trying to get teachers to understand more of the real world of work into which the majority of their pupils were heading:

> ...there was a lot of money poured into training teachers around that period...it was all about showing teachers that they were worth spending all the money on.[32]

Jim Christophers remembered the generous funding arrangements associated with TVEI as well as raised expectations and standards in terms of the delivery of training programmes for teachers, which were intended to model good practice and cutting-edge pedagogy. For Gill Brown, her involvement in leading TVEI projects in her school in Rotherham supported a very different way of working in more innovative ways with children in collaboration with colleagues. She recalled that TVEI brought with it accountability for funding, with more focussed evaluations of the quality of any courses. David Howe was initially sceptical of the TVEI initiative but then warmed to it as he observed more creative headteachers finding ways of interpreting its technical and vocational focus in a broader fashion and take some ownership of what was at first a fairly prescribed national programme.

> I started off being sceptical of a government driven initiative with a narrow agenda until I realised that maybe it influenced a lot of pedagogy for the better. I am sure of that, teachers became much more ready to develop a repertoire of skills rather than the kind of stand and deliver and then write a bit …it gave them pedagogy.[33]

A number of participants were involved in the national training programmes for teachers introduced by the government and delivered by the local education authorities in the late 1980s and early 1990s on the delivery of the new National Curriculum and national assessment programmes. Heavily content based and highly prescribed, these courses, rolled out across schools, were not popular with teachers. Participants deemed this training as 'top-down' with little scope for discussion or challenge of the ideas. There was also a real sense of urgency involved in transmitting the new professional knowledge so that it could be incorporated into the system. Ann Dodd, recently returned to teaching after a career break to raise her family, recalled being trained in the new national requirements. She described a week long training course organised by the LEA during term time:

> Because this National Curriculum was starting to loom I went on a primary language co-ordinators course for the National Curriculum because every week at this school we'd have our normal staff meeting once a week but then once a week after school we were trying to get our heads round these massive ring binders which were the National Curriculum and there were different people on the staff had a role for different important areas of the National Curriculum and we were trying to educate each other on what we'd got to do because you had a deadline and then you had to implement it…[34]

By this time, Joy Kell was a local authority adviser and was required to deliver this training to Cornish teachers. She recalled:

> It was awful for us to do…We had not been given the information in time to prepare it properly, we had two days and then looked at it over and over again at the weekend to try and get, preparation for it. I said, "it's a case of the partially sighted leading the blind but we've got to do it. It's no use spending

the day moaning about it because at the end of the day those children are going to sit those tests and we've got to know what we're doing." Terribly undermining we're talking. But we got through it - but it was demoralising for teachers, it wasn't too good for us either. People who were providing were finding it very difficult at that time…[35]

Andrea Finch recalled the training associated with the National Curriculum as being '…*quite dispiriting for teachers*' with '…*shedloads of folders and everything. It was ploughing through what all of that meant and that was very daunting for people, I think - quite dispiriting actually.*'[36]

With the introduction of the National Curriculum in 1988 also came, for the first time, five annual mandatory training days for all serving teachers in state schools, in addition to their normal teaching workload of 190 days per annum. Known as 'Baker Days' after their namesake Kenneth Baker, then the conservative government's Secretary of State for Education and Science, they were often associated by participants involved in their organisation and delivery with resistance and hostility.[37] Tales of recalcitrant audiences of teachers, resentful of having professional development foisted upon them, emerged from some of the participants' testimony. Cliff Harris, for example, recounted one particular experience of being invited to deliver some training on curriculum development to a primary school in rural Devon:

So I arrive, it was in the days of overhead projectors, and I can see there's a woman knitting, loads of them are marking books, there's loads of them like this, and I'm thinking, this is like stirring cold porridge. And so I started off and I looked and I thought, I'm not going anywhere with this, and my instinct was to just walk out. So I thought, either they're going to walk out or I've got to walk out. So I switched the projector off and I said, "I've seen some cynics in my time, it's the first time I've ever been to (name of place and school)." and they laughed. They started laughing then and I thought, okay, fair do's, you're a victim of this, it's nothing to do with you. And then they were alright.[38]

Jim Christophers had similar experiences and described sessions in which some teachers, present under protest, would sit and mark books or even read newspapers rather than engage with any of the training being delivered. Keith Martin also suggested that, in his experience, for some teachers:

Well you could tell they were there on sufferance. They wanted to go their classrooms and tidy them up. And let you know in no uncertain terms. Yes.[39]

For Jean Firth, as a headteacher, Baker Days could be problematic:

My experience, well I should say that I think a lot of the INSET days that were prescribed either by the authority or by the schools, people did feel were a waste of time. You'd have been better off in your own classroom getting ready for term beginning. They were generally two days at the beginning of term.[40]

For June Rowe, running Baker Days as a headteacher worked better if she ensured that her staff had some dedicated time to prepare their classrooms:

> Baker Days were mostly fine. I mean I used to give them an agenda of what we were going to do for the day but I always made time for them to have preparation time in their classroom. This is before PPA time (Planning, Preparation and Assessment) was brought in so sometimes it was an LEA speaker or a trainer for a couple of hours and then we'd do school stuff for a couple of hours and then they'd have the rest of the day free to get their rooms ready and, for the children because this tended to be the first day of the holidays, term-time or something like that...[41]

For Andrea Finch, Baker Days became more accepted with the passing of time as new generations of teachers came into teaching not having known anything different in terms of expectations around professional development.

> It took a little while. You always have your, what they call the cultural architects that are up for anything don't you, and the ones who moan at the back, but I think my impression was that certainly in the last few years when we were doing it there was an expectation that a day like that would be really worthwhile and if they missed out on it they would be really quite disappointed about that...[42]

INFORMAL/ORGANIC TEACHER DEVELOPMENT

Conversations with participants about their experiences of professional development provoked many memories of 'going on courses' – those many formal opportunities that have been discussed so far in this chapter, which were organised and resourced externally, through various agencies. However, participants also described experiences of professional learning that were informal and often less tangible – influential colleagues who acted as mentors; staffroom discussions and banter, which was nevertheless focussed on immediate problems of teaching and learning or curriculum; the organic formation of groups of teachers seeking to understand better the educational world in which they found themselves.

Cliff Harris, for example, recalled of his early years as a teacher in a secondary boy's school in Brixton in the early 1970s, a real buzz of excitement amongst the young staff in the school who regularly spent time after school discussing educational issues and trying to find ways of addressing the particular needs of the children they taught, who were mainly first generation immigrants from the Caribbean. Though he did not experience any formal professional development opportunities at that time, he regarded the professional engagement with his colleagues as critical for his own development as an educator:

> But we ate education and we'd finish work and we'd go straight to the staff room, all the young teachers, and we'd talk about education philosophy. We'd

then go to the pub and we'd carry on talking about education philosophy. We were concerned about selection. We were concerned about the lack of inclusion of immigrant kids and we managed to establish a thing called The Caribbean Curriculum and it was in all the papers, the red tops took us to town, kind of like all this public money being spent on teachers because we went away to Brighton, I think, to a hotel to construct this.[43]

David Howe described an experience relatively early in his teaching career when he was at his second teaching post at a school in Hull, where he regarded the particular culture of the school as one which actively promoted professional discussion and debate between teachers. The school was, according to David, '...*a spanking new comprehensive school*', and he was invited to join various working parties and development groups where new teaching materials, usually worksheets, were being produced. A rather spontaneous and very organic professional development opportunity arose when the National Union of Teachers (NUT) took strike action. This meant that all teachers not in this union were still required to turn up for work, even though the school had effectively been closed to pupils.

The NUT struck for a fortnight and I wasn't an NUT member and the head said he was going to close the school because half the staff were in the NUT but non-NUT members should work normally. And we came in but we thought was hilarious at first ... to begin with we all came in just before 9.00 and we stayed literally until the bell went. By the second week we'd found masses to do, we thought this is wonderful, and there were meetings going on, discussions taking place and teaching materials being produced for years ahead.[44]

This experience was more than just the practical, operational sorting out of materials for immediate use. For David the experience provided a rare gift of time when teachers could get together and talk about their work.

No it just dawned on us. Isn't this wonderful? Time for each other, with each other which you're not trying to fit in with everything else. So whereas we thought it was a bit of a joke for the first week, we were slow off the mark to realise, think of all the times you've said, "if only we had a bit more time", and you've got it. So, even that was in a school where there was a culture anyway of groups meeting regularly...[45]

Through contacts with other teachers at the Coventry Teachers' Centre, Bill Parkinson was a founder member of an organic teacher-led group known as the 'Primary Natural Science Group'. This is an interesting example of professional development generated by and for local teachers and not part of a more formal, accredited local or national 'top-down' programme:

...we just did it because it was what we needed at that time and we wanted it and I suppose it wasn't anywhere else, it wasn't out there and so we provided it ourselves. I'm making it sound perhaps a bit grander than it was, it was fairly belt and braces but people enjoyed it, it got people involved, it got people from different schools talking and working together, and it wasn't anything hugely innovative - it was just that we were helping each other and learning together.[46]

Through this work, Bill became involved in disseminating some of his ideas, resources and methods in primary Natural Science across Coventry, through the various centres – and most importantly the teachers' centre. He was particularly committed to developing training sessions for teachers which were practical, 'hands-on' and could then be taken by the teachers back to their own classrooms:

You would invite somebody who, sometimes it would be teachers who'd trialled some work and found a good way of doing things and we'd invite them to come and talk to colleagues... I think that was the key to a lot of the things we did. We wanted things that would just make things easier for teachers in that if they wanted to study a piece of land or study a bit of the history of a particular period in Coventry we could guide them to various resources and suggest how they might use that in a way which would involve the children.[47]

Sue Swanson described the value of informal staff meetings during the time in her career when she was an acting deputy head of a primary school in Telford in the early to mid-1980s. She noted the difference between the current formality of staff meetings which are always minuted, to the more informal, *ad-hoc* gatherings of teachers earlier in her teaching career. She recalled a whole staff discussion on how to develop Mathematics in the school and how staff worked together to develop a scheme of work and teaching materials.

In those days it wasn't like that. We didn't have a set staff meeting every week. It was just basically as and when we needed it, when I think about it. We did, yes, we did do things and people had different responsibilities....would lead a staff meeting like there was a girl who did art and craft and she would lead a session on that, but it was very....it was much more informal than it is today.[48]

Gill Brown recalled an experience which began with a group of teachers getting together to try to make sense of new curriculum requirements and to find ways of sharing their practice. This was then taken up by a local authority adviser who then facilitated a more formal working group:

Later on, what happened with this group of heads of departments, there were a few of us who were quite friendly, and when the National Curriculum came in we looked at it and thought, "oh my God how do we do this? We've got to deliver all these new topics, we've got to invent all these resources, it's all stuff we've never done before...What shall we do?" So we got together as a group, I think there six of us to start with. And after we'd had a meeting with the advisor we suggested that we meet more regularly and just share resources because we were all struggling with this whole new thing. And we took the resources and what was good about it is the first person who started off said, "well, I tried this, and here's the resources I produced but it didn't work". Now what was good about it was he said it didn't work because too often you go to these places and people say, "well this is brilliant". But he said it didn't work and started actually talking, really quite consulted about how to make this work. So we moved very much from content to pedagogy and then we went back and we took it back to our departments and said, "try this".[49]

CHAPTER SUMMARY

Throughout this chapter various memories of teacher professional development as experienced by the research participants have been presented. A range of different models have been discussed, including those planned and initiated formally by government, local authorities and schools and those which emerged through more informal, teacher-directed ways. Across this wide and eclectic range of experience are two common characteristics: the *ad hoc* nature of the whole business of teacher professional development; and the way in which it seemed to focus on those teachers who were already committed to a wider professional development agenda. These characteristics will be examined further in the following two chapters which are concerned with questions of quality and impact as well as the wider relationship of professional development to the formation of professional identity.

NOTES

[1] BARDA Project 53026, oral history interview with Ann Dodd, June 2011.
[2] BARDA Project 53026, oral history interview with Gill Brown (p), July 2011.
[3] BARDA Project 53026, oral history interview with Bill Parkinson, May 2011.
[4] BARDA Project 53026, oral history interview with David Howe (1st interview), November 2010.
[5] BARDA Project 53026, oral history interview with Diana Lucas, May 2011.
[6] BARDA Project 53026, oral history interview with Hilary Cox, May 2011.
[7] BARDA Project 53026, oral history interview with Peggy Jones (p), August 2011.
[8] BARDA Project 53026, oral history interview with Joy Kell, May 2011.
[9] Ibid.
[10] BARDA Project 53026, oral history interview with Joy Williams, September 2011.
[11] BARDA Project 53026, oral history interview with Jean Firth, May 2011.
[12] BARDA Project 53026, oral history interview with David Howe.
[13] Ibid.
[14] BARDA Project 53026, oral history interview with Jean Firth.
[15] BARDA Project 53026, oral history interview with Sue Roberts, March 2011.
[16] BARDA Project 53026, oral history interview with Gill Brown.
[17] BARDA Project 53026, oral history interview with Andrea Finch (p), May 2011.
[18] BARDA Project 53026, oral history interview with Joy Kell.
[19] Ibid.
[20] BARDA Project 53026, oral history interview with Graham Jones, May 2011.
[21] Ibid.
[22] BARDA Project 53026, oral history interview with Jack Scott (p), April 2011.
[23] Ibid.
[24] BARDA Project 53026, oral history interview with Valerie Jenkins, September 2011.
[25] BARDA Project 53026, oral history interview with Bill Parkinson.

[26] BARDA Project 53026, oral history interview with Joy Willoughby, May 2011.
[27] Ibid.
[28] BARDA Project 53026, oral history interview with Alan Forster, August 2011.
[29] BARDA Project 53026, oral history interview with Jean Firth.
[30] BARDA Project 53026, oral history interview with Gill Brown.
[31] For further information on the TVEI scheme see Gleeson, D. (1987). *TVEI and secondary education.* Maidenhead: Open University Press; and Dale, R. (1990). *The TVEI Story: Policy, practice and preparation for the workforce.* Maidenhead: Open University Press.
[32] BARDA Project 53026, oral history interview with Cliff Harris (1st interview), April 2011.
[33] BARDA Project 53026, oral history interview with David Howe (2nd interview), February 2011.
[34] BARDA Project 53026, oral history interview with Ann Dodd.
[35] BARDA Project 53026, oral history interview with Joy Kell.
[36] BARDA Project 53026, oral history interview with Andrea Finch.
[37] For further information on Baker days see Cowan, B. and Wright, W., 'Baker Days revisited: An opportunity lost or found? *Education Today*; Chitty, C. (2002). Understanding Schools and Schooling. London: RoutledgeFalmer. Burgess, R. (1993). Implementing In-service Education and Training. London: RoutledgeFalmer. p.108.
[38] BARDA Project 53026, oral history interview with Cliff Harris.
[39] BARDA Project 53026, oral history interview with Keith Martin, May 2011.
[40] BARDA Project 53026, oral history interview with Jean Firth.
[41] BARDA Project 53026, oral history interview with June Rowe, May 2011.
[42] BARDA Project 53026, oral history interview with Andrea Finch.
[43] BARDA Project 53026, oral history interview with Cliff Harris.
[44] BARDA Project 53026, oral history interview with David Howe (1st interview).
[45] Ibid.
[46] BARDA Project 53026, oral history interview with Bill Parkinson.
[47] Ibid.
[48] BARDA Project 53026, oral history interview with Sue Swanson, May 2011.
[49] BARDA Project 53026, oral history interview with Gill Brown.

PART 3

TEACHERS' REFLECTIONS ON PROFESSIONAL DEVELOPMENT

EVALUATING IMPACT: PERSONAL AND PROFESSIONAL PERSPECTIVES

Currently, impact measures on pupil learning are seen as critical to successful teacher professional development, however difficult these are to evaluate and whether or not they are about enhanced teacher professional identity, capacity and expertise. This chapter seeks to evaluate the wider impact of professional development on individuals, in terms of how they believed their professional behaviours and practices were changed as a result of their professional development experience and what purpose they thought it served. The chapter is in three main parts. First, what the idea of impact meant for participants will be examined, with a focus on how participants valued opportunities for putting into practice new ideas from courses; the importance of sharing and disseminating what they had learned with colleagues; and the notion of personal impact. Secondly, how participants conceived of the quality of their professional development will be examined. As might be expected, some experiences were evaluated more positively than others. A number of factors appeared to differentiate the quality of courses, including who delivered them, their professional credibility, the nature and mode of delivery, whether a course was voluntary or mandatory and whether it was accredited or non-accredited. Banal though this might seem on the surface, domestic arrangements were also deemed important in determining the overall quality of experience. Thirdly, the question of who was impacted by professional development is considered. Here, the perennial question of reach, discussed throughout the book, will be explored along a continuum at one end of which was positioned the ever-keen 'professional course-goers' and at the other, the reluctant disengaged teachers who resisted any engagement with professional development opportunities.

MEANINGS OF IMPACT

The question of the wider impact of professional development on individuals was discussed in the interviews, with varying responses. Impact for these participants meant something very different than the way impact is both perceived and measured today – as something with a specific relationship not just with generic school improvement but with pupil learning.[1] The systematic and critical evaluation of professional development courses, in whatever format, appeared to be rather casual in the period before the TVEI initiatives, when there were clear requirements to demonstrate some accountability for the resource expended. Cliff Harris recalled that:

> ...in the early days there was no evaluation of anything, you know you just kind of went along and had a jolly time and then people started thinking well maybe they ought to have these, what do they call them at the end of the course where you...? Evaluations, yes? And most people just said "very good lunch, nice people", that kind of stuff and I think impact has been a big issue in teacher training altogether...[2]

Andrea Finch, on the other hand, did experience a requirement to engage in a much more systematic evaluation of the TVEI training she developed. Investment in good quality resources for teaching and showing teachers how these could be used was, for Andrea, a clear and positive outcome of the TVEI work.

> We had, we had, yes, well we had to evaluate any conference and twilights and things like that and we would look at them and we would change things as a result of that but that was, that was impacting on teacher, on practitioners, on teacher practice and the sort of the art and craft of teaching. It wasn't telling us what GCSE results were happening but we were getting information, well I was getting information about gender. TVEI was very much about opening things up and encouraging girls to look at the whole range of technological careers that they wouldn't have done previously... At least for the first time we knew that the children, the students were actually having high quality resources that were designed to challenge the stereotypes of race and gender whereas before I think it would have been pretty much hit and miss, but I mean I can remember buying, I can't remember again what they were called... an agenda for equality. Anyway some really good spiral bound packs that we brought in and that were being used in schools as well.[3]

Andrea suggested that measures of impact were subtle and that changing teachers' practice was part of a lengthy and complex process.

> But I think, I think we were conscious of the different levels at which change can take place and again I don't think we were beguiled into thinking we've spent two thousand pounds this year putting on conferences and buying resources, therefore it must have worked. We were, well certainly I was conscious of there being the, you have got the input and you've got the process of people going through the training, talking to each other, maybe sharing resources as well and then you've got the outcomes, so for me it taught me that you've got to stand back and look at all of those and not just say, not just deduce that it's been successful because you've successfully spent two thousand pounds, or all of the evaluations have been glowing from every conference that you did, it's much more subtle.[4]

For a number of participants, their idea of impact was associated with an ideal of wanting to be able to put into practice any new ideas they had learned or seen on any courses they had attended. Best intentions were, however, often thwarted by the sheer pressures of time and the day-to-day business of being back in the usual school routine, once their initial enthusiasm had waned. Joy Willoughby considered that courses with a strong practical element as well as some theoretical context were 'easy to absorb' and that she actively tried to use any models of teaching, particularly in specific primary subjects, such as Art, Dance and Drama in her teaching. Gill Brown recalled a local authority RE course that had a profound impact on her teaching because it had built into it the opportunity for teachers to try out new ideas and then go back and discuss these further in follow-up sessions.

> It was really radical… you got taught various ideas to try, you had a go at them and then you went and did the second day three months later and shared what you'd done.

> It was a very good model. I think more of it should be done. I think a lot of people do that in school, as such. I remember we were taught, I was taught about group work, a way of developing group work, about, I remember learning about how group dynamics work whereby you give them a task and they all fall apart and they argue and you have to allow them to work through that.[5]

It was not always straightforward for teachers to put into practice new ideas learned on courses. For example, Cliff Harris, who delivered workshops at teachers' centres throughout the 1970s and early 1980s considered there to have been a real tension between teachers' engaging with new practice and ideas on courses and their ability to apply these properly in the school context.

> I think in the early days of when I was engaged in working on, you know going to the teachers' centres and delivering a programme, workshops, that kind of stuff, I think that people went away completely energised and feeling great about things and then went back to the classroom and I mean, Grantly (Cliff was referring here to a stereotypical cynical teacher characterised in a popular UK TV drama/soap programme on the life of a secondary school) would say, "been on a course then", you know, and I think that there was that phenomenon that people went back, probably enthused and full of good ideas but not able to continue it in the context in which they found themselves.[6]

Sarah Matthews, a primary school teacher who went on to specialise in special educational needs and became a local authority adviser in Somerset, described the importance of courses for teachers having a strong practical element including the provision of good ideas to take forward into practice. She recalled those courses '… *where you just sit down and you listen and there's no practical aspect and you think, oh dear, this is such a waste of time'*. Sarah suggested that a balance of practical and theoretical input on course was the best model and recalled a course she had attended on neuro-linguistic programming that she had found particularly good.

It's got to be practical so that you can use it in school. If it's too, I mean I don't mind theoretical stuff, because I quite thrive on that, but it's no good if you just go there and you've heard a whole load of theory and so on and you can't actually apply it. So to me a good course is one that is practical and will relate itself to your job, yes, and that one was perfect. That was really good. But I have sat through hours of other things and I've thought, why did I go?[7]

As a deputy head teacher of a Devon comprehensive school in the early 1990s, Sue Roberts was a keen advocate of professional development – or 'INSET', as she called it - being school-based and delivered by school staff. She found this model to be far preferable to the earlier 'going out on a course' model because it was properly embedded in the immediate needs of her school and her teachers with much greater potential for effecting real change. She recalled consciously trying to model the best practice that she wanted to bring about in the school through school-based INSET. Responsible for staff development, Sue suggested that this, together with the fact that she herself delivered a lot of school sessions for teachers, had forced her to clarify her own thoughts and to modify her own practice and ideas about teaching as well as those of the staff that the training was actually aimed at.

One obvious extension to this idea that teachers should be able to implement practical changes in school as a result of any professional development opportunities was the cascade model of disseminating new knowledge and understanding to colleagues. This model was based on the principle that one or two teachers from an individual school were invested with the responsibility of attending a course and then bringing back any new ideas or practices and sharing them with other teachers. This was normally done through the formal mechanism of a weekly staff meeting or planned as part of scheduled in-school training days. Ann Dodd noted a change in expectations for staff to disseminate new ideas over the course of her career. In the early days of her career in the 1960s and 1970s she recalled limited opportunity to disseminate or share experiences from courses. However, by the 1980s and 1990s she said it was a common practice for teachers to give brief reports of any courses they had attended to the rest of their colleagues. David Howe observed a similar pattern. In his early years of teaching in the 1960s he suggested that there was not a culture of sharing ideas from courses or workshops in teachers' centres with colleagues. Staff meetings were occasional, short and purely operational. Later on when he became a head of department and responsible for a small group of teachers he found that his colleagues were proactive themselves and would naturally wish to talk about their experiences on courses and whether ideas were possible to implement – though this was done very much on an informal and *ad hoc* basis. David, though responsible overall for his department, had no dedicated budget for staff development, which meant that supply cover was not an option if one member of staff was out on a course. Cover was provided from within the team and shared across the team on an entirely informal basis.

The question of impact was problematic for Joy Kell, especially as she was so committed to ensuring that her staff had generous opportunities to attend courses to avoid becoming 'stale'. As a head teacher responsible for the professional development of her staff, she developed a clear approach which was that two teachers at a time would be sent on the same course to enable them to support each other and monitor each other in implementing new ideas back at school. Joy also believed that twilight or one-off courses were difficult and that focussed residential courses with follow-up sessions had the greatest potential for changing practice in schools.

> ...but courses have lamentably little impact in the classroom and this bothered me because as a provider I wanted to share what I was doing and I suspected it wasn't getting into classrooms and my teachers went on courses, some residential, some twilight and there wasn't a lot of impact. I became very concerned that if a teacher was interested in a course she'd find a colleague in the school who was also interested and they'd both go because if you have been inspired or enthused and you come back the next day or after a week on a course and you do it, tell us, the staff about it at the next staff meeting unless you've got someone who had a slightly different view to you, we all have different opinions don't we? Unless you have someone with you who could share that enthusiasm and say, "no, I don't think that was ... this was meant" there would then be impact which became permanent, if everyone agreed on it...Because I was giving courses and thinking this is so superficial. They'll go away after an hour and a half, they're tired anyway, this was the twilight courses, residential courses had tremendous impact, and I suspected very little went on with it because other teachers were saying, "well, yes very interesting but I'm going down this way and I haven't time to think", but if two of you in the staff are saying, "oh, can we take it over, is anyone else interested in trying it?" It worked. But the impact of two people plus was, and also I encouraged them to go on everything they wanted to go on because in that way you move forward and remember I had a stable staff so I wanted them to have constant outside input because otherwise they would have become stale.[8]

Joy Willoughby regarded it as her professional responsibility to share what she had picked up on any courses she attended both with her teachers, her governing body and also a wider network of nursery headteachers that she belonged to. She described a strong culture of sharing new knowledge and good practice as part of the cascade model. Diana Lucas, as a primary headteacher in Devon in the 1980s expected her teachers to come back from courses and share what they had learned – though she favoured an informal approach to the cascade model in which teachers would disseminate in regular staff meetings.

> Not in a big heavy way, no power points or anything, but yes a little bit about what they'd done, what they'd learnt and what they thought we could do because obviously they went on the course, they knew our situation so how could we actually use what they've learned? Yes, otherwise the value is very limited if it can't be shared.[9]

For June Rowe, in her time as a head teacher of a Coventry primary school, though she valued the cascade model, she recalled certain challenges to managing this properly within staff meetings that were already busy because there were so many of her staff going out on courses and wanting to feedback to colleagues.

> Staff who went on the courses on the whole came back quite inspired, quite enthused and then you've got the opposite problem. You've got the problem that perhaps they had been on a course in a week and they all wanted to focus on their particular thing at the next staff meeting so if you had a weekly staff meeting you've got to divide it into three slots for them to feedback.[10]

As well as thinking about impact in terms of opportunities either to put into practice new understandings or to share this with colleagues, participants also described impact in terms of its personal effect, either because the experience was interesting and enjoyable in its own right or, more particularly, was related in some way to career development and progression.

Valerie Jenkins found the various courses and programmes of study she took part in throughout her career to be fundamental to securing and bolstering her own professional knowledge and understanding. Her description suggests that the courses enabled her to make explicit that which had formerly been tacit in her teaching with an opportunity to see much closer links between theory and practice. This was a source of much personal satisfaction.

> It was like having a firmer foundation that what you were doing you knew more why you were doing it, if you see what I mean. The theory behind what you had possibly done instinctively before.[11]

Diana Lucas also expressed a strong personal commitment and desire to keep learning as a teacher and to help her to improve her own teaching in relation to pupil learning. For her there were clear combined benefits for her personally as well as for the school and the pupils.

> I'd go on anything and everything. I don't mean if it was irrelevant, but you know if it looked good and I thought it would help, I would go on it.[12]

Diana found residential courses to be most beneficial and enjoyable as they offered a real opportunity for teachers to get away from the immediate concerns of the school environment and to take time to think about and engage with new ideas.

> You'd come out and forget you were the Year 2 teacher or whatever, you'd just be yourself and you'd be, you know dying to learn and you'd put your five penneth in. I think that's quite important.[13]

Joy Willoughby claimed to have retained the same basic personal philosophy of teaching from the moment that she left her initial teacher training to her retirement. However, she strongly believed that the professional development she experienced throughout her long career enabled her to firm up and develop her core teaching values.

Yes, I think I had a basic philosophy based on the same ideas really from when I left college, but it enabled me to expand that and to develop it because I'd been on the course that I'd done really.[14]

Residential courses were perceived as popular and by some, such as Joy Kell discussed above, as more effective for teachers. Jack Scott recalled his experience in the early 1980s of auditing a residential course organised by a local authority at Woolley Hall in Yorkshire – an impressive and very pleasant spacious residential venue devoted entirely to a range of courses for teachers. Jack was hard pressed to judge the impact of this kind of professional development experience in terms of current measures related to school improvement and pupil performance. However, he described a very different model which was based on a holistic idea of enhancing the teachers' own experience of learning so that they could go on and do the same for their pupils.

There was a not a tremendous rational way of doing things. I think that's probably unfair but it would be caricatured now as a waste of time, self-indulgent, let them go off - and funding them to go off for the weekend, pay for all the accommodation and so on and no demonstrable outcome in terms of improving children's learning. Certainly what they were trying to do which was to improve the quality of children's experience through improving the quality of the teachers' experience. It wouldn't pay off in terms of any national test results but that's not what the purpose was. The purpose was, the purpose was to, I think it was quite a romantic idea I think, the purpose was to improve the quality in the teachers' experience so that they would want to improve their pupils' experience but it was not set out with objectives or any aims or outcomes or anything, it was designed as a process rather than a set of outcomes so I think it's reasonable to say that it achieved that...[15]

For the teachers involved, Jack reflected on their personal enjoyment.

...my own judgement was that they were going along with playing a game, that they, it's a nice place to be that's the first thing, they get away from family responsibilities for the weekend and the accommodation was very basic but the setting is, have you been? It's stunning, stunning place. I doubt whether in terms of the, one might think I'd know with education accountability, it could demonstrate the effectiveness of value for money. I think that teachers quite enjoyed it, that's the first thing. They liked doing the kind of things that they were doing and they were given an enormous amount of choice. I mean they could just do whatever they wanted for the whole weekend. There was one chap who was a headteacher, I think he was already a headteacher of quite a progressive school who just spent the whole time doing watercolours, so he had a very nice time.[16]

For Jim Christopers there was a very strong personal dimension to professional development.

I think that whatever happened you see, professional development is an internal thing, it certainly happens inside the person. So whatever practice, whatever procedure, whatever framework is used, it's got to do that. It's actually got to deal with the person internally. Which is why in the end, hand on heart, I still believe that the very best professional development, that would do, is that which is done by practitioners within their setting and about their practice.[17]

PERCEPTIONS OF QUALITY

Reflecting on the impact of professional development experiences generated some interesting considerations of quality and the various factors involved. It is perhaps not surprising, given the enormous range of professional development opportunities on offer, that perceptions of quality also varied. General quality indicators seemed to emphasise the importance of an appropriate fit between whoever was delivering a course, its content and its pedagogy. Joy Kell described some poor quality provision and problems of superficiality in relation to opportunities for following up in any depth that which was learned on a course.

It wasn't all good. I felt very often there was a mismatch between the teacher, the course, the pitch, the content, they had, it had often inset had little impact in the classroom, the course, the twilight courses had limited impact, unless they were part of a long course. In a one-off thing they had limited impact because the teachers were teaching all day and unless it's something that is quite a little nugget of something, it doesn't work. So short courses are too superficial, if there's no follow up to a course, to discuss the impact and problems, again it's a problem, its limited.[18]

June Rowe commented on the variability of the various courses she attended throughout her career, with some being very good and others a complete waste of time. For June, the quality of the course tutor or convenor was critical.

Well if the tutor or whoever was running the course was enthusiastic and conveyed that enthusiasm and had a lot of fresh ideas that you could put into practice really. I mean some of them just droned on and on...[19]

Valerie Jenkins described similar experiences and developed the idea that the quality of a course tutor was also very much related to their own ability to teach and to engage with teachers. For Valerie '...*some were excellent, some were dreadful*'. She was particularly sceptical of those who were not actually teachers telling teachers how to teach and was interested in the idea of professional credibility and relevant experience.

It really depended upon who was running them and how effective they were. How effective they were. There were some people, you would sit in a lecture and think if these people were working with children there would be a riot in the classroom, and we're all so polite that we put up with really third rate input and very well paid people which I thought was very poor really. But some were very good.[20]

Valerie found most of the benefit from attending courses to be the opportunity to meet other people and to share ideas.

But the main benefit as such of course is talking to other people. Sharing ideas. Sharing means of dealing with difficult children really…I think a combination of working on one's own and working with a team is quite good really. I'm not sure that the input from outsiders was of any great value. That sounds terribly arrogant, but so often when you hear somebody pontificating about what should go on in the classroom and you can't help but think that well they haven't been doing it and they don't know. Whereas talking with colleagues who are actually working at the chalk face, that seems to me much more valuable.[21]

Joy Willoughby, describing the value of attending a particularly useful Science and Mathematics residential conference, organised by the Department for Education in the early 1980s, also emphasised the importance of working with other professionals as a way of furthering her own thinking.

I think you make closer relationships with other people and because of that, they're fun and you've got the social side of things but that also gives you a bit more depth in your own professional discussions because you've got that intensive time. You know, working together with a shared view on things, it does promote your own thinking and develop your own thinking. No, it's good, I enjoyed them.[22]

Diana Lucas found residential courses to be less likely to be poor quality, largely because of the time investment involved all round.

I think the one's you remember best usually are the residential ones because they are the more concentrated ones…I mostly enjoyed going on courses but sometimes you go on a course and think, "good God I'm wasting my time here, I'd be much better back at school". But I don't think I ever found that on a residential course, maybe they're better thought out, I don't know.[23]

Hilary Cox described her own frustration at what she viewed as a rather drawn out and formulaic approach to courses taken by local authorities and the lack of any input on the part of teachers into the structure and content of courses.

I think one of the things I found frustrating with the some of the courses that I went to in Warwickshire was the rather formulaic method of presenting things. I don't know. Just sort of talking to you and then, well very much often they talked at you, and then perhaps a short discussion time and then coming back and having some comments on that and very often things that you felt you knew already and often taking it at quite a slow pace I think particularly, I mean I went on quite a lot of Maths courses and certainly that was my experience, that it was very slow and certainly when the National Curriculum came in and we had the training. Well I think it was general that we all thought it could have been done in about one and a half days and, it was I don't know, was it three days or five days or something ridiculous? I mean, and when, I mean in a way you felt a bit sorry for the tutors because when they were challenged over it they said, "Oh well we're doing it the way the government says" and I, well my reply was, "Well if you feel that that's not necessary ought you not to be saying something? You know you ought to be saying we don't need to take this long, the people that we're getting on our courses don't need to take three days to do this - you could do it much more quickly".[24]

Andrea Finch offered an interesting perspective from the position of someone who had been responsible for designing and delivering courses for teachers through her involvement with the TVEI initiative. For Andrea, the confidence that her own professional identity was firmly rooted in the reality of the classroom gave her credibility with teachers.

We were not deluded in any way, shape or form, we were very rooted. We were teachers, we weren't academics in that sense. We wanted the best for kids and we were very driven by that sense of this has got to be right for the kids and it's got to change things for young people and it's got to raise aspirations so we were all very much rooted in that's what it's about. We weren't in it for self-glory or anything and we worked with these people, we'd come from schools and we could draw on that.[25]

Andrea described in some detail a particular incident which to her reinforced the significance of her own credibility with teachers.

I remember going over to…a massive school in Birmingham, and actually there was a problem, somebody hadn't turned up or was delayed in traffic or trains or something so giving a, having to kind of busk really, and started off just by giving a very, very potted one minute history of my career to date and that apparently, it hadn't been planned particularly but had gone down well because people thought oh yes, she's a teacher, she's good, she's been a head, she's…, she's done that, she's taught in that school, she's taught in this school, she's been there, that's a hugely important and something that I think, even now, I don't forget because you, I've got to remember that I've been there with my sleeves rolled up dealing with stroppy kids and stroppy parents and having to mark endlessly and write reports and I think that was essential really to be, to be credible.[26]

A number of participants raised the quality of refreshments on courses as something that teachers rated as important – though they did this in a wry, semi-joking way. Passing comments about teachers only being motivated by how satisfying the lunch provided was and using this to gauge overall quality might suggest that for teachers there was a perceived relationship about how they were treated and valued, particularly if they were giving up their own time to attend a course. For Andrea Finch, feeding teachers was a fundamental part of the business of delivering courses.

> But I mean the money helped in those days...We always thought our success was piles of sandwiches actually. Seriously, for twilight sessions we used a fantastic little, it was a post office and it used to put up all these lovely fresh sandwiches and then we'd take them and just drive off to the place that we were working in and just start off the session with that and that really helped and it wasn't meant to be kind of Machiavellian in any way but it was just, look they've had a hard day sorting out all these kids, planning lessons probably doing a duty, got to go home and face, sort out their families, do a whole pile of marking, sort of tomorrow's lessons, let's at least give them a few nice tasty sandwiches rather than just some horrible stale ones...[27]

Peggy Jones believed that the atmosphere and domestic arrangements for courses was very important for teachers and described as '*dehumanising*' those events which provided no refreshments. Gill Brown explained why the free tea and coffee for teachers on local authority courses was seen as an important by the teachers, because there was a sense in that it was the least that could be done to ease the transition of teachers from school into a course.

> At one point the teachers' centre or the council decided that teachers should pay for, it was wrong that they get free tea and coffee and we started to have to pay for it. Which didn't go down very well, as you know, the only perk you got was an afternoon out and then you had to pay for your own coffee which was served really slowly.[28]

Joy Williams, as warden of a teachers' centre in Hampshire, described in some detail how she had been responsible for organising the lunches for teachers attending day courses at her centre.

> We had a big I was going to say industrial oven but a big oven like that and we would bring our own big casseroles in and make chilli con carne or something like that and serve a great plateful of that and an apple which we'd go up to the apple orchards up at the other end of Winchester and I would buy crates, boxes of apples and come down and so they would have chilli con carne and an apple for lunch and that was alright and then we went on with the next thing, so... We did eventually we did get somebody who would come and cook and bring the food in at one moment and then I went up to collect the food from her and I found her cat walking all over the kitchen sink and I thought, no we don't do that anymore. I mean ours might not have been ever so pristine but it was a bloody sight better than the cat walking over the kitchen. But I don't know how we funded it now I come to think about it. We must have got, we must have

got money from the County for doing it. We had to keep it to the minimum, I know we weren't splashing out on anything and of course we had to do it unless we were. But we were all cooks and we'd all fed our families so what's the odds really? And if the, I had two excellent secretaries and they were both very good cooks and so one of them would do the cooking while the other one was answering all the telephones and so on...[29]

Joy Kell described how as a professional development coordinator in Cornwall during the 1980s and 1990s, how important it was for teachers to feel valued either by the venue and location of a course or opportunities for refreshment and time to socialise.

But I always provided sandwiches and a cake and a cup of tea on every course I ran when I was a PDC because they were giving up their time and to arrive and have a dry biscuit and a cup of lukewarm tea, which often was the case, then sit in somebody's classroom.....so when I was organising courses, when I was paid as a PDC, I would use hotels frequently, and they were appropriate. When I was an independent I had to use schools but I would make sure that they had sandwiches and time to eat them and chat because that's always so important...[30]

For both Joys, getting the 'domestics' right was a memorable part of their roles in organising courses or teachers – though it is interesting that none of the other male teachers' centre wardens who participated in this research referred to any of the domestics involved in their roles, suggesting that this may have been a gendered consideration.

IMPACT FOR WHOM? MOTIVATIONS AND REACH

Discussion around perceptions of quality and impact of professional development with participants raised some interesting questions about which teachers were engaging with their own professional development and what was motivating them to do so, as well as those perennial questions about the problem of disengaged teachers. There was a general sense that certainly in the days before mandatory 'Baker Days', it was the keen and enthusiastic teacher who benefited most from the range of opportunities available to them – and that there was always a group of teachers, either in an individual school or within a local authority who were much harder to reach and disenfranchised from the whole process, as demonstrated in Chapter Six.

Bill Parkinson, though firmly committed to organic, teacher-led professional development that enabled and facilitated the sharing of resources and ideas that could then be taken back to the classroom, had an interesting perspective on impact. He suggested that teachers often went on courses on subjects that interested them and that they were already good at – not courses or subjects that they necessarily needed additional help with.

Looking back now I think you probably just reinforced what you liked and what you were good at, rather than developing your areas where you were weaker.[31]

David Howe described something of a phenomenon of the 'professional course goer'. During his time as an adviser and inspector in Warwickshire he claimed to have seen the same core group of teachers time and time again at the various courses organised by the local authority.

But there were regular professional course goers and particularly in primary as well. Which meant of course that if we'd done an analysis, a lot were not being touched but the idea was if we get the right people along, we can train our leaders and then get them to go back to their schools and Teachers' Centres and so on, and lead others, the ones who wouldn't give a weekend up but might come on a Wednesday afternoon after school to the Teachers' Centre.[32]

David believed that this was part of a conscious strategy on the part of the local authority to identify and nurture willing and engaged teachers who were keen to effect change and to use them as change agents in their schools. Aside from the personal enjoyment and the attractions of good food and good company on residential courses David appeared to be describing a particular sort of professional culture and community amongst a group of teachers.

...With primary courses they loved it because they had this food and they were spoilt and they didn't have to do anything and there were teachers who would say where is it and sign up rather than what is it? Obviously if it was something very specialised they wouldn't go but primary school teaching tended to be quite broad so you did have quite a regular clientele coming along at the Teachers' Centres. We looked at the registers once, we found teachers who would come into the Teachers' Centre on four days and we didn't normally have anything on a Friday, coming to anything. So they were almost voracious – for what? I don't know – a social life – but there were some that liked the kind of pampering even if they had families. I think they quite liked a weekend where everything was done for them as far as eating is concerned.[33]

Derek Cloke similarly described a core '*nucleus*' of the same teachers at his centre in Devon and recognised that there was a large group of teachers who did not engage with centre activities. Alan Forster, as a teacher centre leader in Devon also attended a number of local authority courses and conferences outside of his routine centre work. He recalled '...*meeting the same participants and the same leaders every time*...' and described these assiduous 'course goers' as '...*the same old attendant groupies*'. Keith Martin, also involved with a number of teachers as a teachers' centre warden attempted to quantify the split between those teachers who attended centre courses and those who he never ever met. He estimated that he reached about 40% of teachers, but rather like David Howe's observation on reach, that this 40% would spread the ideas they had picked up with their less keen colleagues.

But certainly there were some teachers you didn't reach. Now when I think I might have counted a percentage term, about how many teachers I reached, sometimes I think, gosh that wasn't very many, because I would think it wasn't half. I would think it was just under half.[34]

In reflecting on teachers' motivation to engage with their professional development, links were clearly made with the draw of opportunities for career progression or enhancement. Jim Christophers suggested that were some powerful links between engagement with professional development opportunities and career development, particularly in local authority courses, where advisers and inspectors would identify those teachers they wished to see on such courses.

I think those people that were involved and proactive and so on were probably picked out and groomed if you like.[35]

Jim was very aware of the increasing importance of accredited professional development, normally through university masters' or doctoral programmes, since the early 1990s and that this was a shift in culture from an earlier period in his own career.

But it made me think you see, because of course over the last 15 years or so… there was a time when people were coming into university without necessarily a sense of, this is going to help my career specifically, but with a genuine interest in doing something within that particular field. I think now people are much more aware, if you like, of doing accredited professional development because it's a step towards a career and the sense that if you want to get to really senior positions now within the schools, that having a Master's degree or Master's level qualification, is important.[36]

Joy Willoughby and Juliet Amery, both noted that though they had conscientiously attended numerous interesting and inspiring courses throughout their careers, none of these had carried with them any formal accreditation and that though they had not been unduly concerned about this at the time, recognised that in the current climate they would be more anxious for proper formal accreditation. June Rowe described how she had not set out with any clear career plan, but that her experiences, particularly on university accredited programmes had a direct impact on her own confidence and her own interest in school management.

But I never thought of it, never thought of it like that, you just kind of keep moving forward don't you? So you don't really think about what your end, I mean when I went to Warwick I never dreamt of doing, applying for headships but then when I did this BPhilEd, one of the modules was management of education, I got really interested then, but that was within my role as management of the infant department.[37]

Sue Roberts identified what she regarded as a quite obvious link between those teachers who wanted to develop as professionals and career progression, though it is interesting that she distanced herself from this notion and stressed how much she had been motivated by personal interest.

> I think it just makes you a better teacher. I mean, the bottom line is that the better you are as a teacher the better it is for the students, isn't it? And that has a secondary knock on effect with the school generally and so on, and it tends to be the teachers who are most interested and most enthusiastic and professionally really wanting to do a good job, they are the ones who progress through the system but I didn't have any objective any progressing through the system, I just did it because I was interested and I, and you know I get a buzz out of doing it.[38]

She went on to describe her experiences of attending conferences and meetings as a female secondary head teacher, offering a particular insight on the 'professional course goer' identified by some of the other participants. Sue clearly did not identify with the 'men in suits' and saw them very much as other to herself.

> There's quite a lot of male networking and bonding goes on at these things. If you're the woman at these, a lot of these meetings, certainly when I was going, you could be quite isolated and on your own unless you happen to know somebody else but, so, I think it had an additional role, a networking role for some, certainly what I'd call the Armani suited brigade who ran the big schools, but for us small fish…[39]

At the other end of the spectrum were those teachers who were hard to reach. A number of participants described some of the frustrations associated with their encounters with disengaged teachers, often recounting amusing anecdotes of resistant teachers, particularly where mandatory attendance was involved. Stories of recalcitrant teachers knitting, marking, reading newspapers and generally being present in body but not in mind or spirit at Baker Day events have already been presented in the previous chapter. For David Howe, forcing teachers who did not want to attend to be at course was counter-productive, as he believed that voluntary and willing attendance would bring about the most change in the profession in the long run.

> In my experience people get narked if they didn't want to be there in the first place and they think it's a waste a time. But if they're there voluntarily they possibly anyway, are more amenable to whatever is going to happen.[40]

Jim Christophers, with his many years of experience of delivering professional development courses suggested of some teachers that:

> They just wouldn't, just didn't engage, and I have had conversations with a couple of guys, chaps in the past, and said actually we're going to do this, so you're either with us or you're not, you know, it's that kind of conversation that you need to have. Yes, but you do meet all types…it's people saying,

we can't take that, we're doing enough already, there's, you know, we've got initiative overload, that sort of thing. But also through to people who actually say nothing.[41]

In June Rowe's experience as a head teacher in a Coventry primary school, she found that there were always one or two teachers on her staff who were just not interested in engaging with professional development, though was anxious to stress that these were always in a minority and that the majority of staff were dedicated and professional. For June, the age of the teachers was critical and she found that in her experience older teachers were much more hostile to new ideas and to staying behind after school to discuss how changes might be implemented.

> Some of the schools where I did audit moderating, they didn't want to know about the SATs (Standard Attainment Tests), and I'd be doing an INSET and you'd see them, they were kind of rolling their eyes and they didn't want to know because they were all middle fifties, and they all knew that they were going soon and they just didn't want to introduce this new thing, but it was compulsory, statutory, they had to do it and it was trying to get it over to them in the simplest way so they'd make a start.[42]

Cliff Harris also commented on older teachers being less amenable to new ideas and opportunities.

> ...there was always a gap between, not with all older people because some of them actually did develop themselves intentionally and so on, but there was always this thing when you went into education, particularly in the early days where somebody could train to be a teacher and that was it for forty years and they'd tell you what you were doing, what's right because this is how you do it, and there were lots of occasions like that, I think.[43]

Kate Moorse recalled having been very conscious of the challenge of drawing in those teachers who she regarded as being in most need of the sort of additional curriculum support that she was able to offer through her teachers' centre in London. For Kate, one obvious solution was to work closely in partnership with inspectors and advisers and with head teachers to identify where particular problems might exist and then go in to work with individuals or groups of teachers rather than expect the teacher to come to the teachers' centre voluntarily.

> So we were seeing ways to draw people in who wouldn't otherwise be drawn in. There were some extraordinary recalcitrant teachers actually, around the place, who in a sense you couldn't reach them and there was a whole thing about the inspection routine, the carrot and stick-ness of that whole thing really. So quite often the Inspector would come in and say, I've just had a very interesting afternoon in X department, we need to find a way of getting in there and doing something. So, rather than it being an inset in getting teachers to come out, yes you would try and do that and go to them...[44]

In a similar way to Kate, Andrea Finch believed that a sensible strategy to achieve optimum teacher engagement was through gentle persuasion in the hope that new ideas would eventually filter their way down into the system as a whole.

> But then it was about being realistic and being pleasant and just hoping to influence other people and that maybe drip-feed-wise it would impact on them without them their losing their dignity or feeling as though they're caving in....[45]

Angela drew upon an evocative metaphor of the teaching profession that she herself had heard used by a national TVEI leader called Jack Chambers as a way of making sense of working with reluctant teachers, describing it as 'swamp theory'.

> One image that has remained with me about trying to deal with these recusant staff was, it was called swamp theory. I don't know whether you've come across it and you have a swamp which is marshy and wet and boggy and horrible and then obviously you have dry land and the dry land is all the people that you can work with and the swamp are the people that you can't and because there are grades within that of marshy-ness and dryness there's always the bit at the edge which is not too boggy, that's not completely dry and his metaphor really was about just work at the edges all the time because if you can just reclaim a little bit of land, don't bother, don't worry about the swamp because they're going to stay there, they aren't going to change, they're always going to be there, they won't change and you won't ever change them anyway. Somebody else might but you won't, so those staff, if you think of them as just working, just nibble away and gradually that dry land it, the swamp recedes and you get, you gain more and at the end somebody somewhere may well influence that person and at the end of the day all you can do is be civil to them but you might not change their teaching styles…[46]

In Andrea's view, there was a certain inevitably that there would always be a group of teachers who would remain at the far edge of the swamp – beyond reach. However, there was some hope of reaching those teachers who operated at the edge of the swamp and dry land.

CHAPTER SUMMARY

In this chapter, participants' perceptions of the quality and impact of their professional development experiences has been presented. Meanings and understandings of impact varied between participants, though there was a strong sense that any professional training needed to have practical credibility and application. Disseminating new knowledge and understanding with colleagues and sharing good practice was considered to be important and a valued way of embedding professional development more widely. Personal enjoyment, motivation and fulfilment, in relation to professional development, was also regarded as significant for a number of participants. As with the previous chapter, a whole range of very rich experiences and views on these experiences have been represented. Nevertheless, at the heart of this focus on quality and impact lies a critical issue relating to the historical problem of teacher professional development. This is concerned with the fundamental question of whether or not professional development should be voluntary or mandatory for all teachers, regardless of their personal interests, professional commitments or career plans and what the implications for the quality of the teaching profession might be with the kind of *ad hoc* voluntary model, apparently devoid of any clear overarching strategy for all teachers, described by so many participants in this chapter. This theme will be considered further in the next chapter, which focuses upon the relationship between professional development and professional identity.

NOTES

[1] See Flecknoe, M. (2000). 'Can continuing professional development for teachers be shown to raise pupils' achievement?', *Journal of In-Service Education*, 26(3), 437–457; Flecknoe, M. (2003). 'Measuring the impact of teacher professional development: can it be done?', *European Journal of Teacher Education*, 25(2), 119–134; Office for Standards in Education, (2004). *Making a difference: the impact of award-bearing INSET on school improvement*. London, UK: Ofsted.

[2] BARDA Project 53026, oral history interview with Cliff Harris (1st interview), April 2011.

[3] BARDA Project 53026, oral history interview with Andrea Finch (p), May 2011.

[4] Ibid.

[5] BARDA Project 53026, oral history interview with Gill Brown (p), July 2011.

[6] BARDA Project 53026, oral history interview with Cliff Harris (2nd interview), October 2011.

[7] BARDA Project 53026, oral history interview with Sarah Matthews (p), May 2011.

[8] BARDA Project 53026, oral history interview with Joy Kell, May 2011.

[9] BARDA Project 53026, oral history interview with Diana Lucas, May 2011.

[10] BARDA Project 53026, oral history interview with June Rowe, May 2011.

[11] BARDA Project 53026, oral history interview with Valerie Jenkins, September 2011.

[12] BARDA Project 53026, oral history interview with Diana Lucas.

[13] Ibid.

[14] BARDA Project 53026, oral history interview with Joy Willoughby, May 2011.

[15] BARDA Project 53026, oral history interview with Jack Scott (p), April 2011.

[16] Ibid.

[17] BARDA Project 53026, oral history interview with Jim Christophers, March 2011.

[18] BARDA Project 53026, oral history interview with Joy Kell.

[19] BARDA Project 53026, oral history interview with June Rowe.

[20] BARDA Project 53026, oral history interview with Valerie Jenkins.

[21] Ibid.

[22] BARDA Project 53026, oral history interview with Joy Willoughby.

[23] BARDA Project 53026, oral history interview with Diana Lucas.

[24] BARDA Project 53026, oral history interview with Hilary Cox, May 2011.

[25] BARDA Project 53026, oral history interview with Andrea Finch.

[26] Ibid.

[27] Ibid.

[28] BARDA Project 53026, oral history interview with Gill Brown.

[29] BARDA Project 53026, oral history interview with Joy Williams, September 2011.

[30] BARDA Project 53026, oral history interview with Joy Kell.

[31] BARDA Project 53026, oral history interview with Bill Parkinson, May 2011.

[32] BARDA Project 53026, oral history interview with David Howe (2nd interview), February 2011.

[33] Ibid.
[34] BARDA Project 53026, oral history interview with Keith Martin, May 2011.
[35] BARDA Project 53026, oral history interview with Jim Christophers.
[36] Ibid.
[37] BARDA Project 53026, oral history interview with June Rowe.
[38] BARDA Project 53026, oral history interview with Sue Roberts, March 2011.
[39] Ibid.
[40] BARDA Project 53026, oral history interview with David Howe (1st interview), November 2010.
[41] BARDA Project 53026, oral history interview with Jim Christophers.
[42] BARDA Project 53026, oral history interview with June Rowe.
[43] BARDA Project 53026, oral history interview with Cliff Harris (1st interview).
[44] BARDA Project 53026, oral history interview with Kate Moorse, February 2011.
[45] BARDA Project 53026, oral history interview with Andrea Finch.
[46] Ibid.

PROFESSIONAL DEVELOPMENT AND PERCEPTIONS OF TEACHER PROFESSIONAL IDENTITY

This chapter explores the relationship between the experience of professional development and ideas of teacher professional identity, status and community. It considers the idea of professional learning as something much more fluid and greater than that confined to formal professional development opportunities for teachers and examines the blurring of boundaries between personal and professional development. It also reflects upon the value placed by some teachers upon certain forms of accredited professional development in relation to their own professional status and recognition. Informal learning from others as an integral part of belonging to a diverse professional community of teachers, as well as the notion that being a learner is intimately tied in to the whole business of being a teacher are also discussed. Arguably, these concepts of professional identity, status and professional learning were less tangible and explicit in the participants' testimonies than some of the more detailed and descriptive accounts of memories of 'going on courses' and all that this entailed. However, some of these more nuanced insights into the nature of professional development in its widest sense serve to crystallize a number of recurring themes that have been identified throughout the book. These include tensions between personal and professional development, professional status, autonomy and control and have variously straddled the chronological phases which have defined the history of teacher professional development in England and Wales throughout the twentieth century. The oral testimony presented here provides a distinctive opportunity to consider such themes from a particular professional perspective. The chapter is in four main parts. First, the personal/professional dimension in relation to teacher professional development is examined. Secondly, the stress placed upon the status acquisition of accredited professional development programmes, particularly at degree level is explored. Thirdly, impact of belonging to a wider professional community on professional development is explored. Finally, the idea of learning as a core element of being a teacher is discussed.

PERSONAL AND PROFESSIONAL DIMENSIONS

For a number of participants the distinction between their professional development and their personal development was not clear cut. Some formal professional development experiences, particularly subject focused courses within primary education, either stimulated personal interest and a keenness to develop some of this work further outside of the formal context or teachers chose to engage with these types of opportunity precisely because they already had a strong interest. Sometimes teachers felt that they brought to their professional practice a range of wider interests and skills that they had pursued in their own time but that they considered to be very much related to their teaching identity.

Bill Parkinson, throughout a long career as a teacher, deputy head teacher and head teacher in primary schools in Coventry, attended a number of adult education courses in his own time and at his own cost to develop his interests in pottery, Art, Drama and sport refereeing and coaching. He went on to use these skills in his professional work in schools:

> I did do things for myself, like I went on a pottery course and things, …when I was at my first school…I did do a pottery course because we had a kiln there and things there which I liked doing…That was just an add-on course just for my own interest which I then used in school because I was quite keen to do that. I also did a referee course because I did the games there and I had no training, even at college…[1]

Joy Willoughby, a nursery education specialist described a close connection between her personal interests and hobbies and her work in schools. For her there was a powerful connection between her personal development and her professional development which was holistic and joined up.

> No, I feel I've been really privileged to have the professional development that I have because I don't think it's just developed me professionally, it's developed me as a person, as a whole person. I mean things like my interests in Dance and Drama and Art have been developed by those opportunities and those are the things that I, were a part of me, my own sort of personality and the things that I have done in my own time so it's all sort of dovetailed in together and I'm not sure teachers get that opportunity now.[2]

June Rowe believed that her wider experiences of working with children as a leader of a cub pack, being a member of the National Women's Register, running her own private nursery enriched her own professional identity as a primary school head teacher.

> I never dreamt of being a head actually, but having run a cub pack with thirty six cubs and taking them to camp and everything and run my own nursery with twenty-five children each morning and each afternoon, so I was used to leadership…[3]

When appointing new staff, June recalled having been quite interested not just in their formal professional development experience but their 'outside interests and hobbies as well' – she too valued a more holistic approach.

Derek Cloke had a slightly different perspective on the relationship between personal and professional development. For him, working on an advanced diploma at the Exeter Institute of Education in the late 1950s '...*became your leisure time activity because you had to attend all the lectures and write the essays...*' He claimed that he took this course purely out of personal interest and not because he was looking for promotion or that he had been specifically recommended to do it by a senior colleague. He enjoyed working on the essays and attending lectures during evenings and weekends, paying his own travel expenses and course fees.[4]

Maureen Fletcher, who initially trained as a junior and secondary teacher of Needlework and Geography in the mid-1950s went on to teach in secondary modern schools in Coventry before taking a career break to bring up her family. In the late 1960s Maureen applied for a teaching post in the hospital service in Coventry, working with sick children who needed specialised teaching provision, either in hospital schools, on children's wards or in their own homes. Maureen remained in this role for the rest of her career, eventually becoming deputy head teacher and then acting head teacher of the hospital service, with responsibility for organising professional development for her staff. Maureen offered some interesting observations about how she perceived her own professional status as a hospital teacher in relation to more conventional classroom teachers in schools and implied that she had struggled to be taken seriously as a 'proper teacher' by other professional colleagues. However, Maureen described a very powerful sense of her own professional identity as one in which she consciously sought to develop her own knowledge and understanding of various subjects that she was interested in personally so that she could communicate them more effectively to the children with whom she was working – children who were experiencing their schooling under very difficult and testing circumstances. For example, she attended a an evening gardening course at a local horticultural college, in her own time and at her own expense. She enjoyed gardening and was interested in learning more about it as a personal hobby. However, she also believed in the importance of using this knowledge to stimulate the children. For Maureen, the real professional learning challenge was to find ways of working out how to adapt and translate her own new knowledge to an appropriate and interesting level for the children.

> I've been on gardening courses. Now, it sounds ridiculous to go on a gardening course as a teacher, but you learn all sorts of skills and knowledge that came in useful with these children...I picked up the ability to go out, say for example, identifying flowers. I then knew the different classes, what their unique resemblance to each other was, and I could apply this to children in a much easier, simply way.[5]

Maureen reflected upon this experience and suggested that other teachers might not have viewed it in such a positive fashion, believing that '...*another teacher wouldn't see this, you see*'. But, her philosophy of teaching and learning was very much bound up with finding attractive ways of drawing in those children outside the conventional school system, thinking about the possibilities of applying her own experiential learning to her teaching. She recalled working as a home tutor with one particular boy who had been excluded from school, a boy who was very antagonistic to the whole idea of formal learning, and bringing her own horticultural experience to this situation.

> So I said, "Right, that's it, we'll go and cut grass". So we'd cut grass and I would say, "I wonder how big this lawn is?" So we would measure it. And we would make notes and so English was brought into it. I would say, "Now, go and draw, draw the plan of the garden and put in how it was like when we started and how it is today"…and you know, it all just linked together.[6]

Keeping a broad outlook and having an openness to recognise where the gaps were in her own personal knowledge and understanding motivated Maureen to attend a whole range of courses. She attended more formal courses in Music, Mathematics and English and in a fairly self-directed way was very keen to make links between her own learning and her teaching.

> I just wanted my own professional development to see if I could improve on what I was doing. Was I doing it correctly? Could I do it differently? Could I approach the children differently?[7]

For Maureen, the wide range of ages of children she encountered in her role, as well as their very diverse needs made it even more important for her to have a wide range of interests and expertise herself.

> …but in a hospital and home teaching situation you have to teach other things, other subjects so you need to broaden your outlook. You know, even if you don't like Maths, you've got to enjoy it to teach it, even if you are only teaching infants. You know, you've got to have some enthusiasm.[8]

Valerie Jenkins described in some detail how her own personal interests in drama, drama education and performance had a significant impact on her professional development as a teacher. As a young woman Valerie had aspirations to become an actress, but her mother considered this to be unsuitable as a career choice and urged her daughter to train as a teacher in the late 1950s. Initially trained as a junior teacher and with early teaching posts in a variety of junior and infant schools, Valerie went on to become a Drama teacher in a boys' grammar school in Wisbech, Cambridgeshire. Whilst working in Wisbech in the early 1970s, she met up with some other teachers at the local teachers' centre and they formed a Drama group, putting on their own performances at the teachers' centre or in hired school halls, later purchasing their own building to form a local theatre.

> But we had a teachers' centre in Wisbech which was superb and a group of us who were keen on drama got together at the teachers' centre and initially just sort of put on plays and then we decided we'd like to do some qualifications so we worked to do the Associateship of the Drama Board and we did with funding initially from Cambridgeshire and then Cambridgeshire withdrew the

funding and we funded it ourselves. My recollection is that there were about eight or nine of us...There was a Drama group in the town but they did rather sort of nice comedies...that was alright but we were more interested in modern theatre and avant-garde stuff...[9]

Whilst developing this drama group, there was a strong commitment from its members to gain the formal education accreditation from the national Drama Board Association and to become fully qualified Associates. Though there was some support from the local drama adviser through the teachers' centre, any financial support was, for some reason, withdrawn by the local authority and this group of teachers were left to their own devices to continue working towards this qualification, which took over three years to complete and involved a substantive amount of work. Valerie recalled:

There was a written exam, there was a project, a piece of work. I remember I did costume design and designed and made costumes that had to be shown and I also did make-up. So you had to demonstrate some technical skill and there was a written paper on a wide knowledge of Drama of all sorts of periods and so on, and the third element was running a class on improvisations...[10]

Members of the group supported each other, working after school and at weekends.

....We worked hard, all sorts of hours I guess....We were self-taught really. The History side particularly, because, as I said, we lost the funding, we did this ourselves. So one person would go off and research a particular period ready for this written exam. The improvisation, we went to various courses. I think we had to pay for ourselves, my recollection is that it was all self-funded.[11]

When probed on their motivation to engage in this additional work, Valerie noted that what they were doing was interesting professionally but also stressed the value of gaining some sort of recognition for what they were doing.

I don't know. Just, I just think we all felt that we wanted to have some recognition of what we were doing, I suppose, and also I suppose the idea of possible promotion in the future. Some sort of letters other than Cert. Ed. were quite useful. I think this was the early 1970s. I'm not sure when the movement towards an all degree profession began but I guess it would be about that time?[12]

Valerie's notable professional concern with achieving degree status is something which will be examined further in the next section. However, this story of her and a small group of teachers furthering their own drama interests in a local community and also gaining further Drama Education qualifications on the back of this deep commitment to drama illustrates the blurring of boundaries between the personal and the professional in the development of teacher identity. As a result of family circumstances, Valerie had to move from Wisbech to Leeds and thus began a whole new chapter in her teaching career. However, she continued to pursue her drama work and drama teaching outside of her normal teaching job.

PERCEPTIONS OF STATUS AND ACCREDITED DEGREES

The value of gaining higher degrees or externally accredited qualifications has already been discussed in earlier chapters in relation to models of secondment for teachers and also perceptions of quality and impact. However, for some teachers, the status conferred by such programmes, whether they had engaged with these as part of their formal professional development or as something pursued in their own time and by their own financial means, was deemed to be a very important part of their own sense of professional identity. The demographics of the group of participants who contributed to this research is such that for many, first degrees were not a necessary requirement for their initial teaching qualification, particularly if they had come through the Teachers' Certificate route. However, their teaching careers spanned a period of transition when the move to an all-graduate profession was formalised following the Robbins Report recommendations in 1964 so that new generations of teachers were coming into the profession with B.Ed. degrees or with postgraduate qualifications. There was a perception that those teachers without degrees could fall behind in terms of career opportunities as well as in the wider respect and recognition they might expect to receive from their colleagues and from wider society. Some of these teachers had the opportunity to be seconded mid-career to study part-time for a B.Ed. degree to supplement their teachers' certificate. Others opted to undertake degrees with the Open University or elsewhere. For some teachers, the threshold was not the undergraduate qualification but the Masters or Doctoral Degree which appeared to confer even higher status and value within an increasingly prized currency of professional qualifications.

Attaining a university degree for Ann Dodd was an important part of her personal professional development which she valued in terms of status and career development. Her initial teacher training had been a two-year certificate but she felt that not having a degree held her back both professionally and socially. For Ann, this was a real matter of status:

> ...I really wanted a degree. Everybody I mixed with, apart from quite a few of the teachers, but all my friends outside of school had all got degrees.[13]

Valerie Jenkins expressed a similar view to Ann. Though she had fully immersed herself in her drama education qualifications, described above, it was the completion of a B.Phil. as part of a secondment to study at Newcastle University much later on in her career that really made the difference to Valerie in terms of how she perceived her own professional status. Working as a teacher in a grammar school in the early 1980s, Valerie was acutely conscious of her non-graduate status, in relation to her colleagues:

> And I stayed there for a year and I was very conscious then that I hadn't got a degree and that other people had. And especially of course when it came to speech day and everybody paraded in their gowns. I was very cross with myself really.[14]

Achieving the B.Phil. degree gave Valerie an important boost in terms of professional self-esteem. She later went on to complete a Masters qualification.

> …it wasn't to do with promotion as much as to do with feeling that I wanted to prove that I could do it, you know, that I wasn't a second class citizen really. And whilst the headteachers down the years have always said, "Oh, two year trained teachers, they're the salt of the earth", it wasn't quite the same and I felt a second class citizen I think. Anyway, I did, so I did the B.Phil. and then opted to go on and do an M.Ed. which I did, again in my own time.[15]

Cliff Harris described how he had felt the pressures in the mid-1970s to get a degree and how mindful he had been of the recommendations of the James Report and its recommendations both for continued professional development for teachers but also for an all-graduate profession. This Open University degree, which he took part-time over three years and paid for himself, was difficult to manage with his day job and a young growing family. However, the ideas, theories and models of education and social reform that he came across on his degree went on to shape his future educational interests and career choices.

> I signed up for an Open University degree and a lot of teachers did that then. I paid for that. Yes. There was pressure. You felt that you had to be a graduate to be a teacher. There was a whole lot of what they called in-service B.Eds that people went on…Then I came down here (Cliff moved from teaching in inner-city London to Devon in the early 1970s) and the James Report came in and I became much more conscious of development, you know, professional development. I did an Open University degree and I did it in Sociology and Curriculum Studies and it was very interesting. Again it confirmed to me the unfairness of the whole education system in terms of gatekeeping and access to life chances and so on…[16]

Cliff mentioned the in-service B.Ed. phenomenon, which a number of other participants in this research had experienced. Joy Willoughby, for example, was pleased to have had the opportunity to enrol part-time on a B.Ed. programme with full local authority funding and support. This involved her attending the university two nights a week for four years as well as many long weekends, evenings and vacations spent completing her coursework assignments. On the course she met other teachers in similar circumstances to herself – experienced, mid-career teachers who belonged to that particular generation for whom degree qualifications had not been so widely available at the initial training stage. In fact, Joy had always wanted to complete a degree, but was compelled to undertake a two-year certificate programme because her family and financial circumstances meant that she needed to start working as a teacher as soon as she could and could not then commit to the time required of a four year degree programme. Coming back to do a degree much later on was important for Joy who did not want to be left behind in a profession which was becoming increasingly all-graduate.

159

I wanted a degree. I felt because the profession was becoming a degree profession by that time and I felt I wanted to. I had wanted to do a degree at college because there was an opportunity for me to do a B.Ed. at college and stay on for two extra years, but my personal circumstances were such that wouldn't allow me to do that...Yes, I had to go to work. I couldn't stay. There was no way I could be supported any longer by my parents. My tutors at college wanted me to do it desperately but there was no way that I could do it financially....[17]

Though Joy had mixed feelings about what she learned on her degree programme, judging some of it as bearing no practical relation at all to her day job of running a large nursery and infant school in Warwickshire, completing it was a real personal achievement and source of professional pride.

It was a good thing to have done in terms of the qualifications but also in terms of showing that I could do it. I wanted it and I was able to achieve it at the same time as doing a headship. I do a lot of work with governors now. If I was a governor now looking at a CV of someone who had done that, I'd be quite impressed by that. I'd think that person has obviously really wanted to achieve, so I think it did me a lot of good in that sense really.[18]

June Rowe similarly pursued an in-service B.Phil.Ed. degree in the early 1980s at the University of Warwick, though she recalled having funded this herself through termly fee instalments. She attended two evening classes per week and completed two modules a year, covering such topics as children's literature, management in education, special educational needs in primary schools and then a research-based dissertation. June had fond memories of this experience, which she particularly enjoyed and valued as a form of professional development, but she did emphasise just how much personal motivation was involved. She was particularly proud of the graduation ceremony, held at Coventry Cathedral which involved taking a day off school, supported by the local authority.

They paid for my day off when we had the ceremony – the graduation ceremony. It worked out very well and I think we did get some expenses back from the LEA but on the whole you had to be motivated yourself to do it.[19]

Joy Williams, as a teachers' centre leader in Hampshire in the 1970s, recalled having felt an almost moral imperative to complete an in-service B.Ed.degree so that she was not seen as being less qualified than the teachers with whom she worked on a daily basis. This was not an enjoyable experience for Joy, but she prized the acquisition of the degree at the end of the process and viewed it very much in status terms.

It was bloody hard work and most of it was totally irrelevant. I mean it was three or four nights a week at the college and then there were essays and things which of course I hadn't written forever, readings which I didn't understand two words of them, an awful lot of stuff, as I say which was quite irrelevant. It might have been relevant to some of the teachers I think, but it certainly wasn't to a Teachers' Centre leader. But I just scraped through and that was, I think, I felt that that was my, I'd got there, I had my degree, like all the other teachers.[20]

Bill Parkinson, though he self-funded and completed an Open University degree in Humanities and Social Sciences in his own time, regretted not having had the opportunity to be seconded by Coventry LEA to the University of Warwick to complete a Bachelor's Degree in Education, which was something that he had aspired to and that he knew had happened for other colleagues:

I would have liked to have done a degree and perhaps been seconded because I know people were being seconded at one point in Coventry to go and study at Warwick and I did apply but I didn't, I never got the chance and I would have really liked to have done that.[21]

Moving beyond a Bachelor's degree qualification to higher degree work at Masters or Doctoral level was prized by some participants. Gill Brown relished the intellectual challenge of studying for her MA in History and felt that both her Teaching Certificate and her B.Ed. qualification were viewed very much as second rate qualifications. Encouraged by her deputy head teacher, who himself was studying for a doctorate at the time, Gill enrolled on a part-time MA in History at her local polytechnic college. Though not an education programme, Gill's school was willing to provide some financial support on the understanding that Gill would complete the required work in her own time. Gill felt that her experience of studying for this degree was a way of proving herself and as a way of pushing herself further. There was a sense that she needed the additional stimulation of this work and she enjoyed the challenge and was quite happy to use her weekends, evenings and holidays to study.

I didn't have children, I was bored. The school I was teaching in by then, I could do less preparation, it was much easier. I used to have to do reading every week for the MA...It was great just to do something different and meet other people and just that and be academically challenged really. I really enjoyed that.[22]

For Peggy Jones, the status linked to having a Masters qualification was important. Peggy had very much wanted to extend her three year teachers' certificate to a B.Ed. in the late 1960s but was prevented from doing so because she had not completed two practical 'A' levels. Peggy had a varied teaching career working as a supply teacher in a number of primary schools and then specialising as a Science Coordinator in the late 1980s, as well as leading on Information Technology and student teacher mentoring. Peggy had the opportunity to undertake a twenty day national Science coordinator's course in 1988, accredited by the Open University and was then able to use some of the credits acquired towards an MA in Educational Studies in the mid-1990s. Peggy believed that having an MA qualification would help with her career progression and also with her own professional status. In discussion with her headteacher, who had also recently completed an MA programme at a local university, Peggy joined the programme, which included specialist modules in mentoring and paid half of the fees herself, with the other half being paid by the school. She attended the university each week in the evenings and recalled the challenge of finishing up her work at school, attending staff meetings and then getting out of the school and into her car to get to her classes. Peggy enjoyed the modules, but did find them to be less practical and more academic than she would have liked. When asked what spurred her on to do this programme Peggy suggested:

> Partly, I think, again professional, you know. Progression within my career which didn't happen...I supposed I just wanted something additional, an additional interest. My own children had got older and you'd got time to devote your thoughts to something else.[23]

Peggy admitted to finding her MA a struggle but was glad that she persevered.

> I feel quite good about that. I didn't get the degree but I got the Masters. It was important. Having said all of this about not liking these sorts of status symbols, yes, there is a certain status to it...[24]

The idea of having to struggle to achieve a Masters degree, studying part time and trying to fit it around regular teaching duties was something that Cliff Harris also raised. However, for Cliff, he prized not just his own Masters qualification – but the expansion of Masters provision more generally for teachers. He viewed this as representing a real advancement in professional development for teachers.

> I think actually, to be quite honest, I think the Masters programme has had more impact on the profession than anything else. Whereas I think that the Masters thing is something much more subtle in terms of how it kind of changes things, and I think if you've got two or three people in a school on the programme who were talking to each other, then that makes quite a big difference. I think the value of Masters is that you sparked off a curiosity in these people about their practice, sometimes they never thought of and they worked on it and they researched it and they changed their practice through their own research.[25]

Cliff was ambivalent, however, about the meaning and status of degrees in relation to the professionalization of teaching. He himself had worked hard to achieve his own first and higher degrees and recognised that they were important and that they should be recognised and acknowledged.

> I think accreditation is important. I really do. I think it's a kind of recognition of what you've done and I think that is a case that somebody should be rewarded for what they'd done.[26]

However, he was more interested in the process, the higher level thinking, the opportunity for genuine reflection on the theory and practice of teaching afforded by engagement with degree-level work in higher education rather than just the idea of doing a degree for the sake of it. Unlike some of the other participants for whom their graduation had been particularly significant, Cliff reported that he had successfully completed three degrees in his career and never once attended a graduation ceremony, which he associated with pompous elitism.

A number of participants recalled having completed various accredited professional diplomas as an important stimulus for their own professional development. Jim Christophers found his Advanced Diploma in Geography Teaching at the University of Bristol, which he did part-time at weekends, formed a useful grounding in his subsequent Masters level work on professional development. Ann Dodd was also inspired by her classroom experience of working with children with reading difficulties to undertake a specialised course of study and training in the area of Dyslexia. Ann chose to fund her Diploma at the Dyslexia Institute herself. This experience led Ann to embark on a University degree in Psychology as a mature student. This degree took Ann into an entirely different area of teaching - Psychology at Advanced Level, working with post-16 students.

PROFESSIONAL DEVELOPMENT AND THE WIDER PROFESSIONAL COMMUNITY

The idea that professional development could contribute to and strengthen professional communities of teachers working together was something that a number of participants explored. Earlier discussions about impact and the value of teachers coming together and working together support this. This suggests that professional identity could be shaped in relation to engagement with other teachers. For Joy Willoughby, opportunities to meet with other teachers formed a fundamental part of her own professional development.

> Even if it's not so good in terms of content, meeting other professionals, going into other people's schools and talking to people has got to be valuable. You can't just be in a little isolated bubble…[27]

Peggy Jones also stressed the value of relationships with other teachers.

> I don't know whether it's anything to do with professional development or whether it's just feelings, it's the people that you come in contact with particularly who have, who can have a big influence on you. I think a lot of the people that I've worked with and learnt different things from. Like that first supply teacher job that I did, that way of teaching was completely new to me… it was an interesting experience and certainly, they were using it to great effect. I think the only other thing that I would say is that one of the best things that a youngish teacher can do is actually go on supply, because I think you have to learn so quickly and I think the most interesting thing that I observed was that when you go into different schools, and particularly when it was in the days of the National Curriculum and you were all ostensibly teaching the same thing, relatively speaking the same thing - just how different schools are. Just how

very different they are, particularly as a result of the leadership which I know is obviously highlighted very much more these days, but particularly because of the leadership, how very different the atmosphere can be in a school and how that influences the staff and how the staff interact.[28]

Gill Brown also stressed the value of learning from others as part of professional development.

I think various types of training are important and you need, if nothing else, you need to be refreshed. You need to go out there and learn, get other ideas from other people and talk to other people and bring your ideas back. You need that. It's good for you as personal development and the school was quite in favour of that as well so we could all do some of that.[29]

Joy Kell, as a head teacher developed a very clear philosophy of teacher professional development which relied heavily on her staff working together as a community of teachers to share and improve their practice. This involved her dedicating a set amount of time each week to bring staff together to discuss their practice and through these discussions, to consolidate a shared philosophy of teaching and learning.

I had an evening after school, a twilight session on a Thursday, when we would discuss philosophy and where we were going. Sometimes our auxiliaries joined in if appropriate. We were very very much a team with a common philosophy, but we all had different strengths and weaknesses and I didn't want my weaknesses replicated through every classroom. So they were able, within that framework, to develop our general philosophy with different emphases really.[30]

Sue Roberts, as a very young and inexperienced Geography teacher, believed that she benefitted particularly from meeting with other staff in her department and working together with them in the shared ambition of improving their practice.

We did some team teaching and tried things out and we'd decide whether it worked or not and lots of good professional discussion. There were three of us – eventually we became very good friends so we'd meet up anyway and we'd have meals together and so it was like an ongoing conversation generating ideas.[31]

A major catalyst for Sue, as well as a number of other participants, in learning from the wider profession, was the interest and support of more experienced teachers. Sue's head of department, who she described as a '...*really good teacher*' also acted as a '...*really good mentor*' to her and she remembered having learned a lot from him.

I loved it, it was great and I certainly moved on quite rapidly in my understanding of the job as a result of this particular head of department. He was just inspirational really. That was just luck and if you end up with somebody like that I think it's a really good start.[32]

Learning from others, particularly heads of departments, deputy heads and head teachers, who could share their professional expertise or just encourage less experienced teachers towards meeting other people, making connections with local authority advisers and promoting certain opportunities, was an important part of their professional development for a number of participants. Sue Swanson recalled having been '...*taught such a lot, an awful lot...*' by a headteacher in her early days of teaching. Like Sue, Jean Firth felt that she benefited from careful mentoring by her head teacher in her first few years of teaching.

> But the head was extremely interested in us as individuals and sometimes protected us from inspectors and people who were not terribly nice to young teachers. And sometimes she just pushed us forward to meet important people from the authority and to get on courses and things.[33]

BEING A TEACHER, BEING A LEARNER

For a number of participants there was something very important about being a learner and the enjoyment of being a learner, in its broadest sense, which was intimately connected with their professional identity as teachers. Gill Brown captured this idea when she said:

> I think at different stages of your career you want different things and not everybody wants to be stimulated and moved forward but they should because that's what teaching's about. It's about learning isn't it? Never lose the habit of learning.[34]

Gill described herself as a lifelong learner, wholly committed to her own ongoing development and improvement.

> ...otherwise you get stale and you get stuck. I mean I don't think, I very rarely taught the same lesson exactly the same every time because you just get, you want to, maybe my early training always taught me that it's all about development and improving. You can always do it better.[35]

June Rowe reported a similar view:

> I think everywhere you go you pick up something to add to your, well, your progression and profession. You're always learning aren't you?[36]

Joy Willoughby recalled her professional development experiences as being very enjoyable and important to her.

> I always enjoyed...I owe a lot to the in-service training that I did because it was almost part of my social life. I made a lot of friends. I've always done a lot of in-service training because I enjoyed it so much, so it never seemed like a chore to me, quite the reverse really.[37]

For Ann Dodd, her early career involvement London teachers' centres in the late 1960s and early 1970s, where she regularly spent evenings and weekends socializing with other teachers and preparing teaching materials and resources was very much part of her professional identity as a teacher.

> I was still in my early twenties, hadn't got children or anything, John was at work all that time and it was my job. And I liked being a teacher. I liked the whole thing, so it was just part of the job.[38]

Diana Lucas recalled her absolute eagerness to learn as a teacher when she attended the various residential courses that she found so useful and how this somehow nourished and stimulated her personal and professional development and her confidence.

> You'd come out and forget you were the Year Two teacher or whatever. You'd just be yourself and you'd be, you know dying to learn ....[39]

Professional learning as part of being a teacher and as part of a drive to do the job of being a teacher better was also described by some as needing certain elements of fun, passion and joy. Jean Firth, for example, stressed the importance of fun for her learning and for the children she taught.

> So I have had some good opportunities. I mean, I don't know if people get these sorts of opportunities now. I fancy that they might not be as fun. We did have fun and I think you learn and that's how children learn as well. You've got to keep a little bit of fun there haven't you for, to learn.[40]

For Sarah Matthews, time spent on her own professional development was not just enjoyable – it was worth it in terms of difference she felt she could make as a teacher to the children she worked with, regardless of some of the other possible benefits in terms of her career development.

> I gave up my Sundays. Oh dear. Yes, I did, I did. And yes, ok, I never got to be at the dizzy heights I wanted to be, but I still enjoyed it and I still, I've got a lot of people who respect what I've done and so that's great. And a lot of children at the end of the day, I still meet a lot of parents and they come to me and say, 'Thank you for what you did for my children', and that's brilliant.[41]

Joy Kell described how, throughout her career, she had been strongly motivated by her love for what she was doing.

> I loved what I was doing. I felt passionately about it and I tried in every way to improve my own input and help other people. The thing which drove me to stay in it was my passion for it, not because I had to do it and I think that's different.[42]

Joy did, however, describe what she regarded as a fundamental threat to the joy and passion of teaching, brought about by the numerous national initiatives of the 1980s and 1990s.

It just worked, we were all very different and also the thing which I found very sad as my career progressed, teachers stopped or were prevented from having fun because of the weight on change, the volume of change, the degree of change, the endless tick lists that nobody ever read them anyway and I firmly believe in fun and we had fun. Children respond, teachers respond because life is too short not to and we had a lot of fun but we had very high standards, very high.[43]

For Joy, like Sarah above, teachers becoming better teachers through their own professional learning was ultimately all about the children. '… *Everything I ever did was because I wanted to get it better for children and so did teachers.*[44]

Derek Cloke offered a slightly different perspective on teachers as learners, though his ideas still focused on the relationship between teacher learning and benefits for children. He regarded the routine, daily engagement of teachers with their pupils as a fundamental process of professional learning.

The school is an educational unit and among the people learning there are the teachers. Now they don't have a curriculum and course or lessons and all of that, but every time they go into that classroom, when they come out they're different people, something's bound to have changed in them in that three quarters of an hour, and it's that change which is what I was interested in.[45]

The challenge, however, was to ensure that teachers were able to take stock of this learning and to capture it so that it could be recognized as professional learning.

I always thought these teachers dealing with their particular children in school, they were learning things and they were changing as a result of their experience. If they could only specify it, articulate it, define it, then we could qualify it…It's putting your experience into some sort of package and then getting an award for it.[46]

CHAPTER SUMMARY

In this chapter participants' observations on the relationship between their personal and professional development, as part of a holistic development of themselves as teachers, has been presented. The value placed upon externally accredited degree programmes as an important indicator of professional status has also been examined. The idea of being a teacher and being a learner – whether as part of a wider community of professionals, learning from each other, or through a strong personal commitment to learning has also been discussed. The majority of the participants who took part in the oral history interviews were long retired from their formal teaching careers. Nevertheless, it was striking to observe a significant proportion of this cohort, in their retirement, continuing to be involved on a voluntary basis with teaching and learning – either in local educational institutions or in wider community-based projects. Examples of this ranged from continuing to hear children read in the local primary school, serving on school governing bodies, volunteering for adult literacy projects, helping out with costumes and props for local children's drama productions, unpaid private tuition for pupils struggling with their A level revision, working to support young carers as part of a community scheme. For these participants their identity as 'teacher' had not simply disappeared once they had retired. Rather, it was intricately connected with their personal and professional sense of who they were and what they valued in terms of learning. Professional development was very much about personal improvement, about getting better at being a teacher as well as being a learner.

NOTES

[1] BARDA Project 53026, oral history interview with Bill Parkinson, May 2011.
[2] BARDA Project 53026, oral history interview with Joy Willoughby, May 2011.
[3] BARDA Project 53026, oral history interview with June Rowe, May 2011.
[4] BARDA Project 53026, oral history interview with Derek Cloke, May 2011.
[5] BARDA Project 53026, oral history interview with Maureen Fletcher, May 2011.
[6] Ibid.
[7] Ibid.
[8] Ibid.
[9] BARDA Project 53026, oral history interview with Valerie Jenkins, September 2011.
[10] Ibid.
[11] Ibid.
[12] Ibid.
[13] BARDA Project 53026, oral history interview with Ann Dodd, June 2011.
[14] BARDA Project 53026, oral history interview with Valerie Jenkins.
[15] Ibid.
[16] BARDA Project 53026, oral history interview with Cliff Harris (1st interview), April 2011.
[17] BARDA Project 53026, oral history interview with Joy Willoughby, May 2011.
[18] Ibid.
[19] BARDA Project 53026, oral history interview with June Rowe.
[20] BARDA Project 53026, oral history interview with Joy Williams, September 2011.
[21] BARDA Project 53026, oral history interview with Bill Parkinson.
[22] BARDA Project 53026, oral history interview with Gill Brown (p), July 2011.
[23] BARDA Project 53026, oral history interview with Peggy Jones (p), August 2011.
[24] Ibid.
[25] BARDA Project 53026, oral history interview with Cliff Harris (2nd interview), October 2011.
[26] Ibid.
[27] BARDA Project 53026, oral history interview with Joy Willoughby.
[28] BARDA Project 53026, oral history interview with Peggy Jones.
[29] BARDA Project 53026, oral history interview with Gill Brown.
[30] BARDA Project 53026, oral history interview with Joy Kell, May 2011.
[31] BARDA Project 53026, oral history interview with Sue Roberts, March 2011.
[32] Ibid.
[33] BARDA Project 53026, oral history interview with Jean Firth, May 2011.
[34] BARDA Project 53026, oral history interview with Gill Brown.
[35] Ibid.
[36] BARDA Project 53026, oral history interview with June Rowe.
[37] BARDA Project 53026, oral history interview with Joy Willloughby.
[38] BARDA Project 53026, oral history interview with Ann Dodd.

39 BARDA Project 53026, oral history interview with Diana Lucas, May 2011.
40 BARDA Project 53026, oral history interview with Jean Firth.
41 BARDA Project 53026, oral history interview with Sarah Matthews (p), May 2011.
42 BARDA Project 53026, oral history interview with Joy Kell.
43 Ibid.
44 Ibid.
45 BARDA Project 53026, oral history interview with Derek Cloke.
46 Ibid.

CONCLUSION

In 2004, Philip Adey, then a leading contemporary researcher in the field of teacher professional development posed the question, '*Why has the professional development of teachers already exercised so many good minds for so long?*' and argued that the crucial link between educational improvement and the quality of teachers requires constant attention and re-examination because it has never been properly resolved.[1] More recently, Tim Brighouse and Bob Moon, in an excoriating critique of the current state of teacher professional development in England have drawn on studies which have painted a bleak picture of a '*haphazard, poorly planned and poorly assessed*' *system*, '*lacking in any overall coherence*' *and* '*unstrategic, disjointed and erratic*', *desperately in need of some fundamental reform*.[2] Throughout this book the historical narrative of teacher professional development in England and Wales across much of the twentieth century has revealed that though the context in which the various models, opportunities, policies and practices have been played out has been subject to inevitable processes of change over time, there are a number of core themes and challenges which have characterised experiences of professional development for successive generations of teachers. Indeed, such issues remain at the heart of current discourse, research and policy making on teacher professional development in the wider international landscape.[3]

The historical case studies and oral history testimony presented here suggest a substantive variation in the quality of experience and opportunities available for teachers across the century with a very *ad hoc*, highly differentiated and uneven picture emerging. At the same time, however, professional development for teachers was clearly on the professional and policy agenda right from the earliest period under review, though there were fundamental problems with its funding and prioritisation which contributed to a persistent imbalance between supply and demand. This in turn impacted on the reach of professional development, how it was controlled evaluated and valued and which teachers benefited most. The relationship between teachers' professional and personal development was often blurred in practice and how this balance shifted at different periods revealed much about professional expectations and understandings as well as notions of entitlement and need at system level. Arguably a contested history, fraught with inadequacies, this analysis has, however, uncovered some important examples of what might be regarded as successful or constructive practice in which the process of professional development brought teachers together and contributed to the strengthening of the idea of a shared professional community in which professional learning and professional identity were inextricably linked. In drawing together the various strands of professional development examined in the book, this concluding chapter will focus upon three dominant themes and consider them both for their historical significance and in their relationship to current debates in the field: resourcing, control and reach; personal and professional dimensions of professional development for teachers; and professional development and professional identity.

RESOURCE, CONTROL AND REACH

Sandra Gray's comprehensive report on the state of continuing professional development for teachers in England and Wales, published in 2005, drew upon three influential contemporary research studies[4]: a 2003 EPPI report on the impact of collaborative professional development on classroom teaching and learning[5]; MacBeath and Galton's book *A Life in Secondary Teaching*, published in 2004[6]; and Soulsby and Swain's 2003 report to the Teacher Development Agency on accredited and award-bearing continuing professional development for teachers in England.[7] This work was able to identify what evidence-based models and forms of teacher professional development were considered to be most effective for improved teacher learning and impact on pupil learning in a twentieth-century educational context. These included professional development that is collaborative, classroom-based and research-informed. However, they argued that there was a real gulf between ideals and reality for most teachers. Gray described a highly complex, unregulated, diverse and chaotic picture of teacher professional development, and found it impossible to undertake any meaningful national audit of provision or teacher engagement. She cited a MORI survey undertaken almost a decade earlier in 1995, which had uncovered a very similar picture.[8] For Gray, the nub of the problem was systemic, with a lack of sustained long-term investment in teachers' learning, skills and professionalism. Christopher Day and Judyth Sachs, in their extensive research on the discourse, politics, policies and processes of continuing professional development of teachers internationally, have identified very similar issues. They have argued that in spite of increasingly bureaucratised and centralised control of teacher professional development, with greater accountability where considerable investment has been made by governments, some of this investment has been misplaced because it does not properly relate either to the professional needs of teachers or to school improvement – and it, *'serves the interests of some groups better than others'*.[9] Brighouse and Moon have argued that in England '...*on resources in general, the situation is opaque, verging on chaotic*', with many schools not having a professional development budget and thousands of teachers unable to access what disparate resources are available.[10] These current concerns have a long historical legacy. Drawing together the different historical strands examined in this book, a very strong theme which characterised the whole period under review concerned the difficult relationship between available resource, which was limited, lack of systemic planning and the associated take-up of professional development opportunities by teachers.

Any accurate quantification of teacher engagement in centrally funded as well as other types of professional development provision has eluded generations of civil servants and researchers, with Gray's 2005 report representing a more recent manifestation of a deeply entrenched problem. Various surveys were conducted over the years, but there was never total confidence that the true volume of activity had been captured. In the mid-1960s when the Department was seeking to develop an expanded and more coherent strategy for in-service training, there was no record of how many courses were being organised across the country – just a sense that something urgent needed to be done.[11] A report to a Council of Europe seminar on in-service training in 1966, suggested that '...*an analysis of the total participation of teachers in courses is simply not possible.*'[12] By the early 1980s the matter remained unresolved, when a series of parliamentary questions on spending on teacher education noted that '...*apart from these occasional surveys the Department has no complete information about the volume of in-service training.*'[13] Whilst it is possible to pinpoint some numerical data at different stages in the development of provision and to arrive at approximate estimates of numbers of teachers participating at any one time, the overall picture is patchy and riddled with gaps and inaccuracies. However, in spite of these difficulties, it is possible to demonstrate two very clear and pronounced characteristics of in-service provision. These were the low numbers of teachers attending courses, relative to the whole teaching population; and constant problems with unfulfilled demand and oversubscription of available programmes.

In an attempt to address the challenge of identifying just how many teachers were attending in-service courses, data was plotted from annual Board of Education reports, together with statistics on annual cohorts of teachers to generate some understanding of the numbers of teachers involved.[14] The result, whilst using existing material in a new way, reflects the partial and fragmented nature of the figures given in the primary reports, reflecting some of the methodological challenges of engaging with quantitative sources identified by economic historian, Vincent Carpentier.[15] In the inter-war period, for example, the Board of Education recorded the numbers attending short full-time courses, such as vacation courses, and the numbers attending part-time courses, though full figures are not available for the years before 1927. A gap in the data for the eight years, 1938–1946, reflects the upheaval of war. After the war, the presentation of statistics changed, meaning that it is not possible to fully compare like-for-like with the 1920s and 1930s. It has only been possible to work with the material that was collected and collated at the time and it is not possible, for example, to say whether each case of a teacher taking part in courses recorded in these statistics was a different teacher or whether some teachers might have attended more than one course, either Board or LEA-focussed, in the same year. It is also not possible to determine from the information available what percentage of the teaching workforce was absent from school at one particular time attending in-service training courses. Nevertheless, this is still a useful exercise in building a clearer picture of the volume of teacher participation and also in raising questions about patterns of teacher engagement. The figures below show the recorded numbers for:

1. Teachers taking part in courses (organised by the Board of Education and LEAs) compared to total numbers of teachers, 1927–1938.
2. Teachers attending Ministry of Education courses and LEA courses, 1947–1957.
3. Numbers of men and women teachers attending in-service training courses (organised by the Board and LEAs) versus the total numbers of men and women teachers in public elementary and grant maintained secondary schools, 1927–1938.
4. Men and women teachers attending LEA courses versus total numbers of men and women teachers, 1947–1957.
5. Teachers attending various types of in-service training, 1964–1975.

It is interesting to note an almost steady pattern of engagement across the period under review, the obvious attrition of the war years aside, with a maximum of only two per cent annually, a tiny minority of the national cohort of teachers, participating in centrally organised in-service provision from the 1920s to the mid-1960s. A paper on professional development in the mid-1960s suggested that out of a total of 325,274 serving teachers in maintained schools eligible to take part in professional

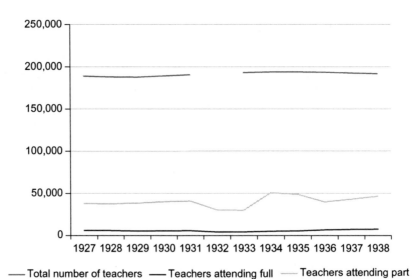

Figure 1. Teachers taking part in courses (organised by the Board of Education and LEAs) compared to total numbers of teachers, 1927–1938.

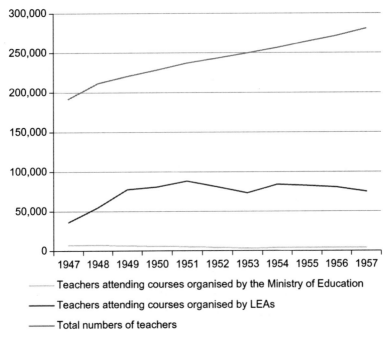

*Figure 2. Teachers attending Ministry of Education courses and LEA courses,
1947–1957.*

development courses, very small numbers were actually involved. Given a split
between a wide variety of opportunities at national, regional, area and local level,
it was reported that at this time only 6,000 teachers were taking part in nationally
organised courses.[16] This figure is slightly under 2% of the teacher workforce. Any
estimate of teacher engagement with professional development has to be treated
carefully as national-level reporting would not necessarily reflect the whole
spectrum of activity at local level, through voluntary organisations, in universities
and professional subject associations. By the early 1970s, the government was
still unclear as to the exact numbers of teachers engaging with central and locally
provided in-service training. A further concern was the extent to which existing
provision matched current demand. On 1 November 1973, the DES issued a press
notice endorsing its commitment to increasing in-service training courses for
teachers, promising an immediate 50% increase in one-term courses for 1974/5 and
a 20% increase in one-year courses. As part of the consultation and debate leading
to the publication of the White Paper, 'Education: A Framework for Expansion' in
1974, the main proposals for expansion included an ambition to aim for a 3% release
of the teaching workforce at any one time in the school year by 1981.[17]

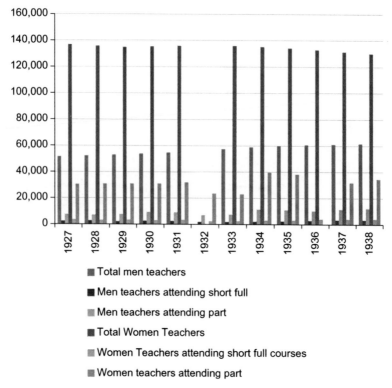

■ Total men teachers

■ Men teachers attending short full

▨ Men teachers attending part

■ Total Women Teachers

▨ Women Teachers attending short full courses

▨ Women teachers attending part

Figure 3. Numbers of men and women teachers attending in-service training courses (organised by the Board and LEAs) versus the total numbers of men and women teachers in public elementary and grant maintained secondary schools, 1927–1938.

Resource

It is difficult to trace accurately and cumulatively exact details on the annual expenditure by the Education Department on teacher professional development. However, what is clear from the patchy evidence available is that this expenditure was the source of much negotiation and wrangling between civil servants for Education and those in the Treasury for the whole period under review. Though we know from Carpentier's research that educational expenditure as a proportion of all public expenditure grew during the twentieth century, with varying spurts and troughs, depending on wider economic prosperity, the picture for targeted spending on teacher professional development is not clear cut.[18] The Education Department had continuously to justify its expenditure on this area of work and make good cases for increased spending. The impression given from the often terse exchanges noted in letters between the Treasury and Education Department

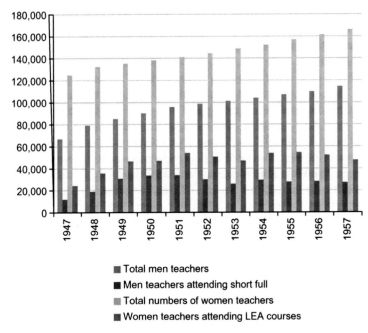

Figure 4. Men and women teachers attending LEA courses versus total numbers of men and women teachers, 1947–1957.

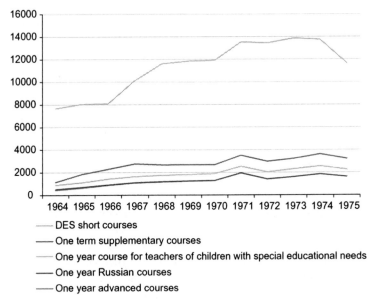

Figure 5. Teachers attending various types of in-service training, 1964–1975.

177

was that funding for in-service provision was highly restricted and given low priority and that wherever possible savings and cost-cutting measures had to be made, even if these required teachers to subsidise their attendance at courses out of their own pocket.

Aldrich, Crook and Watson's study of the Board of Education and its relationship with the Treasury, as well as local authorities, supports these findings about long-standing disputes over funding and responsibility for teacher professional development.[19] An illustration of this tension can be found in one of the earliest records of provision. In 1912 the Treasury sanctioned, for the first time, funding for short courses. However, the Board of Education was required to reapply for funding every year, with no formal entitlement to an established budget, which made forward planning difficult. In 1917 the Board of Education wanted to develop a series of gardening courses for teachers, at a time of national food shortage. This generated considerable debate on the nature and amount of the government grant that should be allowed for this purpose, right down to the fine detail of supporting teachers' travel to and from the course.[20] Another example can be found in a 1924 attempt by the Treasury to withdraw all funding for Board of Education short courses, arguing that provision should be at the discretion of LEAs and that it should also be left to individual teachers to meet the costs of their own in-service training. The Board of Education, already subject to budget cuts in preceding years due to the impact of 'Geddes' axe', vehemently resisted this attempt as a false economy, whilst also taking the opportunity to push for grant-aid recognition of short courses to be made a permanent part of its provision, with free tuition for teachers and £1.00 per week maintenance.[21] There were fears that without a proper fully-funded model of provision, teachers would not engage with the short courses and would not be willing to find themselves out of pocket.

Within this longstanding deficit funding model, was an assumption that teachers should make a financial contribution. This could either be through paying for travel, accommodation or maintenance costs or through the use of their own time, unpaid, outside of normal working hours, during evenings, weekends and holidays. An illustration of the challenges raised by this expectation can be found in a 1937 resolution to the Board of Education from the Association of Teachers in Technical Institutions which argued that courses were not attracting younger teachers or married men because of the additional burden of costs to participants. Whilst the courses were free, '....*Teachers have to give up some of their holiday or dip into their own pockets to meet the cost of fares and maintenance.*'[22] The popular vacation courses discussed in Chapter Three, though often partially subsidised by local authorities, were reliant on teachers paying fairly substantive contributions towards costs, either for maintenance, travel or course fees. Advanced courses for experienced teachers were developed during the 1950s and '...*in fixing the maintenance grant for these courses the Ministry intended that the teacher should make some financial sacrifice in order to take a course, particularly in view of the better prospects which satisfactory completion of it would give him.*'[23]

Assumptions about the ability of teachers to personally subsidise their attendance at courses carried particular implications for women. First, it was assumed that unmarried women teachers could well afford to subsidise their attendance at courses, as they had no dependants, unlike their married male counterparts. Secondly, where tuition and maintenance support was on offer, as for special advanced courses for serving teachers, maintenance was means tested to include a consideration of any additional household income beyond the teacher's salary from her husband's wages.[24] An illustration of this can be found in a letter from the Treasury to the Board of Education in July 1924 which argued that '...*teachers now receive very good salaries. The majority are women, and though these are no doubt gradually getting over their embarrassment at the amount of money dealt out to them, they should easily be able to pay the expenses of courses of instruction which improve their market value...The teachers must be fully alive to the financial benefit to them of improving their qualifications.*'[25] The barriers faced by women seeking to access professional development opportunities were an extension of those they encountered in other areas of their work during this period.[26] The tradition that teachers should be expected to contribute to the cost of keeping themselves up-to-date, persisted throughout the 1960s, and this argument was used against any proposal to incentivise teachers through full funding. During the late 1960s and early 1970s HMI conducted a series of surveys on regional provision of in-service training. Ongoing issues about inadequate resourcing and the need for teachers to dig into their own pockets and make financial and time-based contributions remained unresolved and were raised time and again in reports.[27] At the heart of this assumption, that it was the professional duty of teachers to subsidise their own professional betterment, lay a fundamental problem which continues to vex the enterprise to this day – the reluctance of the less enthusiastic, time-pressed and vulnerable teacher to engage with professional development activity. Emergent patterns of professional development really only supported those teachers who were keen, willing and able to afford the associated financial or time costs. The oral history testimony presented in Part Three suggests that for a number of teachers, there remained tradition of '...*beg, borrow or steal*', in relation to accessing funding for professional development courses, though by the 1980s and 1990s, grant-related professional development, funded by government, was perceived to be very generous.[28]

Control

In a context of relatively low participation and limited resource, it is perhaps not surprising that the Department sought to keep very tight control of any centrally organised professional development activity. This control encompassed all aspects of provision, from the selection and monitoring of candidates, decisions about course content and pedagogy and inspection of provision. HMI were the lynchpin of this central control and acted as valuable mediators between central government and local authorities. Communication between the hierarchy of Inspectors, from

Senior Chief Inspectors, to Divisional HMI down to District HMI was important and enabled a close monitoring of provision. From the early days, HMI played a key role in the selection of teachers for courses. They were expected to select strong candidates who, '...*in order to be eligible, should show marked promise and should have enough knowledge of their subject and experience in teaching it to make it clear that they can profit by observing and holding intercourse with more experienced teachers.*'[29] A memorandum on short courses in 1928 illustrates the critical role played by HMI.[30] Once a course had been approved by a Senior Chief Inspector and funding agreed, the Divisional Inspector of an area would take on responsibility for instruction on these courses and became the 'Director of Studies', though they could draw on the assistance of external lecturers if necessary. Any funded courses had stringent selection criteria, involving the close involvement of HMI in the identification and selection of candidates and the follow-up of candidates once back in school. Special care was taken to ensure that the 'right' kind of candidate was chosen for the courses, including short courses, weekend and vacation courses and the longer advanced courses; and teachers were selected by District Inspectors in consultation with LEAs and finally approved by the centre. A note to Inspectors in 1938, on short courses for teachers, advised that '...*in selecting teachers for recommendation to the Board ... only those teachers should be considered whose work would directly benefit by a Course of the kind proposed. What is aimed at is the bringing together of a body of teachers who may under the stimulus of the Course return to their schools with a new orientation and a richer equipment.*'[31] Right from the start the idea that already strong practitioners were best placed to receive further training so they might influence their less able colleagues was prevalent.

Inspectors were keen to examine the longer-term impact of courses on teachers. For example, an inspection report on Derby Vacation Course in the early 1920s suggested that '...*the success of this course is beyond question, and the effects upon the schools from which the teachers are drawn have doubtless been most useful.*'[32] Inspectors of Welsh courses in the 1920s were encouraged to '...*do something in the way of following up the teachers who have already had the advantage of attending the Courses, and seeing whether they are profiting by the suggestions given by the Courses and are putting to practical use the knowledge they have gained at them.*'[33]

In the post-1945 period, there was some recognition that teachers should be made to feel more involved with the process, with discussion about the 'broader appeal' of the courses on offer, pedagogical approaches which allowed for discussions and more practical work. Changes to the recruitment policy were also introduced, which allowed teachers to apply but still left the decision-making on acceptance to HMI, in consultation with LEAs. The idea that some control should be ceded to the teachers was more widely accepted by the late 1960s, though was still contested. It was argued that '...*increasingly teachers are being given a "doing-role", as opposed to a "listening-only role" on courses.*'[34] This shift in emphasis possibly also reflected more liberal approaches to pedagogy and curriculum which characterised the discourse in the wider education system at this time. At a time when it was considered a matter of urgency that the profession should be updated in new knowledge, curriculum developments and school organisation, it was recognised that those teachers who had previously been overlooked in the narrow processes of central selection needed to be drawn in. By this time there was growing recognition that in-service training could not just be the reserve of the able and privileged few – but needed to reach out to the whole profession.

Reach

Against such an entrenched background of inadequate funding, limited places on courses and tight regulation and control, it is perhaps not surprising that provision across the period under review was the preserve of a very particular type of teacher. This teacher was specially chosen and deemed worthy and deserving of additional professional development. Various reports and memos in the archives interrogated for this book reflect the use of some interesting descriptive language by HMI and policy-makers which, though confined to a relatively restricted range of primary sources, does offer an evocative perspective on how this model teacher might have been perceived and constructed. Described as 'chosen'[35], 'cream' and 'elite'[36], 'high calibre'[37], and 'missionary'[38] this model teacher underpinned a powerful ideology of excellence mixed with one of salvation. This allowed a limited resource to be maximised because it invested in the ideal model teacher the responsibility for improving the rank and file of the profession. From the early 1920s teachers were selected who would '... *make their own enthusiasm felt in the schools.*'[39] The regeneration of refresher courses in the post-1945 period planned for selected teachers to be ambassadors – returning from Ministry courses and setting up local conferences to share new knowledge and ideas, '...*to aid in making the knowledge and experience necessary for the successful handling of the teaching more quickly available to fellow teachers.*'[40] Special advanced courses for experienced teachers were explicitly designed to improve leadership in the profession, disseminate good practice and to generate new teacher educators, and were regarded as the 'crown' of the service.[41] Discussions about in-service training within the Ministry of Education in the early 1960s were explicit about the need to build up a spearhead of staff able to provide refreshment for other teachers, through the development of high level courses for the very best teachers. These teachers were very much positioned against the '...*so many indifferent teachers...*' and it was hoped that the general quality of teaching would be impacted by an investment in excellence.[42]

This model was not unproblematic. Aside from being overtly elitist, it also contained certain contradictions about the ideal teacher for investment. In addition to exhibiting the rather altruistic and pure qualities ascribed above, the successful teachers were often also ambitious for their own career development, and attendance at courses was regarded as an important vehicle for promotion. There was, however, some reservation about the overt use of courses for promotion purposes, as though this were rather sordid. For example, in the late 1940s, when advanced courses were being set up in the universities, the motivation of potential applicants was thoroughly questioned – and those interested only in promotion rather than being true 'educationists' were regarded as potentially 'dangerous' – yet, ironically, at the same time these very courses were being developed so as to generate leadership and access to higher positions in teacher education.[43] Of course bright, ambitious and 'keen' teachers, willing to sacrifice their own time and income, would logically be ideal candidates for selection on courses, and would also be the very type of teachers likely to be promoted within the profession. This idea that teachers attending courses might be tainted with ruthless ambition, set apart from the wider population of teachers warrants further investigation, as do more general links between career promotion and in-service training, perceived or real. Some of the oral history participants described what they regarded as the 'professional course goers', those teachers who were part of an elite group within a local authority context who had either been selected or who had put themselves forward to be groomed for school leadership positions.

Another fundamental problem with this elite ideology is that it did not ultimately reach the very teachers who really most needed additional support. By the early-1960s it was becoming obvious that it was all very well targeting resource at the keen and willing enthusiast, the already excellent teacher – but this was doing nothing, in the words of the Ministry, '...*to attract the inferior and apathetic teacher*.'[44] The evocative language used to describe the 'model' teacher in a selection of primary sources described above, was also reflected in the starkly contrasting language found in government memos from the early 1960s, which described the 'lame ducks', the 'less enthusiastic', 'inferior', 'uninspired', 'un-enterprising' and 'less distinguished' members of the profession.[45] A Ministry meeting to discuss in-service provision in Science, Mathematics and English in December 1961 reported, 'Not much was done at present to attract the inferior or apathetic teacher.'[46] An unpublished discussion paper entitled 'The Professional Development of Teachers During Their Service' neatly captured the problem; '...*not only is too little spent on courses and too small a proportion of teachers enabled to attend them....they have the inherent disadvantage that they attract those teachers whose need for further professional development is least pressing – those who are already keen, in touch, and anxious to find out more*.'[47] No longer could the business of teacher professional development be left to the select core of able, dedicated professionals, willing to pay their own expenses, give up their holidays, and sacrifice their own time. No longer could this special group be expected to reach out and 'save' their colleagues – the bulk of the profession which, in a rapidly expanding system and changing professional landscape, was apparently found wanting. Discussions about incentivising teachers, addressing the financial inadequacies, removing obstacles, and relying less on good-will and personal sacrifice began to challenge established assumptions about which teachers should be involved with professional development opportunities, who should benefit from them and the very purpose of the endeavour. Judging by a number of government-commissioned studies in England in recent years, it is clear that this extended reach has never been fully managed or properly integrated at system level. As a bare minimum, teachers in England, for the last two decades, have been required as part of their working conditions to attend five compulsory in-service training days per year. The oral history testimony presented in Part Three indicated a fairly widespread dislike of these compulsory days, with dubious quality and impact reported which is similarly reflected in a series of formal reports by Ofsted as well as key research studies.[48] Day and Leith's research, for example, found that much of what happens in the formal five days is very closely connected with the delivery of national government strategies, with a formulaic transmission 'scripted' model of delivery.[49] What happens outside of this requirement remains a very mixed picture, as described in Opfer and Pedder's influential "state of the nation" study of teacher professional development in England, commissioned by the Training Development Agency in 2009, which found that on the whole professional development is largely down to the motivation and interest of individual teachers.[50] The English five day requirement is on average ten days fewer than the international average identified by the OECD in its 2008 TALIS 'Teaching and Learning International Survey', in which twenty eight countries participated.[51] In this study over half of the teachers surveyed considered their professional development opportunities to be inadequate and not to be meeting their professional learning needs. The reach of teacher professional development continues to thwart the endeavour and as Brighouse and Moon argue, this is because '...governments, from as far back as the well-received James report in 1971, have just not been good at following through from advocacy to the creation of realistic implementation strategies.'[52] Devolved funding from central government to local authorities and more recently to individual schools has added further complexity and differentiation to this picture. This book shows that a fundamental failure on the part of successive governments to follow through idealistic aims and ambitions to create a systemic fully-resourced entitlement, or mandatory requirement, for all teachers to career-long professional development can be traced as far back as the 1925 Departmental Committee. This possibly says as much about the contested history of teaching being perceived and valued as a profession than anything else – a subject outside of the scope of this book, but one that has been addressed elsewhere by a number of other authors.[53]

Thus far, in drawing together past and more recent perspectives on the state of teacher professional development, a picture has emerged of a structure and a process fraught with inadequacies. Nevertheless, both this historical analysis as well as more current research does also suggest some more positive and beneficial aspects of teacher professional development, which make its pursuit worthwhile and which serve to strengthen teacher professional identity, status and impact. From the historical research this focuses on the importance of the relationship between professional and personal development and the relationship between professional development and professional communities of practice.

PROFESSIONAL AND PERSONAL DEVELOPMENT

The historical analysis in this book has suggested that professional development for teachers was closely bound up with personal development, with the professional and personal boundaries and motivations for learning often difficult to distinguish. Much current discourse on teacher professional development suggests that the top-down, politically driven professional development agendas of the last two decades have tipped the balance between meeting professional and personal development needs too far away from the personal, with system and school-level needs being prioritised at the expense of individual teacher need.[54] This perceived imbalance in focus and priority has also been played out against arguments that teaching, on the one hand, has been subject to a deliberate de-professionalisation and, on the other, to a different kind of re-professionalisation agenda.[55] This has raised important questions about what kind of professionalism for teachers is fit for purpose in the twenty-first century, with researchers such as Judyth Sachs and Nicole Mockler arguing for new forms of democratic professionalism to counter what they see as the prevailing model of managerial professionalism.[56] Significantly, these current discourses about new models of teacher professionalism have at their very heart the idea that teacher professional learning is critical for any professional transformation.

In evaluating the history of teacher professional development in England it is important to recognise that some of the earlier forms of professional development – the 'refresher courses', vacation courses and even the paid secondments to undertake formal periods of study, were intended, in part, to go some way to compensate for inadequacies both in the general education of teachers prior to them becoming teachers and also in their initial training, as well as to respond to social and technological changes which might impact on curriculum and pedagogy. The long shadow of apprenticeship training for would-be elementary teachers which had characterised the nineteenth and early twentieth-century expansion of the state education machinery, combined with the tendency for elementary teachers both to be drawn from the same social class background as their pupils and to be predominantly female, contributed to a powerful status anxiety for the emergent profession of school teaching, which has been widely discussed elsewhere.[57] Teaching was not an all-graduate profession until the 1970s. Whilst teachers in the independent and grammar schools would have been educated to degree level at the very least, the majority of teachers in elementary/primary and secondary modern/comprehensive schools would have remained in formal education themselves until the age of eighteen years and then undertaken a two or three year period of teacher training at a training college. In the first half of the twentieth century, there were real concerns about the narrowness of outlook and experience of elementary school teachers in particular, which would have been compounded by working in isolated rural communities where opportunities to engage with wider social, cultural and educational activities would have been limited. As discussed in Chapter Two, early provision of 'refresher courses' for teachers by the Board of Education in the 1920s was specifically targeted at teachers regarded as vulnerable to being isolated and cut off not just from other members of their profession but also new ideas and developments. Milestone government reports on teacher professional development, also discussed in Chapter Two, successively revisited the idea that teachers needed to be refreshed and invigorated on a regular basis – with a combined objective of ensuring that teachers were kept updated on subject knowledge and pedagogic skills together with a commitment to ensuring that they were stimulated at a personal level. The James Report was explicit in its recommendation that teachers should be able to extend their personal education and experience whilst at the same time improving their professional skills and understanding.

In Chapter Four the implications for the vacation course model in relation to attitudes and understandings of teacher professionalism at that time in the 1920s and 1930s was examined. It was suggested that the vacation course model embodied a merging of the personal and the professional to generate something quite important for those teachers involved – the potential creation of new forms of professional understanding, identity and community. This idea was revisited again in Chapter Six with the discussion of the teachers' centres in the 1960s and 1970s. Though *ad hoc* and hugely varied there is clear evidence that for some teachers, teachers' centres became a highly valued focus for professional identity and community. They were places of professional learning but also brought teachers together for wider social and cultural engagement.

Oral history testimony presented in Part Three revealed some interesting insights into perceptions of professional and personal learning. Informal professional learning involving extended discussions with colleagues outside of work and in social settings was not uncommon and suggests a blurring of the personal and professional in the experiences of some teachers. The idea that professional development could be part of a more holistic all-round development of the teacher which involved personal enjoyment and would benefit both the teacher and their teaching was widely discussed by participants. In Chapter Eight various examples of how teachers explicitly described the close connections between their personal interests and even 'hobbies' and their professional development were presented. Joy Willoughby's reflections capture this commitment to the idea of joined-up, holistic development when she said, '...*I feel I've been really privileged to have the professional development that I have because I don't think it's just developed me professionally, it has developed me as a person, as a whole person.*'[58] Ann Dodd, reflecting on the amount of time she spent voluntarily at her local teachers' centre in the early 1970s, either on formal courses or just mixing socially with other teachers in the community, considered this to be just '...*part of the job*'.[59]

Historically, teacher professional learning has had a strong personal dimension which may have been lost in more recent years. This historical analysis would suggest that the personal for teachers at different times could have multiple meanings and emphases with blurred boundaries between personal and professional. For example, it could relate to personal learning through advanced study at a university or college; it could be an extension of personal interests or hobbies; it could be about personal refreshment and reinvigoration through social contact with other teachers and education professionals. It is significant that current research has identified that the 'personal' and possibly the 'professional' dimensions of teacher professional development has been overshadowed with national initiatives, school and pupil-level improvement priorities dominating the agenda. This critique of a 'centre-periphery' or 'top-down' perspective on teacher professional development views teachers as having no real personal or professional ownership of their own learning – something very undermining and damaging for the profession.[60] In 2007, *Teachers Matter: Connecting Lives, Work and Effectiveness*, was published to present findings from a large research project initiated by the then Department for Education and Science. The VITAE project, 'Variations in Teachers' Work, Lives and their Effects on Pupils', amongst many other things, sought to fundamentally relocate teachers, *'...right back into the centre of the equation and in this act of moral re-centring hopes to reinvigorate an educational enterprise which at the moment seems to be too often unfocused and unfulfilling for the teaching force...'*[61] Significantly, this study also highlighted the complex interaction between teachers' personal and professional lives and argued strongly for a need for a better recognition of this if the educational reform agenda was to be reconceptualised and revisioned to succeed. It is hoped that this longer historical perspective might inform some of the current debates and theorising around teachers' professional lives and identities.

PROFESSIONAL LEARNING AND PROFESSIONAL IDENTITY

Related to the idea discussed above, that teacher professional development is closely bound up with personal development and identity, was the importance both of formal and informal professional development experiences to the formation of communities of practice between teachers. This was a consistent theme running throughout the historical analysis, right from the early years of the vacation courses in the 1920s and 1930s, through to the valuing of teachers' centres by teachers in the 1960s and 1970s, and in the testimony of oral history participants.

In Chapter Two, some of the early Board of Education organised courses for rural elementary school teachers were discussed, where there was a deliberate intention built into their development to provide opportunities for those teachers most at risk of professional isolation to meet with other colleagues and to simply exchange ideas about their teaching. During the 1920s and 30s this focus on courses as facilitating and supporting discussions and exchanges of ideas between teachers continued to be strong and was viewed as an important element of the rationale for expanding professional development opportunities. The elaborate social and cultural programmes which formed a core component of vacation courses for teachers, discussed in detail in Chapter Three, and echoed again in the preference expressed by oral history participants for intensive residential programmes, suggest that professional networking was an important part of the overall experience. In

Chapter Five, the role that teachers' centres played in creating formal and informal opportunities for teachers to meet and share their experiences was highlighted as a particular feature of the teachers' centre model. In Chapter Eight some of the perspectives of oral history participants on the value of professional development in strengthening professional identity and communities of teachers working together were presented.

Rather as the relationship between professional and personal development and how this might be experienced by teachers had multiple meanings and a certain amorphous quality in the historical narrative, so too was the idea of professional development, professional identity and the formation of professional networks and communities of practice. Indeed, it could be argued that bringing teachers together in groups to experience different forms of professional development would inevitably lead to an exchange of ideas, discussions about practice and a shared sense of purpose and identity – that this would be an entirely natural part of the process. In Chapter Four, some of the historical debates around teacher professionalism and how this might have been to some degree externally engineered through the different kinds of social and cultural expectations placed upon teachers, exemplified in the vacation course model, as 'top-down', rather than organic and 'bottom-up', were examined. It was suggested that professional development for teachers in the 1920s and 1930s could be interpreted as having been specifically designed to help shape a new form of teacher professionalism and identity, which served the ideological aspirations of the political establishment for teaching to be a distinctive form of civic service. It was also argued that such an interpretation might be deemed rather narrow, given that so many teachers both voluntarily participated in, benefited from and clamoured for more professional development opportunities and experiences than were readily available. As demonstrated earlier in this chapter, across the whole period under review, supply was never able to meet demand. There is also strong evidence to suggest that across the different chronological phases identified in this book, there was a consistent proportion of the teaching force which sought out, enjoyed and actively engaged in continuing to develop their professional expertise and identity through professional development opportunities. Historically, the relationship between teacher professionalism, identity and professional development was clearly highly complex and subject to an iterative dynamic of political and personal force.

More recent theories of social and professional learning both resonate with and offer some useful frameworks for making sense of this aspect of the long historical tradition uncovered in this book. In 2004, reflecting on his many years of experience of working with teachers on in-service courses, Philip Adey recalled, '...*the best experiences that teachers have in in-service courses is talking with other teachers.... they learned far much more from each other than they ever did from us.*'[62] Adey's emergent model of teacher professional development had at its heart the idea that teacher professional learning should be collegial and social, '...*it seems clear that teachers' concepts about the nature of teaching and learning will be heavily influenced by the type of 'mutual sharing and assistance' they encounter, and that in a positively collegial atmosphere there will be safe opportunities for reflection and so an increased chance of building new strategies into intuitive practice.*[63] Etienne Wenger's well-regarded work on professional 'communities of practice' has argued that teaching is a social profession and that engagement in social practice is the fundamental process by which teachers learn and achieve a sense of professional identity.[64] Wenger's five-dimensional model of professional identity which brings together the social, cultural and political aspects of identity formation for teachers has contributed to the reconceptualization of teacher professional development by other researchers in the field.[65] This reconceptualization describes the potential for teacher professional development and teacher professional learning to be transformative in such a way that it can bring coherence to those potentially competing dimensions of personal development, professional development and educational reform which have characterised more recent history.

This book began with a brief outline of current international debate on the primacy of teacher professional development as a lever for educational reform and suggested that this is a complex and contested field. The 'problem' of teacher professional development – its funding, its purpose, its content and focus, and most importantly its reach to the whole profession remains unresolved and continues to exercise researchers and policy-makers across the world. In drawing this historical analysis to a close, this chapter has examined a number of key themes and considered them both for their historical significance and in their relationship to current debates in the field. It has been argued that the twentieth- century history of teacher professional development in England and Wales, though delivering certain notable examples of excellence, particularly for the individual teachers involved, can broadly be characterised as a history of unfulfilled promise, ongoing problems of underfunding and scarce resource and incoherence. This historical analysis has suggested that successive governments have paid lip-service to the idea that a teaching profession needs and requires continuous renewal to maintain both professional and personal standards and quality – as something not just reserved for a small elite group, but for all teachers. With a dominant focus on initial teacher preparation, supply and demand, there has been an inadequate conceptualisation of career-long teacher professional development at the political level and at the level of policy.

At the current juncture, looking both backwards and forwards, what contribution might this book offer to existing research and theory around teacher professional development and to current research imperatives for a major redefining of the field?[66] First, it can be argued that in this field where there is such a dearth of detailed historical analysis, there is scope to better understand the evolution of the current 'problem' of teacher professional development through a more focussed historical lens. Secondly, it can be argued that some of the historical constructions and meanings associated with teacher professionalism and teacher professional development might enrich wider historical and understandings of this highly complex dynamic. One of the important questions arising from this historical analysis is whether the limited reach of professional development was caused just by inadequate funding and therefore limited opportunity – or whether there were more complex patterns of professional resistance and self-selection, with certain groups or 'types' of teachers identifying with dominant discourses of professional development and others excluding themselves, or even being excluded. More research is needed to probe these questions further – and ideally should incorporate comparative historical studies of the evolution of teacher professional development in other countries. Thirdly, it can be argued that some of the organising concepts developed throughout the book to examine models and ideologies of professional development for teachers may prove suggestive for a historical analysis of professional development amongst other professions.

NOTES

[1] Adey, P. (2004). *The professional development of teachers: Practice and theory*. Dordrecht: Kluwer Academic Publishers. pp. 2–3.

[2] Brighouse, T., & Moon, B. (2013). '*Taking teacher development seriously: A proposal to establish a National Teaching Institute for Teacher Professional Development in England*'. London, UK: New Visions for Education Group.

[3] Little, J. (2003). 'Professional development in a climate of educational reform', *Educational Evaluation and Policy Analysis*, 15, pp. 129–151.

[4] Gray, S. (2005). *An enquiry into continuing professional development for report*. London, UK: Esmee Fairburn Foundation.

[5] Cordingley, P., Bell, M., Rundell, B., & Evans, D. (2003). '*The impact of collaborative CPD on classroom teaching and learning*'. London, UK: Research Evidence in Education Library, EPPI-Centre. See also a more recent report in Cordingley, P., & Bell, M. (2012). '*Understanding what enables high quality professional learning: a report on the research evidence*'. London, UK: Centre for the Use of Research Evidence in Education (CUREE): Pearson School Improvement.

[6] MacBeath, J., & Galton, M. (2004). *A life in secondary teaching: Finding time for learning*. Cambridge: National Union of Teachers.

[7] Soulsby, D., & Swain, D. (2003). '*A Report on the Award-bearing INSET Scheme*'. London, UK: Training and Development Agency, Department for Education and Science.

[8] Market and Opinion Research International (MORI). (1995). *Survey of continuing professional development*. London, UK: MORI.

[9] Day, C., & Sachs, J. (2004). *International handbook on the continuing professional development of teachers*. Maidenhead: Open University Press. P. 27.

[10] Brighouse and Moon, *'Taking teacher development seriously'*, p. 1.

[11] The UK National Archives (hereafter TNA), ED 86/379, memo by C.H.B on 'The Suggested Programme of Action on In-service Training, 2 April 1965.

[12] TNA, ED 86/380, Report for England for a Council of Europe Seminar on Further (In-Service) Training of Teachers, 12–19 August 1966.

[13] TNA, ED34/235, Sir Thomas McNally: To ask the Secretary of State for Education and Science what was the total expenditure on: (a) in-service training and (b) initial teacher training in England in each of the past five years, Nov 15th 1982.

[14] The statistics used to compile the figures presented in this paper have been collated from the Annual Reports of the Board of Education, the Ministry of Education and the Department for Education and Science, issued between 1927 and 1965: these are available as House of Commons Command Papers. For the period 1966–1975, the statistics used here were collated from annual volumes of *Statistics of Education* (London: HMSO, 1966–1976).

[15] Carpentier, V. (2008). 'Quantitative sources for the history of education', *History of Education, 37*(5), pp. 701–720.

16 TNA, ED 86/380, Report for England for a Council of Europe Seminar on Further (In-Service) Training of Teachers, 12–19 August 1966.
17 DES, *Teacher education and training: A report by a committee of inquiry appointed by the secretary of state for education and science under the Chairmanship of Lord James of Rusholme*, (London: HMSO, 1972), p.12; TNA, ED 281/18, Advisory Committee on the Supply and Training of Teachers, Sub-committee on Induction and In-Service Training: meetings and papers, 1973–1978.
18 Carpentier, V. (2003). 'Public expenditure on education and economic growth in the UK, 1833–2000', *History of Education, 32*(1), pp. 1–15.
19 Aldrich., R., Crook, D., & Watson, D. (2000). *Education and employment: The DfEE and its place in history*. London, UK: London University Institute of Education.
20 TNA, ED 23/449, Letter from the Secretary of the Board of Education to the Treasury, 7 September 1917.
21 Aldrich, Crook, and Watson, *Education and employment*, p. 59; TNA, ED 22/449, Letter from the Treasury to the Secretary of the Board of Education, 10 November 1925.
22 TNA, ED 86/11, Paper from Association of Teachers in Technical Institutions, Conference Resolution, 1937.
23 TNA, ED 86/222, Letter from Stevenson to Dorset, 5 April 1948.
24 TNA, ED 86/222, Letter from Stevenson to Miss Weddell, Principal of the Training College of Domestic Economy, 17 February1949.
25 TNA, ED23/449, Letter from the Treasury to the Secretary of the Board of Education, 29 July 1924.
26 Partington, G. (1976). *Women teachers in the twentieth century in England and Wales*. Windsor: NFER.
27 See for example: TNA, ED 25/37, HMI report on in-service courses for teachers in East Sussex, 1968–9; TNA, ED 77/303, Survey of courses for teachers sponsored by the local education authority, East Riding of Yorkshire 1962–1964; TNA ED 77/279, Survey by HMI of residential courses for teachers conducted by Manchester Education Authority, 1957–1958.
28 Two oral history participants, Joy Kell and Gill Brown specifically used this language of having to 'grovel and beg' to describe the struggle to access resources for professional development.
29 TNA, ED 22/45, Memo to Inspectors regarding the selection of teachers for observation visits and short courses, 3 August 1917.
30 TNA, ED 22/103, Memo to Inspectors no. 299, 'Weekend Refresher Courses for Elementary School Teachers'.
31 TNA, ED 22/226, Report on courses for teachers in Wales, 1938.
32 TNA, ED 82/126, Inspection report on Derby Vacation Course, 10 August 1923.
33 TNA, ED 22/175, Memo attached to list of teachers who attended short courses of instruction for teachers in Wales, 1922–1924, by Alfred T. Davies, 24 February 1925.
34 TNA, ED 86/380, Report for England for a Council of Europe Seminar on Further (In-Service) Training of Teachers, 12–19 August 1966.
35 TNA, ED86/223, Letter to Miss C. Bell from Professor W. R. Niblett, 12 March 1952.
36 See TNA, Ed 86/222, Note on the issue of funding for Special Course for Experienced Serving Teachers, dated 21 July 1951, '…we want these courses to attract the cream of the teaching profession. We should be training a small elite....'.
37 TNA, ED 86/378, Minute detailing draft paper on 'In-service Training for Qualified Servicing Teachers: Proposals for Development', June 1961.
38 TNA ED 10/204. Memo on Physical Education courses for teachers, 19 December 1919.
39 TNA, ED 22/176, Memo to Inspectors (Wales) no. 355, 1925.
40 TNA, ED 86/111, Memo to Inspectors on short courses, 1944.
41 TNA, ED 86/380, Report for England for a Council of Europe Seminar on Further (In-Service) Training of Teachers, 12–19 August 1966.
42 TNA, ED 86/378, Minute detailing draft paper on 'In-service Training for Qualified Servicing Teachers: Proposals for Development', June 1961.
43 TNA, ED 86/222, Notes dated 9 October 1947.
44 TNA, ED 86/378, Minute detailing draft paper on 'In-service Training for Qualified Servicing Teachers: Proposals for Development', June 1961.

45   TNA, ED 86/378, Correspondence regarding draft paper on 'In-service Training for Qualified Servicing Teachers: Proposals for Development', June 1961; ED 86/379, Letter to A. T Beecher from Mr Long, 20 July 1964; ED281/18, Advisory Committee on the Supply and Training of Teachers, Sub-committee on Induction and In-Service Training: meetings and papers, 1973–1978.

46   NA, ED 86/378, Minute detailing draft paper on 'In-service Training for Qualified Servicing Teachers: Proposals for Development', June 1961.

47   TNA, ED 86/380, Report for England for a Council of Europe Seminar on Further (In-Service) Training of Teachers, 12–19 August 1966.

48   Office for Standards in Education (hereafter OFSTED), *The logical chain: Continuing professional development in effective schools* (London: OFSTED, 2006); OFSTED, *Good professional development in schools*, (London: OFSTED, 2010); R. McCormick, 'The state of the nation in CPD: a literature review', *The Curriculum Journal*, 24, 4 (2010), pp. 395–412.

49   Day, C., & Leith, R. (2007). 'The continuing professional development of teachers: issues of coherence, cohesion and effectiveness'. In T. Townsend (Ed.), *International Handbook of School Effectiveness and Improvement*. Dordrecht, The Netherlands: Springer. pp. 468–83.

50   See Pedder, D., Storey, A., Opfer, V., & McCormick, R. (2009). '*Schools and continuing professional development (CPD) in England – state of the nation research project: Synthesis report*'. London, UK: Training and Development Agency for Schools.; Pedder, D., et al. (2010). 'Schools and continuing professional development in England – "State of the Nation" research study: Policy; context; aims and design', *The Curriculum Journal*, *21*(4), pp. 365–394; Opfer, V., & Pedder, D. (2011). 'The lost promise of teacher professional development in England', *European Journal of Teacher Education*, *34*(1), pp. 3–24.

51   Organisation for Economic Co-operation and Development (hereafter, OECD), *Preparing teachers and developing school leaders for the 21st century – Lessons from around the world* (Paris: OECD, 2012).

52   Brighouse and Moon, *Taking teacher development seriously*, p. 3.

53   See for example, Hargreaves, A. (2003). *Teaching in the knowledge society: Education in the age of insecurity*. Maidenhead: Open University Press.; Ozga, J., & Lawn, M. (1981). *Teachers professionalism and class*. London, UK: The Falmer Press.; Ogren, G. (1953). *Trends in English teachers' training from 1800: A survey and an investigation*. Stockholm: Esselte.

54   See for example, Hopkins, D. (1986). *Inservice training and educational development: An international survey*. Dover, NH: Croom Helm.; and Guskey, T., & Huberman, M. (Eds), (1995). *Professional development in education*. New York, NY: Teachers' College Press.

55   See Sachs, J. (2001). 'Teacher professional identity: Competing discourses, competing outcomes', *Journal of Education Policy*, *16*(2), 149–161.

56   Mockler, N. (2005). 'Trans/forming teachers: New professional learning and transformative teachers professionalism', *Journal of In-Service Education*, *31*(4), 733–746.

57   See Robinson, W. (2003). *Pupil teachers and their professional training in pupil-teacher centres in England and Wales, 1870–1914*. New York, NY: Edward Mellen Press.; Robinson, W. (2004). *Power to teach: Learning through practice*. London, UK: RoutledgeFalmer.; Cunningham, P., & Gardner, P. (2004). *Becoming teachers; texts and testimonies 1907–1950*. London, UK: Woburn Press.

58   BARDA Project 53026, oral history interview with Joy Willoughby, May 2011.

59   BARDA Project 53026, oral history interview with Ann Dodd, June 2011.

60   See Hopkins, D., *Inservice training and educational development: An international survey*, p. 8.

61   Day, C., Sammons, P., Stobart, G., Kington, A. & Gu, Q. (2007). *Teachers matter: Connecting lives, work and effectiveness*. Maidenhead: Open University Press. P. xiii.

62   Adey, *The professional development of teachers*, p. 10.

63   Adey, *The professional development of teachers*, p. 167.

64   Wenger, E. (1998). *Communities of practice: Learning, meaning and identity*. Cambridge UK: Cambridge University Press.

65   Wenger, *Communities of practice: Learning, meaning and identity*, p. 149.

66   Neufeld, J. (2009). *Redefining teacher development*. London, UK: Routledge.

SELECT BIBLIOGRAPHY

ARCHIVE SOURCES

The National Archives, Kew, England
ED 10/204, Handwritten memo from R.S. Wood on possible camping short course, 1919.
ED 22/45, Circulars and Memoranda, 1917.
ED 22/64, Short, full-time, or vacation courses for teachers, 1920.
ED 22/95, Short, full-time, or vacation courses, 1921.
Ed 22/103, Weekend refresher courses for elementary school teachers, 1928.
ED 22/108, Short courses for science teachers in senior schools, 1938–40; Also, short courses for handicraft teachers.
ED 22/109, Elementary Inspectors' File, 1934.
ED 22/129, Course in physical education at Eastbourne, 1925.
ED 22/130, Physical training courses at Eastbourne, August 1926, 1926.
ED 22/134, Physical training courses at Eastbourne, 1930; Short courses for secondary school teachers.
ED 22/139, Inspectors' Files, 1935–1938.
ED 22/144, Short courses of instruction for teachers with supplement, 1924.
ED 22/159, Full and part-time studentships for teachers, 1923.
ED 22/173, Short courses (Wales), 1923.
ED 22/175, Short courses (Wales) and list of attendees, 1925.
ED 22/176, List of teachers who attended 1925 short courses, 1926.
ED 22/177, Short courses: Wales; list of teachers who attended 1927 short courses, 1927.
ED 22/184, Short course in physical training for Welsh speaking teachers at Aberystwyth, 1934.
ED 22, 203, Circulars and Memoranda, 1937.
ED 22/204, Courses for teachers, 1938.
ED 22/217, Reports on short courses for teachers, 1937.
ED 22/225, Circular 1453: Courses for teachers.
ED 22/231, Short courses for teachers, 1939.
ED 23/449, Regulations for training of teachers (Short Courses) No.24, 1915–1925.
ED 23/984, Correspondence on the art of calligraphy with particular reference to Mr Alfred J Fairbank and his employment as a lecturer on short courses of training for teachers, 1951–52.
ED 24/1810, City of London Vacation Courses in Education for teachers: papers, 1922–1935.
ED 24/1870, Short courses for teachers of building subjects, 1926.
ED 34/235, Sir Thomas McNally: To ask the Secretary of State for Education and Science what was the total expenditure on: (a) in-service training and (b) initial teacher training in England in each of the past five years, Nov 15th 1982.
ED 54/245, Vacation courses, 1960–1967.
ED 54/246, Vacation courses: abroad, 1950–1959.
ED 54/247, Vacation courses: abroad, 1960–1967.
ED 54/248, Vacation courses: England and Wales, 1960–1963.
ED 54/249, Vacation courses: England and Wales, 1964–1967.
ED 54/340, Correspondence and background to committee papers: vacation courses, 1964–1968.
ED 54/461, Working party on transfer of responsibility for vacation courses, 1969–1970.
ED 54/462, Working party on transfer of responsibility for vacation courses, 1969–1970.
ED 76/8, Hull and Leeds Universities, Joint Committee (North Yorkshire Vacation Committee), 1931–1955.
ED 76/17, Oxford University, tutorial classes committee (Reading Vacation Courses), 1930–1939.
ED 76/28, North Wales University College and Manchester University, Joint Committee for Tutorial Classes, 1934–1955.

ED 77/196, Weekend refresher courses for rural elementary school teachers.

ED 77/279, Survey by HMI of residential courses for teachers conducted by Manchester Education Authority, 1957–1958.

ED 77/303, Survey of courses for teachers sponsored by the local education authority, East Riding of Yorkshire, 1962–64.

ED 77/352, Survey of in-service teacher training, 1968–1970.

ED 82/110, Scarborough Summer School Physical Training Course for Teachers, 1921–1932.

ED 82/122, Brighton Course for Teachers of the Deaf, 1924–1929.

ED 82/126, Derby Training College Vacation Courses for teachers, 1921.

ED 82/158, Aberystwyth Summer School Teachers' Course, 1922–1931.

ED 86/111, Board of Education expenditure on short courses, 1936–1945.

ED 86/126, Women Teachers, 1950.

ED 86/222, Special courses for experienced serving teachers, 1947–1951.

ED 86/223, Special courses for experienced serving teachers, 1952–1953.

ED 86/378, Student grants, in-service training, 1961–1964.

ED 86/379, In-service training, 1964–1965.

ED 86/380, In-service training, 1965–1967.

ED 86/443, Special courses for experienced serving teachers, 1957–1965.

ED 94/63, Harrison, Miss M. J., Additional grant not payable in respect of vacation course at the Alliance Francaise, 1950; 1949–1955.

ED 94/109, Stubbington, Miss J. M., Grant for additional attendance and vacational courses, 1951; 1948–1952.

ED 94/111, Winterbottom, Miss J., Student required to spend 6 months in France including summer term at the Sorbonne, 1951; 1950–1953.

ED 94/226, Miller, Miss E. A., Student on vacation course in France held up for one week and put to additional travel expenses because of rail strike, 1953; 1952–1955.

ED 94/17, Plack, R. L., Approval of travel grant to student in respect of vacation course in Isle of Man, 1947–1950.

ED 94/42, Johnson, C. L., additional grant for vacation course not reduced on account of financial assistance, 1947–1950.

ED 94/82, Kirk, P. M., Calculation of tuition fees where student on overseas vacation course, 1948–1951.

ED 94/119, Hargreaves, Miss. S. P., Not Ministry practice to pay claims for vacation courses in retrospect, 1947–1951.

ED 94/120, Wright, Miss. H. J., Student assisted, exceptionally with expenses of a vacation course, 1950–1951.

ED 94/178, Canon, R. C., Student intending to do research on completion of approved course, 1950–1953.

ED 94/203, Wiley, D. A., Student visiting Greece on a travelling scholarship, 1949–1953.

ED 94/251, Hallam, A., Additional grant for vacation course, 1951–1955.

ED 94/253, House, G. R., Oil tour of Britain undertaken by student of geology, 1953–1954.

ED 94/258, Piette, I. R., Student Awards, 1952–1953.

ED 94/259, Ringrose, B. S., Student awards for vacation course, 1951–1955.

ED 114/1336, Residential courses for teachers sponsored by Manchester Education Authority 1957–1958.

ED 114/1630/10, Aspects of provision at Manchester Polytechnic: in-service training at the School of Education, 1987.

ED 121/3, Short courses for teachers on American history: bibliography, 1941.

ED 121/4, Short courses for teachers on American history: reports, 1941–1943.

ED 121/11, Proposed attendance of French teachers at the City of London Vacation Course on Education and its inclusion in the Board of Education list 180, 1938–1940.

ED 121/42, Lecture courses for teachers on health education, 1939–1943.

ED 121/405, Brief pamphlet on short courses for teachers in England and Wales, 1947.

ED 135/7, Emergency training: special courses, 1947.

ED 135/11, List of supplementary courses, 1951–1952.

ED 135/29, LEA support for teachers on in-service training, 1969–1970.

ED 135/41, Memorandum to Inspectors (In-Service Training: Long Courses for Teachers, and HMI and Courses for Teachers), 1970s-80s.

ED 143/22, Special courses, handicraft teachers, 1944–1948.

ED 143/23, Special courses, handicraft teachers, 1944–1951.

ED 143/24, Special courses, arts and craft, 1943–1949.

ED 143/29, Special courses, general, 1946–1951.

ED 143/30, Special courses in Wales for Welsh students, 1946–1947.

ED 143/31, Special courses, selection and assessment of students, 1944–1949.

ED 176/1-6, Courses run by the Ministry, 1945–1947.

ED 181/55, In-Service training of teachers: cost-effectiveness, 1967–1968.

ED 189/25, In-Service training of teachers, 1966–1967.

ED 192/140, In-service teacher training in science and mathematics Royal Society and DES joint committee, 1967–1973

ED 212/112, James Report on Teacher Education and Training: response to recommendations and consultations with concerned bodies, 1972.

ED 233, Department of Education and Science and predecessors: HM Inspectorate: Unregistered papers from Regional Offices, 1840–1978.

ED 233/13, In-Service training of Modern Language teachers, 1967–8.

ED 233/14, Reports of discussions about teachers' centres at HMI (Schools) conferences, 1972.

ED 235/7, In Service courses for teachers in East Sussex, 1968–9.

ED 235/21/20, In service training undertaken by staff of Ealing Technical College and Southall College of Technology, 1972–1973.

ED 235/22/2, Home economics in-service training in Hertfordshire, 1972–1973.

ED 235/82/1, In-service training for adult education teachers in Northamptonshire, 1990–1991.

ED 250/55, Working party on transfer of responsibility for vacation courses, 1969.

ED 250/56, Working party on transfer of responsibility for vacation courses, 1970.

ED 272/3/1, Some aspects of in-service training for teachers of mathematics in the North West Division, 1969–1978.

ED 272/30/2, In-service training in Beverley and Market Weighton, 1967–1973.

ED 272/33, In-service training of teachers, 1970–1971.

ED 281/17-22, Advisory Committee on the Supply and Training of Teachers, Sub-committee on Induction and In-Service Training: meetings and papers, 1973–1978,

ED 281/23, Advisory Committee on the Supply and Training of Teachers: papers, and National Conference on In-Service Training at Bournemouth, 1978.

ED 281/54, Council for Accreditation of Teacher Education: meetings, papers and letters, 1984.

ED 281/55/1-4, Council for Accreditation of Teacher Education: meetings, papers and letters, 1985.

ED 281/56, Council for Accreditation of Teacher Education: meetings, papers and letters, 1986.

Ed 281/57, Council for Accreditation of Teacher Education: meetings, papers and letters, 1987.

Ed 281/58-62, Council: Reporting groups A, B, C, D: papers on group proposals for various courses, 1988.

ED 281/63-66, Council: Reporting groups A, B, C, D: papers on group proposals for various courses, 1989.

ED 284/11, Committee of Inquiry into the Teaching of Mathematics in Schools (Cockcroft Committee): Working Group on In-Service Training and other support service; meetings, agendas and papers, 1979–1981.

The Bodleian Library, University of Oxford
Teachers World and Schoolmistress, 1920–1940.
The Times, 1920–1940,

Special Collections, University of Bristol,
DM2076/Box 4/File 1, Board of the Institute of Education, Minutes.
DM2076/Box 4/File 2, Annual Reports on Advanced Courses.
DM2076/Box 8/file 1: 'Relationship between Advanced Certificate, Diploma in Education and M.Ed.', dated 11/11/1963.

SELECT BIBLIOGRAPHY

DM2076/Box 8/File 2: 'A Revised Structure for Advanced Courses', October 1968.
DM/2076/Box 8: File 5.
DM2076/Box 74 – Prospectuses 1925–1969

Derbyshire Record Office
DER RO, D6845/Box 34/5, Derby Training College Vacation Course.

Institute of Education Archives, University of London
DC/DG/A/1
DC/AF Amelia Fysh papers
DC/CS/M/1: Institute of Education courses
IoE/DC/CS/M/2
HR/6/32: Harry Ree papers
SCC/P/22: Knowsley Teachers' Centre, 1981–1982
SCC/175/385/01: Teachers' Centres, role and functioning, 1978–79.

Jesus College Archives, University of Oxford
BU.COR.2CN, Alfred T Davies papers.

King's College Archives, University of London,
Archives of the Nuffield Foundation Science Teaching Project.

OFFICIAL PUBLICATIONS

Board of Education. (1925). *Report of the departmental committee on the training of teachers for public elementary schools.* Cd. 2409.
Board of Education. (1919–1944). *Annual reports and statistics of education.*
Board of Education. (1944). *Teachers and youth leaders: Report of the committee appointed by the president of the board of education to consider the supply, recruitment and training of teachers and youth leaders (McNair).* London, UK: HMSO.
Department of Education and Science (hereafter DES). (1964). *Course of further training for teachers* (Circular 7/64). London, UK: DES.
DES. (1967). *Statistics of education, survey of in-service training for teachers.* London, UK: HMSO.
DES. (1972). *Teacher education and training: A report by a committee of inquiry appointed by the secretary of state for education and science under the chairmanship of Lord James of Rusholme.* London, UK: HMSO.
DES. (1972). *Education: A framework for expansion* (Cd. 5174).
DES. (1973). *Development of higher education in the non-university sector* (Circular 7/73). London, UK: DES.
DES. (1984). *Initial teacher training: Approval of courses* (Circular 3/84). London, UK: DES.
DES. (1984). *The in-service teacher training grants scheme* (Circular 4/84). London, UK: DES.
Ministry of Education. (1947–1960). *Annual reports and statistics of education.*
Office for Standards in Education (hereafter OFSTED). (2004). *Making a difference: the Impact of award-bearing INSET on school improvement.* London, UK: OFSTED.
OFSTED. (2006). *The logical chain: Continuing professional development in effective schools.* London, UK: OFSTED.
OFSTED. (2010). *Good professional development in schools.* London, UK: OFSTED.

PUBLISHED BOOKS AND ARTICLES

Adams, E. (Ed.). (1975). *In-service education and teachers' Centres.* Oxford: Pergamon Press.
Adey, P. (2004). *The professional development of teachers: Practice and theory.* Dordrecht: Kluwer Academic Publishers,

Aldrich, R. (2002). *The institute of education 1902–2002: A centenary history.* London, UK: Institute of Education.

Aldrich, R., Crook, D., & Watson, D. (2000). *Education and employment: The DfEE and its place in history.* London, UK: London University, Institute of Education.

Altenbaugh, R. (1992). *The teacher's voice: A social history of teaching in twentieth century America.* Lewes: Falmer Press.

Bassett, R. (1922). *Streatham county secondary school for girls: Dalton plan assignments compiled by the staff of Streatham county secondary school for girls.* London, UK: G. Bell and Sons.

Bates, T., Gough, B., & Stammers, P. (1999). The role of central government and its agencies in the continuing professional development of teachers: An evaluation of recent changes in its financing in England. *Journal of In-Service Education, 25*(2), 321–335.

Bax, S. (2002). The social and cultural dimensions of trainer training. *Journal of Education for Teaching, 28*(2), 165–178.

Bocko, H. (2004). Professional development and teacher learning: Mapping the terrain. *Educational Researcher, 33*(8), 3–15.

Brighouse, T., & Moon, B. (2013). *Taking teacher development seriously: A proposal to establish a national teaching institute for teacher professional development in England.* London, UK: New Visions for Education Group.

Bridgwood, A. (1996). Consortium collaboration: The experience of TVEI. In D. Bridges & C. Husbands (Eds.), *Consorting and collaborating in the education market place.* London, UK: Falmer Press.

Burchell, H., Dyson, J., & Rees, M. (2002). Making a difference: A study of the impact of continuing professional development on professional practice. *Journal of In-Service Education, 28*(2), 219–229.

Burd, J. (1978). INSET in the USA. *Insight, 2*(2), 19–22.

Burgess, R. (1993). *Implementing in-service education and training.* London, UK: RoutledgeFalmer.

Carpentier, V. (2003). Public expenditure on education and economic growth in the UK, 1833–2000. *History of Education, 32*(1), 1–15.

Carpentier, V. (2008). Quantitative sources for the history of education. *History of Education, 37*(5), 701–720.

Chitty, C. (2002). *Understanding schools and schooling.* London, UK: Routledge Falmer.

Copelman, D. (1996). *London's women teachers: Gender, class and feminism 1870–1930.* London, UK: Routledge.

Cordingley, P., Bell, M., Rundell, B., & Evans, D. (2003). *The impact of collaborative CPD on classroom teaching and learning.* London, UK: Research Evidence in Education Library, EPPI-Centre.

Cordingley, P., & Bell, M. (2012). *Understanding what enables high quality professional learning: A report on the research evidence.* London, UK: Centre for the Use of Research Evidence in Education (CUREE): Pearson School Improvement.

Cowan, B., & Wright, N. (1990). Two million days lost: What teachers do on Baker Days. *Education, 175*(5), 117–118.

Cox, G. (2001). Teaching music in schools: Some historical reflections. In C. Philpott & C. Plummeridge (Eds), *Issues in music teaching* (pp. 9–20). London, UK: RoutledgeFalmer.

Craft, M. (1971). Social process, social change and English teacher education. *International Review of Education, 17*(4), 425–441.

Croll, P., Abbott, D., Broadfoot, P., Osborn, M., & Pollard, A. (1994). Teachers and education policy: Roles and models. *British Journal of Educational Studies, 42*(4), 333–347.

Crook, D. (1995). Universities, teacher training, and the legacy of McNair 1944–1994. *History of Education, 24*(3), 231–245.

Crook, D. (2011). In-service education and professional development for teachers in England: Historical perspectives from the late twentieth century. *History of Education Researcher, 87*, 4–12.

Cunningham, P. (1992). Teachers professional image and the press 1950–1990. *History of Education, 21*(1), 37–56.

Dale, R. (1990). *The TVEI story: Policy, practice and preparation for the workforce.* Maidenhead: Open University Press.

Darling-Hammond, L., & Sykes, G. (2005). *Teaching as the learning profession: A handbook of policy and practice.* San Francisco, CA: Jossey-Boss.

197

Davis, R. (1979). How to involve teachers in their own in-service work through a teachers' centre. *British Journal of In-Service Education, 5*(2), 30–38.

Davies, R., & Preston, M. (2002). An evaluation of the impact of continuing professional development on personal and professional lives. *Journal of In-Service Education, 28*(2), 231–255.

Day, C. (1999). *Developing teachers: The challenges of lifelong learning.* London, UK: Routledge Falmer.

Day, C., & Leith, R. (2007). The continuing professional development of teachers: Issues of coherence, cohesion and effectiveness. In T. Townsend (Ed.), *International handbook of school effectiveness and improvement.* Dordrecht, The Netherlands: Springer, 468–483.

Day, C., & Sachs, J. (2005). *International handbook on the continuing professional development for teachers.* Milton Keynes: Open University Press.

Day, C., Sammons, P., Stobart, G., Kington, A., & Gu, Q. (2007). *Teachers matter: Connecting lives, work and effectiveness.* Maidenhead: Open University Press.

de Vroede, M. (1981). The history of teacher training. *History of Education Society Bulletin, 10*(1), 1–8.

Dent, H. (1977). *The training of teachers in England and Wales, 1800–1975.* London, UK: Hodder and Stoughton.

Dobson, M. (1951). *1851–1951: The first hundred years of the Diocesan Training College Derby.* West Bromwich: Kenrick & Jefferson.

Edelfelt, R., & Hruska, M. (1982). British-American exchange on teachers' centres. *British Journal of In-Service Education, 9*(2), 80–87.

Eggleston, J. (1979). Teacher's centres: A British development in further professional training. *European Journal of Education, 14*, 351–357.

Evans, L. (2002). What is teacher development? *Oxford Review of Education, 28*(1), 123–137.

Finch, R. (1923). *A.& C. Black's world-wide geography pictures.* London, UK: A. & C. Black.

Flecknoe, M. (2000). Can continuing professional development for teachers be shown to raise pupils' achievement? *Journal of In-Service Education, 26*(3), 437–457.

Flecknoe, M. (2003). Measuring the impact of teacher professional development: Can it be done? *European Journal of Teacher Education, 25*(2), 119–134.

Friedman, A. (2000). *Continuing professional development in the UK: Policies and practices.* London, UK: PARN.

Gardner, P. (2003). Oral history in education: Teacher's memory and teachers' history. *History of Education, 32*(2), 175–188.

Gardner, P. (2007). The Life-long draught: From learning to teaching and back. *History of Education, 36*(4), 465–482.

Gardner, P. (2010). *Hermeneutics, history and memory.* Oxford: Routledge.

Gardner, P., & Cunningham, P. (2004). *Teachers: Texts and testimonies 1907–1950.* London, UK: Woburn Press.

General Teaching Council. (2003). *Teachers' professional learning framework.* London, UK: General Teaching Council.

Gilpin, A. (1997). Cascade training: Sustainability or dilution? In I. McGrath (Ed.), *Learning to train: Perspectives on the development of language teacher trainers.* Hemel Hempstead: Prentice Hall.

Gleeson, D. (1987). *TVEI and secondary education.* Maidenhead: Open University Press.

Gleeson, D., & McLean, M. (2004). Whatever happened to TVEI?: TVEI, curriculum and schooling', *Journal of Education Policy, 9*(3), 233–244.

Glover, D., & Law, S. (1996). *Managing professional development in education.* London, UK: Kogan Page.

Gosden, P. (1972). *The evolution of a profession.* Oxford: Basil Blackwell.

Gosden, P. (1976). *Education in the second world war: A study of policy and administration.* London, UK: Methuen.

Gough, B. (1975). Teachers' centres as providers of in-service education. *British Journal of In-Service Education, 1*(3), 12.

Gough, B. (1989). 20 years or so of teachers' centres. What have we learned? What can we share? *British Journal of In-Service Education, 15*(1), 51–54.

Gough, B. (1997). Teacher's centres as seen through the pages of the *British Journal of In-Service Education. British Journal of In-Service Education, 23*(1), 23–29.

Gray, S. (2005). *An enquiry into continuing professional development.* London, UK: Esmee Fairburn Foundation.

Guskey, T., & Huberman, M. (Eds.). (1995). *Professional development in education.* New York, NY: Teachers' College Press.

Hargreaves, A. (2003). *Teaching in the knowledge society: Education in the age of insecurity.* Maidenhead: Open University Press.

Hargreaves, A., & Fullan, M. (1992). *Understanding teacher development.* London, UK: Cassell.

Hayes, D. (2000). Cascade training and teachers' professional development. *English Language Teaching Journal, 54*(2), 135–145.

Hopkins, D. (1986). *Inservice training and educational development: An international survey.* Dover, NH: Croom Helm.

Hoyle, E., & John, P. (1995). *Professional knowledge and professional practice.* London, UK: Cassell.

Humphreys, D. (1976). *The University of Bristol and the education and training of teachers.* Bristol: University of Bristol School of Education.

Humphries, S. (1984). *The handbook of oral history: Recording life stories.* London, UK: Inter-Action.

Jennings, A. (1985). Out of the secret garden. In M. Plaskow (Ed.), *Life and death of the Schools Council.* London, UK: Falmer Press.

Jenkins, E. (1979). *From Armstrong to Nuffield: Studies in twentieth-century science education in England and Wales.* London, UK: John Murray.

Jones, G., & Roderick, G. (2003). *A history of education in Wales.* Cardiff, UK: University of Wales Press.

Jones, G. (1982). *Controls and conflicts in Welsh secondary education, 1889–1944.* Cardiff, UK: University of Wales Press.

Jones, K. (2003). *Education in Britain: 1944 to the present.* Cambridge: Polity Press.

Jones, L. (1924). *The training of teachers in England and Wales: A critical survey.* Oxford, Oxford University Press.

Kahn, H. (1982). Teachers' centres their aims, objectives and philosophy: A Commonwealth perspective. *British Journal of In-Service Education, 9*(2), 75–80.

Khan, H. (1991). *Teachers' resource centres.* London, UK: Commonwealth Secretariat.

Kerry, T. (1993). Baker days revisited: An opportunity lost or found? *Education Today, 43*(1), 26-30.

Knamiller, G. (Eds). (1999). *The effectiveness of teacher resource centre strategy.* London, UK: Department for International Development.

Knox, H. (1951). The study of education in British universities. *The Universities Review, 24*, 34–40.

Labaree, D. (2004). *The trouble with Ed Schools.* New Haven: Yale University Press.

Lawn, M. (1987). *Servants of the state: The contested control of teaching 1900–1930.* London, UK: The Falmer Press.

Little, J. (2003). Professional development in a climate of educational reform. *Educational Evaluation and Policy Analysis, 15*, 129–151.

Lowe, R. (1997). *Schooling and social change 1964–1990.* London, UK: Routledge.

MacBeath, J., & Galton, M. (2004). *A life in secondary teaching: Finding time for learning.* Cambridge: Cambridge Printing.

McCormick, R. (2010). The state of the nation in CPD: A literature review. *The Curriculum Journal, 24*(4), 395–412.

McCulloch, G. (2004). *Documentary research in education, history and the social sciences.* London, UK: RoutledgeFalmer.

McCulloch, G., & Richardson, W. (2000). *Historical research in educational settings.* Buckingham: Open University Press.

Manzer, R. (1975). The secret garden of the curriculum. In R. Bell & W. Prescott (Eds), *The schools council: A second look* (pp. 9–15). London, UK: Ward Lock Educational.

Martin, P. (1981). The role of teachers' centres. *Insight, 4*(2), 22–28.

Mockler, N. (2005). Trans/forming teachers: New professional learning and transformative teachers professionalism. *Journal of In-Service Education, 31*(4), 733–746.

Morant, R. (1978). Re-appraising the role of teachers' centres. *British Journal of In-Service Education, 4*(3), 198–205.

Moreland, N. (1988). Grist to the mill: Emergent practices and problems in the grant-related in-service training system – A perspective from a providing institution. *Innovation in Education and Training International, 25*(2), 129–135.

Market & Opinion Research International (MORI). (1995). *Survey of continuing professional development.* London, UK: MORI.

Midwinter, E. (1974). Teachers' centres: The facilitators. *British Journal of In-Service Education, 1*(1), 10–14.

Musset, P. (2010). *Initial teacher education and continuing training policies in a comparative perspective: Current practices in OECD countries and a literature review on potential effects.* Paris: Organisation for Economic Co-operation and Development (hereafter, OECD).

Neufeld, J. (2009). *Redefining teacher development.* London, UK: Routledge.

Newman, C., Shostak, R., & Sollars, R. (1981). Teachers centres: Some emergent characteristics. *Professional Development in Education, 8*(1), 45–50.

OECD. (1998). *Staying ahead: In-service training and teacher professional development.* Paris: OECD.

OECD. (2005). *Teachers matter: Attracting, developing and retaining effective teachers.* Paris: OECD.

OECD. (2009).*Teaching and learning international study.* Paris: OECD.

OECD. (2011). *Building a high-quality teaching profession: Lessons from around the world. Paris,* OECD.

OECD. (2012). *Preparing teachers and developing school leaders for the 21st century – Lessons from around the world.* Paris: OECD.

Ogren, G. (1953). *Trends in English teachers' training from 1800: A survey and an investigation* Stockholm: Esselte.

Opfer, V. & Pedder, D. (2011). The lost promise of teacher professional development in England. *European Journal of Teacher Education, 34*(1), 3–24.

Opfer, V., Pedder, D., & Lavicza, Z. (2008). *Schools and continuing professional development (CPD) in England- state of the nation research project: A report for the Training and Development Agency for Schools.* London, UK: Training and Development Agency for Schools.

Ozga, J., & Lawn, M. (1981). *Teachers professionalism and class.* London, UK: The Falmer Press.

Patrick, H. (1986). From cross to CATE: The universities and teacher education over the past century. *The Oxford Review of Education, 12*(3), 243–261.

Partington, G. (1976). *Women teachers in the twentieth century in England and Wales.* Windsor: NFER.

Pedder, D., Storey, A., Opfer, V., & McCormick, R. (2009). *Schools and continuing professional development (CPD) in England – State of the nation research project: Synthesis report.* London, UK: Training and Development Agency for Schools.

Pedder, D., Storey, A., Opfer, V., & McCormick, R. (2010). Schools and continuing professional development in England – state of the nation research study: Policy; context; aims and design. *The Curriculum Journal, 21*(4), 365–394.

Percy, L. E. (1958). *Some memories.* London, UK: Eyre and Spottis.

Perks, R. (1998). *Oral history: Talking about the past.* London, UK: Historical Association and Oral History Society.

Perks, R., & Thomson, A. (Eds.). (1998). *The oral history reader.* London, UK: Routledge.

Pinfield, B. (1975). Manchester Teachers' Centre. *Mathematics in school, 4*(1), 2–3.

Plaskow, M. (1990). It was the best of times, *Education,* August 3, 1990, p. 90. In C. Chitty & J. Dunford, (Eds.). *State schools: New Labour and the Conservative legacy* (p. 22). London, UK: Woburn Press.

Plummer, K. (2001). *Documents of life 2: An invitation to critical humanism.* London, UK: Sage.

Purdon, A. (2003). A national framework of CPD: Continuing professional development or continuing policy dominance? *Journal of Education Policy, 18*(4), 423–437.

Pyrs, G. (1996). The countryside as educator: Schools, rurality and citizenship in inter-war Wales. *Journal of Historical Geography, 22*(4), 412–423.

Redknap, C. (1977). *Focus on teachers' centres.* Windsor: NFER Publishing Company.

Rich, R. (1933). *The training of teachers in England and Wales during the nineteenth century.* Cambridge: Cambridge University Press.

Richards, C. (1972). Teachers' centres - A primary school view. *Trends in Education, 25*, 31–33.

Riding, P. (2001). Online teacher communities and CPD. *Teacher Development, 5*(3), 283–295.

Robinson, W. (1993). Pupil teachers: The Achilles heel of higher grade schools 1882–104. *History of Education, 22*(3), 241–253.

Robinson, W. (1996). Expert and novice in the pupil teacher system of the later nineteenth century. *Journal of Educational Administration and History, 28*(2), 129–141.

Robinson, W. (1999). In search of a plain tale: Rediscovering the champions of the pupil-teacher centres 1900–1910. *History of Education, 28*(1), 53–71.

Robinson, W. (2002). Towards a bi-centenary review? Historiographical reflections on the 1902 Education Act. *Oxford Review of Education, 28*(2), 159–172.

Robinson, W. (2003). Frocks, frills, femininity and representation of the woman teacher in *The Woman Teacher's World*: Reconstructing the early twentieth century English 'schoolmarm. *Journal of Educational Administration and History, 74*(2), 87–99.

Robinson, W. (2003). *Pupil teachers and their professional training in pupil teacher centres in England and Wales, 1870–1914*. New York, NY: Edwin Mellen Press.

Robinson, W. (2004). *Power to teach: Learning through practice*. London, UK: Routledge Falmer.

Robinson, W. (2008). Teacher education in England and Wales. In T. O'Donoghue & C. Whitehead (Eds.), *Teacher education in the English speaking world: Past, present and future* (pp. 45–61). Charlotte, NC: Information Age.

Robinson, W. (2010). Revisiting teacher professional development: Past and present models 1920–2008. *History of Education Researcher, 85*, 28–34.

Robinson, W. (2011). 'That great educational experiment' the City of London Vacation Course in Education 1922–1938: A forgotten story in the history of teacher professional development. *History of Education, 40*(5), 557–575.

Robinson, W., & Bryce, M. (2013). Capturing the willing enthusiasts and lame ducks: Central government and the history of teacher professional development in England and Wales 1920–1975', *Paedagogica Historica, 49*(3), 345–360.

Rousmaniere, K. (1997). *City teachers: Teaching and school reform in historical perspective*. New York, NY: Teachers College Press.

Rutherford, T. (1981). The teachers centre leaders: A partner in education. *Insight, 4*(3), 8–12.

Rust, B. (1973). Teachers' centers in England. *The Elementary School Journal, 73*(4), 182–192.

Sachs, J. (2001). Teacher professional identity: Competing discourses, competing outcomes. *Journal of Education Policy, 16*(2), 149–161.

Sandbrook, D. (2006). *White heat: A history of Britain in the swinging sixties*. London, UK: Little, Brown.

Selby-Bigge, L. (1927). *The Board of Education*. London, UK: G. P. Putnam's Sons.

Simon, B. (1974). *The politics of educational reform 1920–1940*. London, UK: Lawrence & Wishart.

Simpson, D. (1998). Not yet a dodo: The LEA teachers' centre. *History of Education Society Bulletin, 62*, 96–104.

Soulsby, D., & Swain, D. (2003). *A report on the award-bearing INSET scheme*. London, UK: Training and Development Agency, Department for Education and Science.

Stabler, E. (1976). Teachers' centres: A comparative view. *Canadian Journal of Education / Revue canadienne de l'éducation1, 2*, 37–50.

Thompson, F. (Ed.). (1990). *The University of London and the world of learning 1836–1936*. London, UK: The Hambledon Press.

Thomson, P. (1988). *The voice of the past: Oral history*. Oxford, Oxford University Press.

Thornbury, R. (Ed.). (1973). *Teachers' centres*. London, UK: Darton, Longman & Todd.

Thornbury, R. (1974, June 27). Teachers' centres. *New Society, 28*, 761.

Timperley, H. (2008). *Teacher professional learning and development: Best evidence synthesis iteration*. Brussels: UNESCO/International Bureau of Education.

Tonkin, E. (1992). *Narrating our pasts: The social construction of oral history*. Cambridge: Cambridge University Press.

Todd, F. (Ed.). (1987). *Planning continuous professional development*. London, UK: Croom Helm.

Tropp, A. (1957). *The school teachers*. London, UK: William Heinmann Ltd.

Van Praagh, G. (1988). *Seeing it through: Travels of a science teacher.* Crawley, England: Frognal Publishers.

Waring, M. (1979). *Social pressures and curriculum innovation: A study of the Nuffield Foundation Science Teaching Project.* London, UK: Methuen.

Weindling, D., Reid, M., & Davis, P. (1983). *Teachers' centres: A focus for in-service education* Methuen Educational.

Wenger, E. (1998). *Communities of practice: Learning, meaning and identity.* Cambridge, Cambridge University Press.

Whitehead, K. (2003). Postwar headteachers perspectives of good teachers. *Journal of Educational Administration and History, 35*(1), 23–35.

Widdowson, F. (1980). *Women and elementary teacher training 1840–1914.* London, UK: Women's Research and Resources Centre.

Widdowson, F., & de Lyon, H. (1989). *Women teachers: Issues and experiences.* Milton Keynes: Open University Press.

Williams, J. (1981). Teachers centres in the United Kingdom: An Antipodean view. *British Journal of In-Service Education, 7*(2), 132.

Wiseman, S. (1953). Higher degrees in education in British universities. *British Journal of Educational Studies, 2,* 54–66.

Woodward, S. (1985). The teachers centre's INSET role: A primary headteacher's perspective. *School Organization, 5*(3), 217–220.

Wooldridge, A. (1994). *Measuring the mind: Education and psychology in England 1860–1990.* Cambridge: Cambridge University Press.

UNPUBLISHED WORK

Brand, J. (1972). *The in-service education role of teachers' centres.* Unpublished Dip. Ed. Thesis, University of Nottingham.

Davis, R. (1979). *A study of the Kendal Teachers' Centre in Kendal with special reference to the views of users.* Unpublished MSc. Thesis, University of Lancaster.

Ravenhall, R. (1971). *Teachers' centres and their role in the pattern of in-service education for teachers.* Unpublished Dip. Ed. Thesis, University of Exeter.

Townsend, H. (1968). *The in-service training of teachers in the city of Wakefield.* Unpublished MEd. Thesis, University of Manchester.

Selby, D. (1976). *The concept and growth of the teachers' centre movement, with special reference to the Lancashire area.* Unpublished MEd. Thesis, University of Manchester.